IMAGES
of America

Patrick Henry's Red Hill

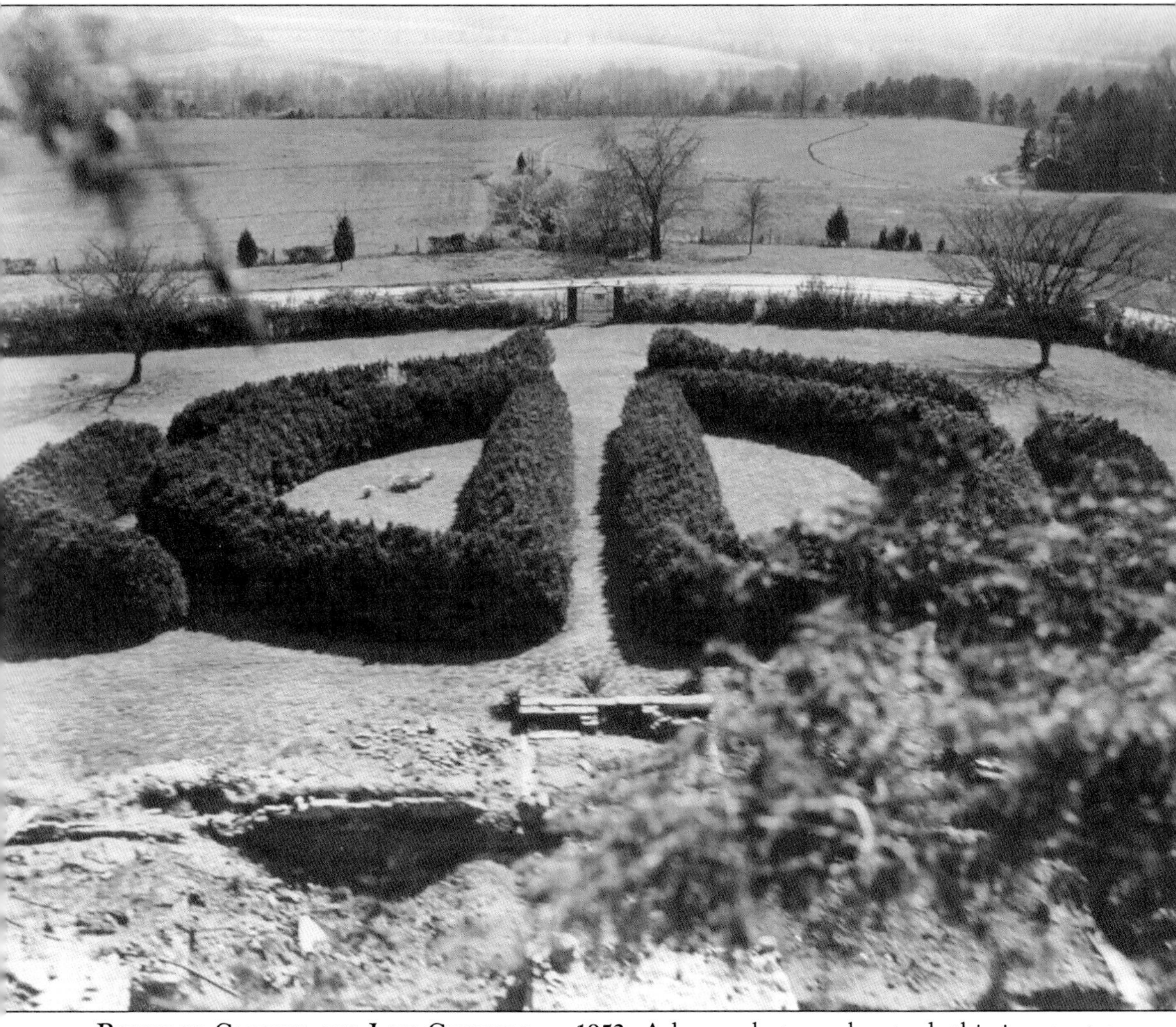

Boxwood Gardens and Low Grounds, c. 1952. A brave photographer took this image atop a tree at Red Hill, showing a view largely unchanged since the 18th century. The ruins of the burned Henry family mansion, a century-old boxwood garden, and sprawling farmlands symbolize resilience and continued progress, rising above destruction and adversity. (Courtesy of the Patrick Henry Memorial Foundation.)

On the Cover: Visitors at Red Hill, c. 1972. This publicity image shows visitors enjoying the restored grounds of Patrick Henry's final home and burial place at Red Hill. Since its founding as a museum in 1945, Red Hill's pastoral location and historic collections have continued to attract visitors worldwide. (Courtesy of the Patrick Henry Memorial Foundation.)

IMAGES
of America

PATRICK HENRY'S RED HILL

Cody Youngblood, Mark Couvillon,
and Patrick Henry Jolly

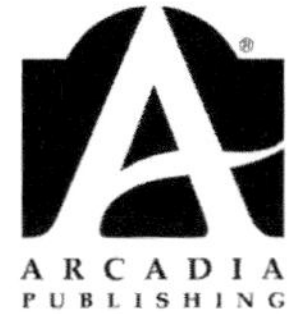

ISBN 978-1-4671-6293-7
Published by Arcadia Publishing
Charleston, South Carolina

Printed in the United States of America

Library of Congress Control Number: 2025941960

For all general information, please contact Arcadia Publishing:
Telephone 843-853-2070
Fax 843-853-0044
E-mail sales@arcadiapublishing.com

Visit us on the Internet at www.arcadiapublishing.com

To the past, present, and future stewards of Red Hill
who endeavor to illuminate its remarkable story

Contents

ACKNOWLEDGMENTS

Since the creation of the Patrick Henry Memorial Foundation in 1944, hundreds of volunteers and staff devoted to education and historic preservation have supported the restoration and care of Red Hill. It is impossible to thank all of them individually, but without their hard work in making this small nonprofit a success, this book would not have been possible. Many of the images in this volume would not exist today without the dedicated efforts of Edith C. Poindexter, "Miz P," who worked for decades as the foundation's curator and genealogist.

The authors wish to thank the following institutions for providing images and historical information: Amherst College (AC), Colonial Williamsburg Foundation (CWF), Library of Congress (LOC), Library of Virginia (LVA), Maryland Center for History & Culture (MCHC), Mount Vernon Ladies' Association (MVLA), Museum of Fine Arts Boston (MFA), New York Public Library (NYPL), Reynolda House (RH), Smithsonian Institution (SI), Stratford Hall (SH), The Valentine (TV), University of Maryland, Baltimore County (UMBC), US Air Force (USAF), Virginia Museum of History & Culture (VMHC), and Wellcome Collection (WC). Also, thanks go to Lucia Butler and Courtney Hollingsworth, who assisted with scanning photographs and helped bring this project over the finish line.

No part of this book could have been completed without the steadfast support of Hope E. Marstin, chief executive officer of the Patrick Henry Memorial Foundation, who graciously allowed the use of its collections at Red Hill to bring these images into publication for the first time. Unless otherwise noted, all images appear courtesy of the Patrick Henry Memorial Foundation.

Introduction

"I know no way of judging of the future but by the past." These words, spoken by Patrick Henry during his famous "Liberty or Death" speech in March 1775, encapsulate history's role in guiding the future. Standing before a gathering of Virginia's delegates, Henry had just delivered a rallying cry for people on the eve of a revolution that would fundamentally alter the course of history. Though spoken more than 250 years ago, Henry's assertion remains as relevant today as it was then, especially when reflecting upon the enduring legacy of the place where he spent his final years: Red Hill.

Here, on the banks of the Staunton River in southern Virginia, Henry retired from public life, spending his days looking after his "little flock" and enjoying life's simple pleasures. Here, while walking the tranquil grounds, the aging patriot reflected on the political battles he had fought and prepared his final public address to save the new republic from civil unrest and disunion. But it was also here that he died in 1799, at the age of 63, leaving behind a family and a complicated legacy. Red Hill, with its rolling hills and expansive views of the Virginia countryside, serves as a silent witness to this legacy, characterized by idealistic words of liberty yet actions of enslavement.

Red Hill is not just the home of a prominent Founding Father; it is a repository of stories that stretch back before European colonization—Archaic- and Woodland-period Indigenous sites on fertile farmland document the centuries-old home of the Saponi peoples. The size of these villages rivaled that of Henry's later estate. Excavated Dan River Ware ceramic vessels, clay pipes, stone projectile points, and animal bones point to advanced hunting methods and artistic knowledge.

A physical reminder of Indigenous existence stands just feet from Patrick Henry's house in the form of North America's largest Osage orange tree. Although native to present-day Oklahoma, the North Indian trade network contributed to the passing of tree cuttings to the Saponi, who may have been responsible for this tree's introduction to the Staunton River valley. This tree witnessed the historical events documented in this book and represents resilience despite the uncertainties of the future.

Richard Marot Booker no doubt gazed upon this tree when he ordered the construction of his new home at a place he named Red Hill, which he inherited after his father's death in 1760. Located near ferries and tobacco warehouses, Red Hill served as the seat of Booker's family, who introduced the institution of slavery to this land. By 1789, Booker sold off property, and in March 1794, Patrick Henry purchased the 700-acre tract from him. Henry added to the parcel, eventually owning 2,965 acres in Campbell and Charlotte Counties. Henry also purchased Seven Islands plantation from Booker's brother William across the river in Halifax County.

Why Red Hill? Henry arrived in nearby Campbell County in 1792 with the purchase of Long Island from Henry Lee III. Located about 13 miles upriver, Long Island felt too far removed from society, much to the consternation of Henry's daughters. Upon their move to Red Hill, Henry remarked, "They will be relieved from this Solitude, as that is a more public place." Nearby lived a number of relatives and friends, and the fertile soil provided an additional source of income, which enabled the aging patriot to rid himself of debt.

Patrick Henry's large family was only a small portion of the Red Hill populace. A month following Henry's death, an estate inventory recorded that he had 67 enslaved African Americans at Red Hill—a mixture of children, teenagers, adults, and elderly men and women. By 1802, the number of enslaved people had risen slightly to 69. Both inventories lack detailed identifying information for individual enslaved people, yet a small number of family groups are identified with mothers and their young children. Maintaining enslaved families would have provided Henry with a consistent means of sustaining and increasing his enslaved labor force.

Enslaved Blacks continued to toil at Red Hill when, in 1810, the widow Dorothea Henry gave the estate to her two youngest sons, John and Edward Winston Henry. The brothers soon divided the property upon coming of age in 1814. John Henry married in 1826 and brought his new wife, Elvira McClelland, to Red Hill. Edward settled east of the original estate and renamed his portion Windstone.

John Henry called his father's old cottage home and, in 1832, hired builders to expand it into a suitable living space. Elvira oversaw the landscape and ordered the construction of an orangery to plant expensive orange and lemon trees, a symbol of wealth in Victorian America. Enslaved gardeners planted D-shaped boxwood gardens and other shrubs. Elvira's enthusiasm for landscaping caused one of her husband's older siblings to complain "that young wife of John is ruining Red Hill."

Following the deaths of John and Elvira Henry in 1868 and 1875, respectively, their son William Wirt Henry inherited the estate. William's successful law practice kept him in Richmond, and farm operations were relegated to his brother, Thomas Stanhope Henry. Thomas ensured agricultural success following the nationwide emancipation of enslaved people in 1865. Many freed Black sharecroppers and domestics remained at Red Hill, and their labor continued to provide for the Henry family.

The turn of the 20th century brought unprecedented change with William Wirt Henry's death in 1900. Despite being excluded from the will, his daughter, Lucy Gray Henry Harrison, purchased the shares of Red Hill from her mother and siblings. Lucy left an indelible mark on the property when she expanded her grandfather's modest home into a Colonial Revival mansion, remodeled the gardens, and allowed both a railroad and state highway to pass through. This Red Hill renaissance only lasted eight years when, in 1919, the mansion burned to the ground, and Lucy's troubled finances left her with little choice but to move into her great-grandfather's expanded law office. Lucy died in 1944, the last of Henry's descendants to live at Red Hill.

The next chapter began in 1945 when the newly formed Patrick Henry Memorial Foundation purchased 960.61 acres from Lucy Harrison's estate. With a mission to restore the estate and preserve Patrick Henry's burial place, the foundation embarked on an ambitious project to reconstruct lost buildings and welcome visitors as a public museum. Following its restoration, Congress recognized Red Hill as the Patrick Henry National Memorial in 1986.

Today, Red Hill is both a living monument and a place of reflection where the past and present converge. It serves as a testament to Patrick Henry's legacy and the complex history of the land, its Indigenous peoples, the institution of slavery, and the generations that shaped and were shaped by it. From the Saponi peoples to Henry's transformative role in the new republic, from the painful realities of slavery to the eventual preservation of the estate as a national memorial, Red Hill embodies America's diverse and complex story.

One

Patrick Henry 1736–1799

Patrick Henry (1736–1799) was a lawyer, orator, and statesman whose life, career, and influence spanned the founding of the United States.

Born in 1736 on a plantation in rural Hanover County, Virginia, Henry's modest upbringing allowed for a few years of elementary schooling outside the home, followed by tutoring from his college-educated father until the age of 15. Success was not guaranteed to Patrick as he struggled to support his young family with a poorly producing farm and failed attempts as a merchant. He then pursued a career in law, studying independently for a short time. His reputation as a spokesman for the people and against unchecked authority was catapulted in 1763 with his successful involvement in the Parsons' Cause.

In 1765, Virginians elected Patrick Henry to the House of Burgesses, beginning his lifelong dedication to politics. Eleven years before the colonies would separate themselves from Great Britain, he spoke against the Stamp Act in an event that Thomas Jefferson later said "gave the first impulse to the ball of revolution."

For the next decade, Henry led Virginia through the volatile waters toward independence. He served as delegate to the first and second Continental Congresses (1774–1775) and commander-in-chief of the Virginia forces (1775–1776), and he attended four of the five Virginia Conventions. It was at the Second Virginia Convention that Henry delivered his historic words "Give me liberty or give me death!" while simultaneously grappling with his role as a lifelong enslaver of people.

In 1776, Henry became Virginia's first elected governor, an unprecedented and challenging position that he held for five terms (1776–1779 and 1784–1786). With the creation of a new national government, Henry fiercely decried the proposed US Constitution and believed it created a government too centralized and too distant from its citizens. As a member of the House of Delegates (1780–1784 and 1787–1791), his efforts in the 1788 Virginia Ratifying Convention ensured the inclusion of the Bill of Rights.

"The Voice of the Revolution" retired to Red Hill, his final home, and died there in 1799. But for the Henry family and Red Hill, the story was just beginning.

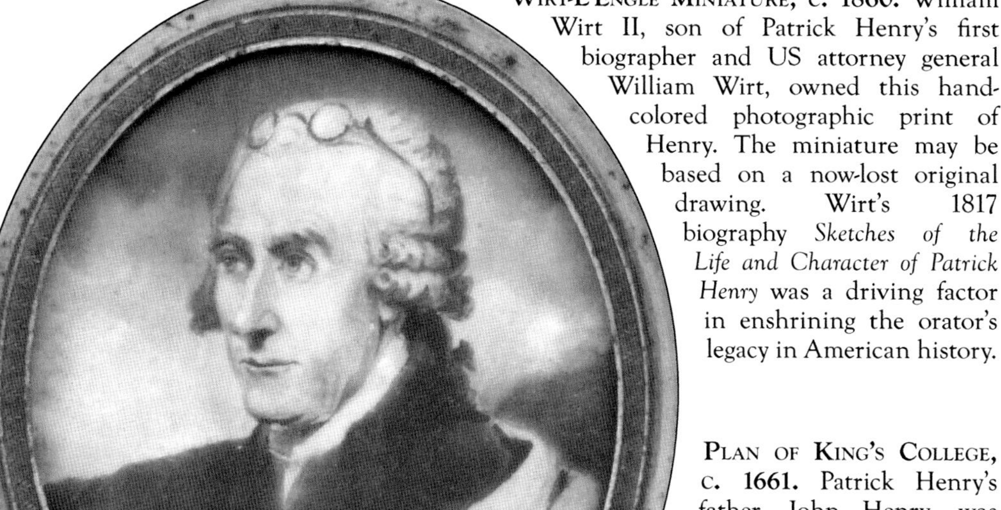

Wirt-L'Engle Miniature, c. 1860. William Wirt II, son of Patrick Henry's first biographer and US attorney general William Wirt, owned this hand-colored photographic print of Henry. The miniature may be based on a now-lost original drawing. Wirt's 1817 biography *Sketches of the Life and Character of Patrick Henry* was a driving factor in enshrining the orator's legacy in American history.

Plan of King's College, c. 1661. Patrick Henry's father, John Henry, was born in Scotland in 1704. At the age of 15, he won a Latin scholarship to King's College, Aberdeen. After four years of study, he left college to find his fortune in Virginia. Following his marriage to Sarah Winston Syme in 1733, John was appointed a vestryman, a justice of the peace, and colonel of the county militia. (WC.)

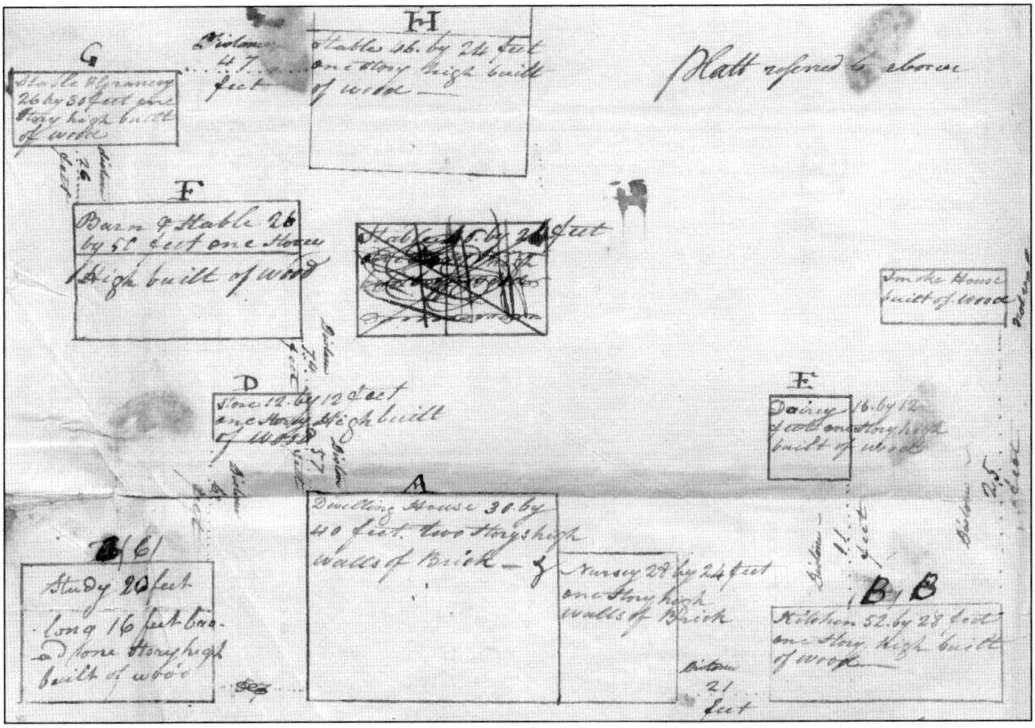

Studley, Mutual Assurance Policy, 1796. On May 29, 1736, Patrick Henry was born at Studley, a 600-acre tobacco plantation located eight miles northeast of Richmond in Hanover County, Virginia. Henry's birth home was a two-story brick structure measuring 40 by 30 feet. Built around 1720, a fire destroyed the house in 1807. When Henry was a teenager, his father moved his family to Mount Brilliant, 20 miles northwest of Studley. (LVA.)

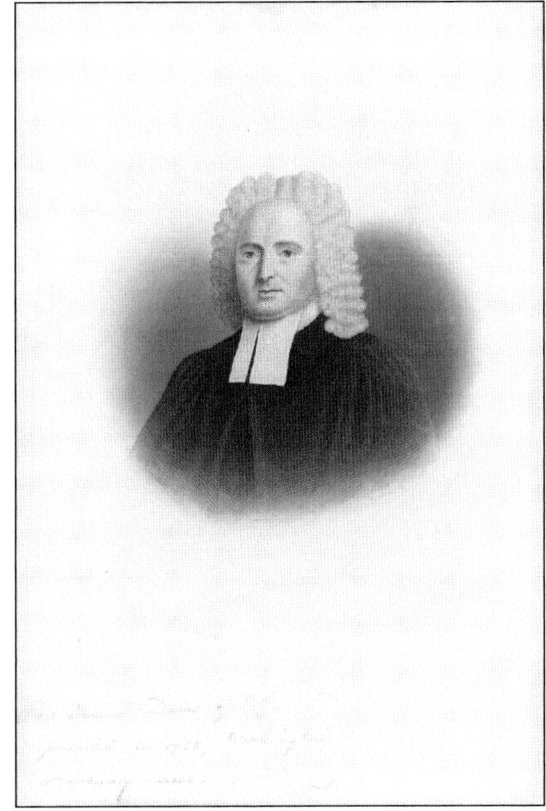

Rev. Samuel Davies, 1840. The Presbyterian evangelist Samuel Davies (1723–1761) played an important role in forming Patrick Henry's early religious views as well as his oratorical skills. During his adolescence, Henry attended the Reverend Davies's services with his mother. In later years, Henry declared Davies to be "the greatest orator he ever heard." In 1759, Samuel Davies left Hanover to become president of Princeton University. (NYPL.)

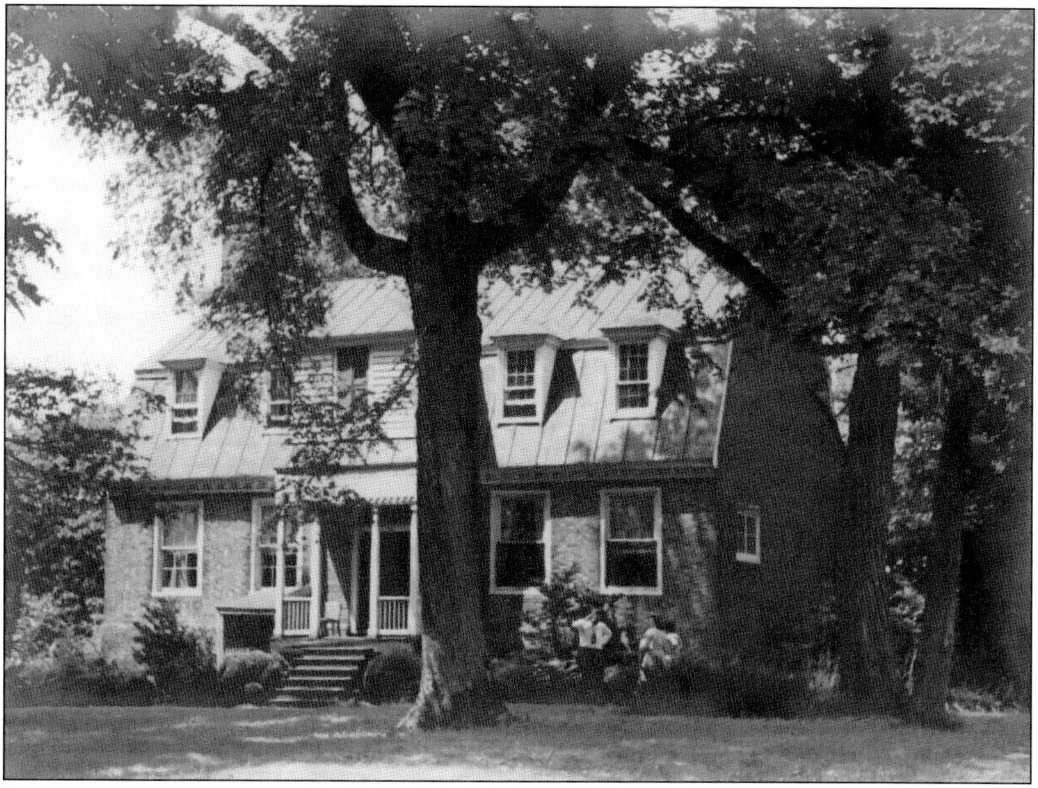

RURAL PLAINS, 1947. Situated four miles west of Studley plantation, Rural Plains was the childhood home of Patrick Henry's first wife, Sarah Shelton. The home was built by Sarah's grandfather John Shelton in 1725 and remained in the Shelton family until 2006. The house and grounds are now owned by the National Park Service as part of the Richmond National Battlefield Park.

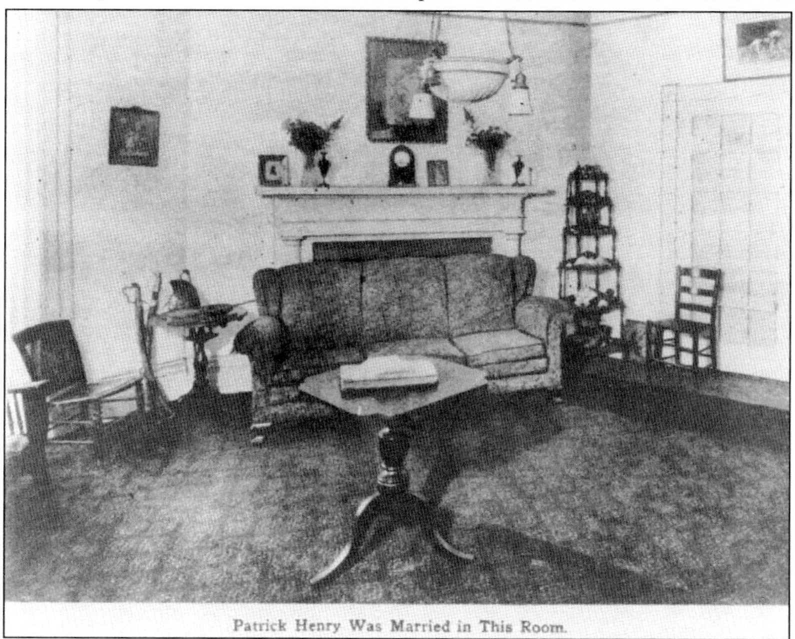

Patrick Henry Was Married in This Room.

PARLOR AT RURAL PLAINS, 1928. In 1754, at the age of 18, Patrick Henry married 16-year-old Sarah Shelton. According to family tradition, their marriage occurred in the parlor of his father-in-law's home, Rural Plains, which stands 12 miles northeast of Richmond. Sarah Henry would die in 1775, leaving behind her husband and six children.

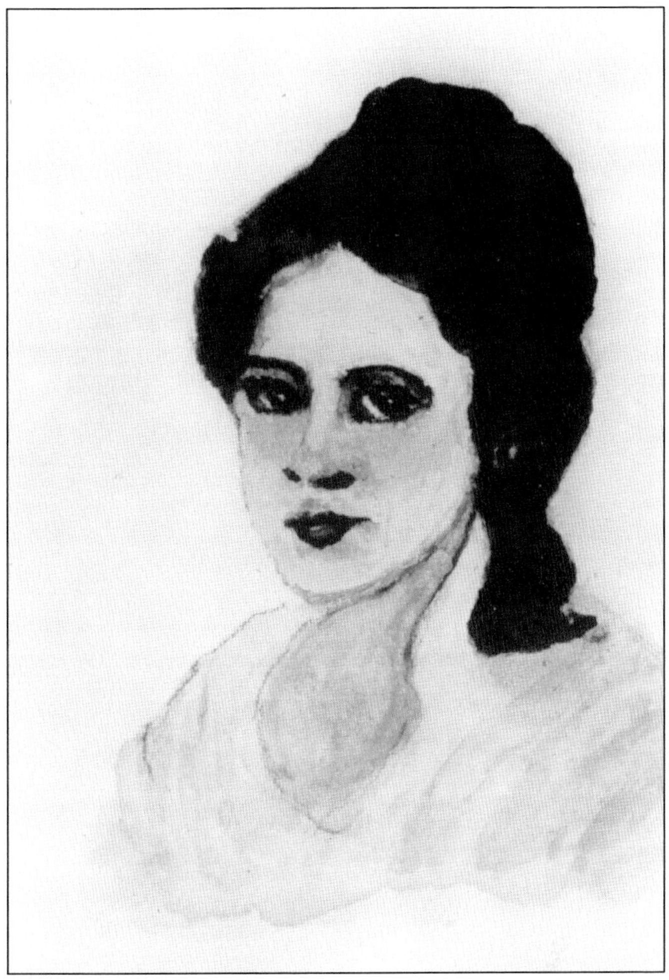

Sarah Shelton Aylett by A.L. Matthews, c. 1830. Sarah Shelton Aylett (1811–1876) was said to have greatly resembled her grandmother Sarah Shelton Henry. In 1832, Sarah married her cousin William Spotswood Fontaine, and they had five children. This portrait of Sarah hung in the passageway of Rural Plains and showcases the "Shelton features" of dark hair and even darker eyes.

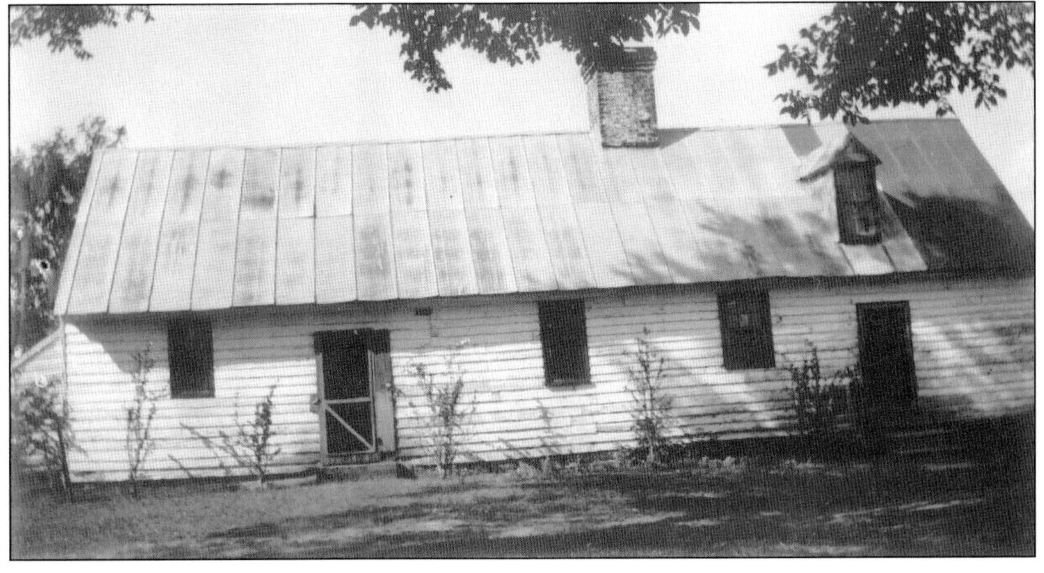

Overseer's Cottage at Piny Slash, c. 1935. As part of his wife's wedding dowry, Patrick Henry received from his father-in-law a 300-acre farm known as Piny Slash and six enslaved African Americans to work the fields. In 1757, a fire destroyed the couple's home, and according to tradition, the Henrys moved into an unoccupied overseer's house on the property. Built in 1751, the story-and-a-half wooden structure still survives. (LVA.)

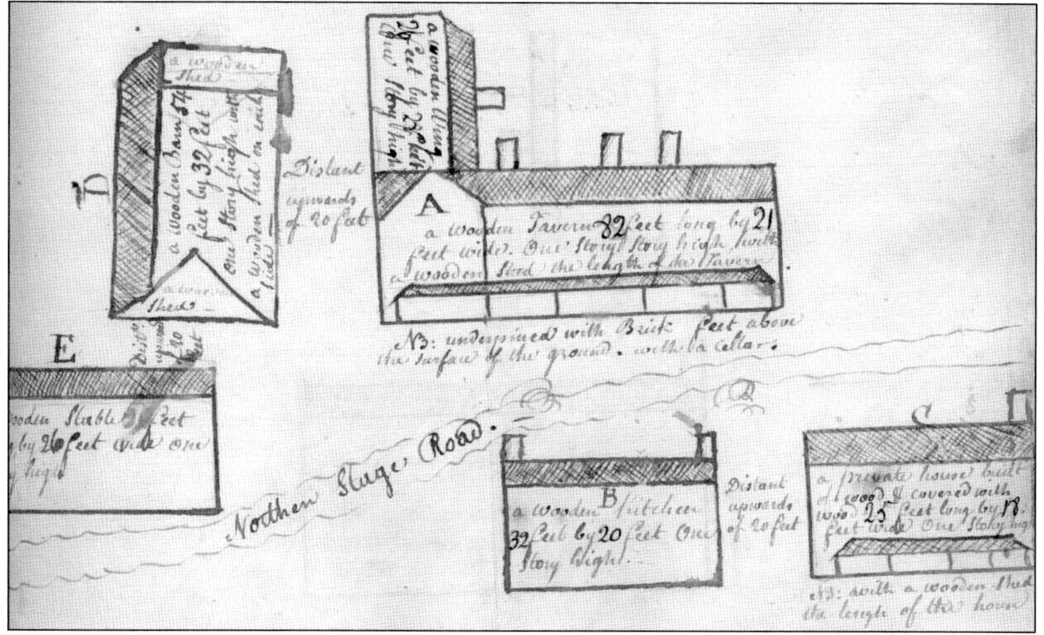

HANOVER TAVERN, MUTUAL ASSURANCE POLICY, 1801. In 1758, Patrick and his family moved into his father-in-law's tavern near Hanover Courthouse. It was here that Patrick Henry's interest in the law blossomed, and in 1760, he became a lawyer. In 1764, Shelton was forced to sell the tavern due to debt. Described as a "Tolerable handsome inn," the tavern survived into the mid-19th century. (LVA.)

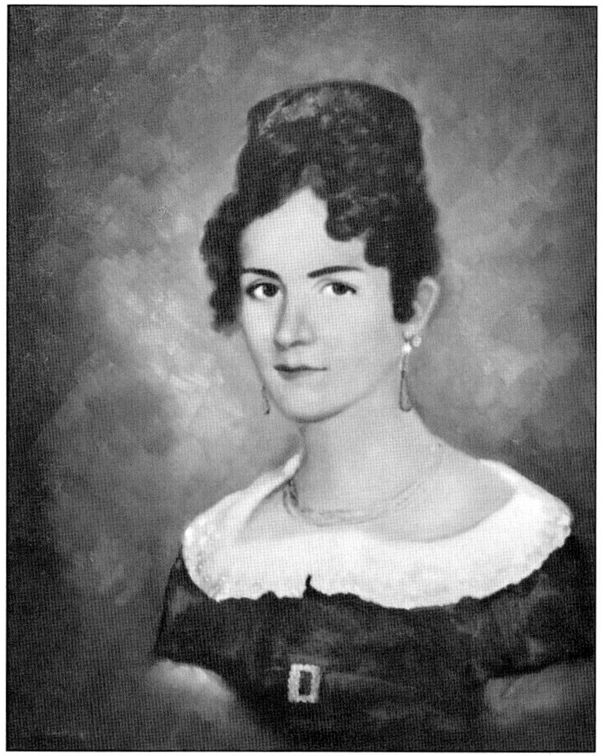

***ELIZABETH HENRY AYLETT* BY UNKNOWN, C. 1800.** This is a watercolor portrait of Patrick and Sarah Shelton Henry's daughter Elizabeth "Betsey" Henry Aylett. In 1786, Elizabeth married Philip Aylett, and they had 13 children. The pearl belt buckle, said to have been a wedding gift from her father, is now in the Red Hill collection. Elizabeth died in 1842 at the age of 73.

HANOVER COURTHOUSE, C. 1920. Hanover Courthouse was where Patrick Henry's eloquence first appeared in a civil case known as the Parsons' Cause. Henry's philippic against the king for nullifying a "good law" passed during a time of financial strife earned him a reputation as a spokesman for the common man. Completed by 1740, the arcaded brick courthouse still stands.

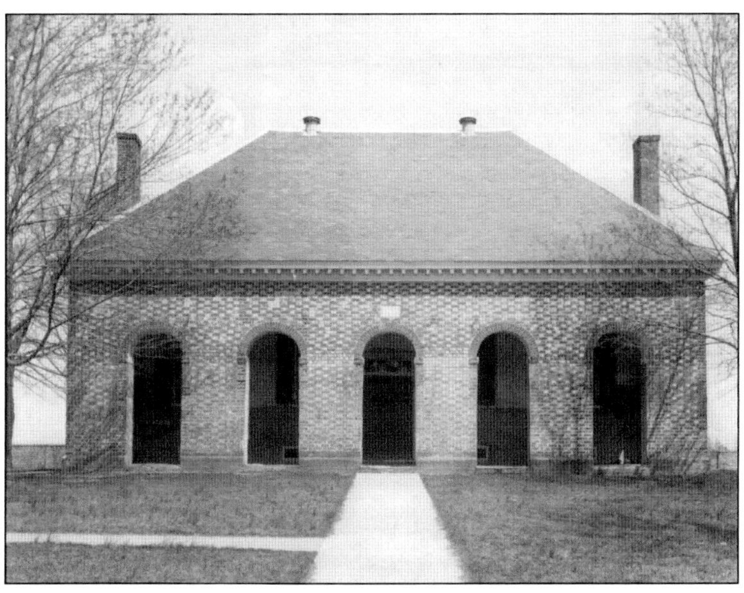

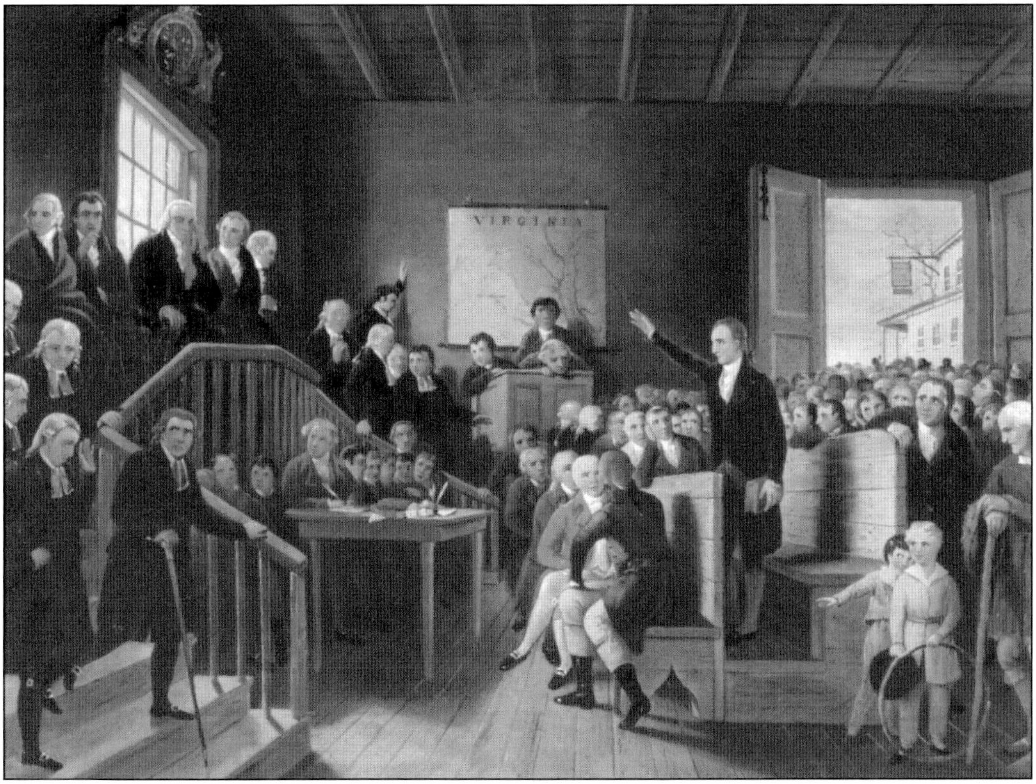

***PATRICK HENRY ARGUES THE PARSONS' CAUSE* BY GEORGE COOKE, C. 1834.** This oil painting by artist George Cooke depicts Patrick Henry denouncing the Anglican clergy during the Parsons' Cause for their greed and avarice. His father, the chief magistrate, is seen on the bench weeping with pride as Anglican clergymen descend the stairs and file out of the courtroom. Hanover Tavern can be seen through the open doors. (VMHC.)

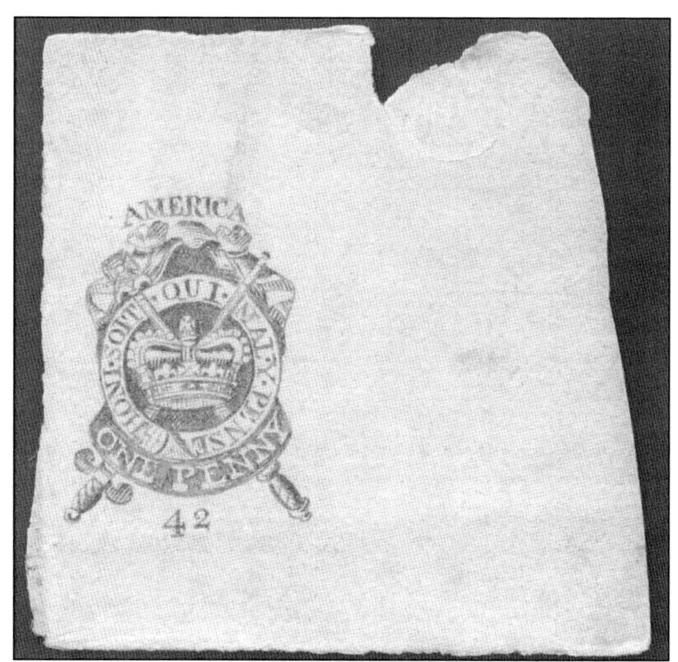

Stamp Act Proof, 1765. The Stamp Act of 1765 taxed colonists without representation in the British Parliament. Newspapers, legal documents, and even playing cards were required to have an official paper stamp purchased by the colonists. Patrick Henry led Virginia's official resistance to the illegal tax and, according to Thomas Jefferson, "gave the first impulse to the ball of revolution." (SI.)

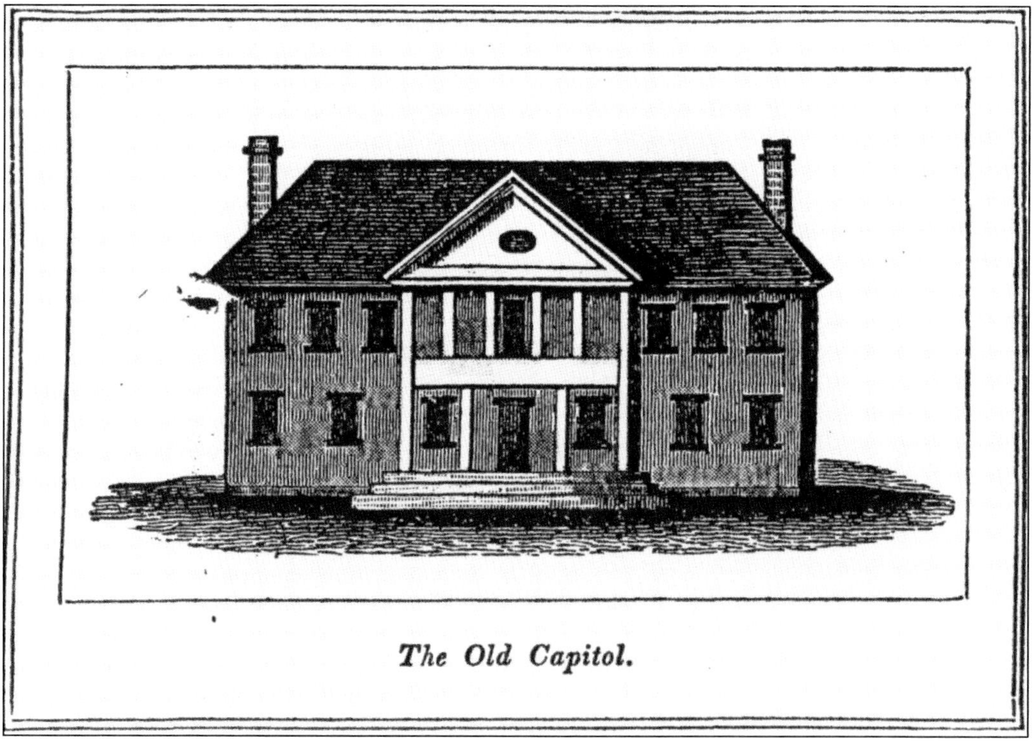

The Old Capitol.

Second Williamsburg Capitol, 1845. This engraving by Henry Howe depicts the capitol building of Virginia that stood from 1753 to 1832. It was in this building that Patrick Henry introduced his history-changing resolutions against the Stamp Act in 1765. It was also the site where the Fifth Virginia Convention declared the colony "free and independent" from Great Britain on May 15, 1776.

Resolved

That the first Adventurers and Settlers of this his Majesties Colony and Dominion brought with them and transmitted to their Posterity and all other his Majesties Subjects since inhabiting in this his Majesties said Colony all the Priviledges, Franchises & Immunities that have at any Time been held, enjoyed & possessed by the People of Great Britain.

Resolved

That by the two royal Charters granted by King James the first the Colonists aforesaid are declared entitled to all the Priviledges, Liberties & Immunities of Denizens and natural born Subjects to all Intents and Purposes as if they had been abiding and born within the Realm of England.

Resolved.

That the Taxation of the People by themselves or by Persons chosen by themselves to represent them who can only know what Taxes the People are able to bear and the easiest Mode of raising them and are equally affected by such Taxes themselves is the distinguishing Characteristick of British Freedom and without which the ancient Constitution cannot subsist.

Resolved That his Majesties liege People of this most ancient Colony have uninterruptedly enjoyed the Right of being thus governed by their own Assembly in the Article of their Taxes and internal Police and that the same hath never been forfeited or any other Way given up but hath been constantly recognized by the Kings & People of Great Britain.

Resolved Therefore that the General Assembly of this Colony have the only sole exclusive Right & Power to lay Taxes & Impositions upon the Inhabitants of this Colony and that every Attempt to vest such Power in any Person or Persons whatsoever other than the General Assembly aforesaid has a manifest Tendency to destroy British as well as American Freedom.

VIRGINIA RESOLVES, 1765. According to many of his contemporaries, Patrick Henry's actions against the Stamp Act of 1765 created the initial chasm in the relationship between the colonies and Great Britain. The relationship would never recover. He was a new member of the prestigious House of Burgesses, and on May 30, 1765, he argued the validity of the tax, which was placed by Parliament upon the American colonies. His arguments in defense of the resolutions, which eventually passed by a single vote, resulted in the accusation of treason by the house speaker. After Patrick Henry's death, a page was found among his papers, sealed and thus endorsed: "Inclosed are the resolutions of the Virginia Assembly in 1765, concerning the Stamp Act. Let my executors open this paper." On the reverse page, Henry wrote, "Upon offering them to the house violent debates ensued." This manuscript remained at Red Hill until sold at auction in 1910. (CWF.)

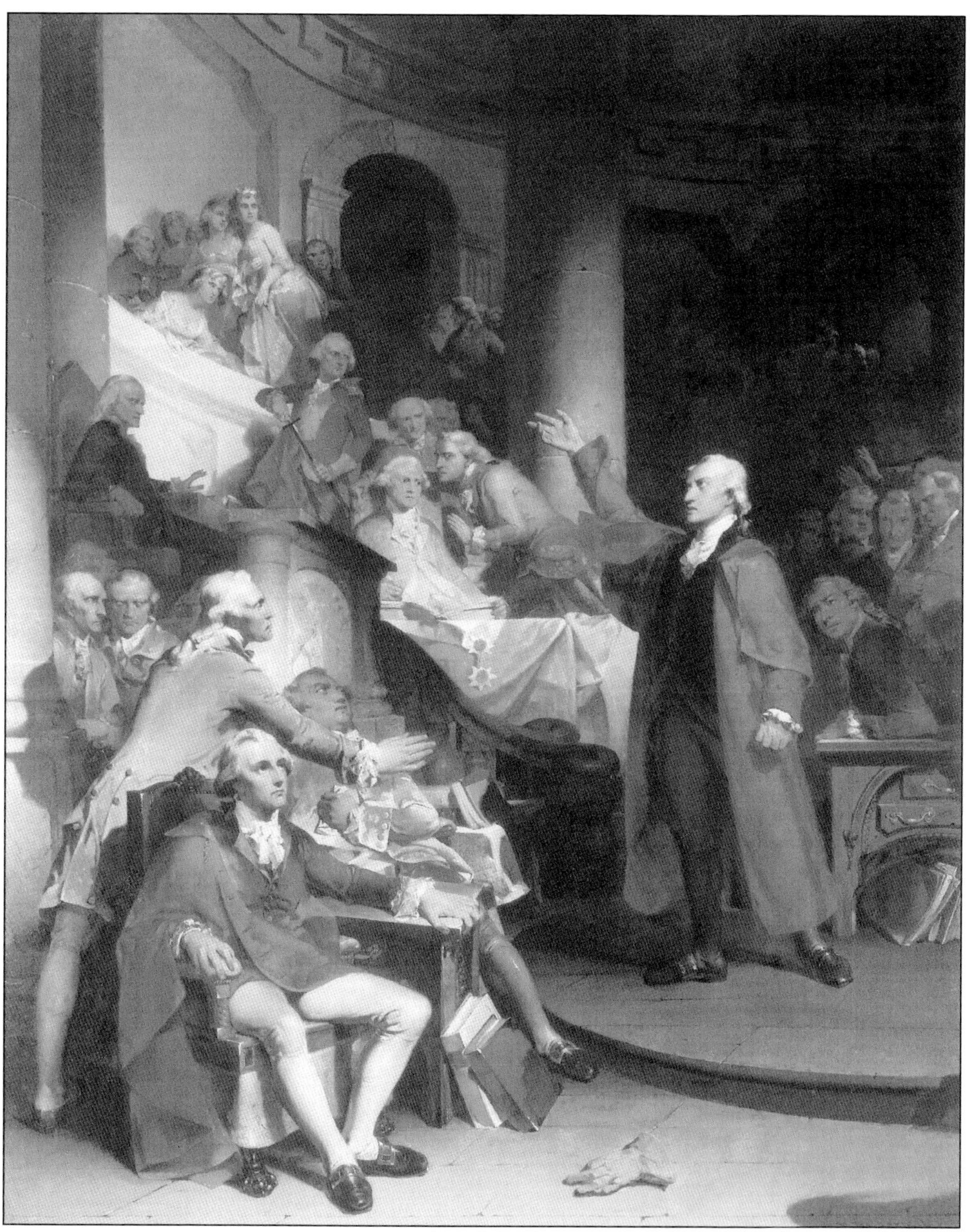

PATRICK HENRY *BEFORE THE* VIRGINIA HOUSE *OF* BURGESSES BY PETER F. ROTHERMEL, 1851. Patrick Henry's rise to fame climaxed with his Virginia Resolves in 1765. As a junior member of the House of Burgesses, Henry introduced five resolutions against the recently passed Stamp Act. Henry provoked cries of "Treason!" from the more conservative delegates when he declared: "Tarquin and Caesar had each his Brutus, Charles the First his Cromwell, and George the Third may profit from their example . . . if this be treason, make the most of it!" These immortal words were illustrated in this painting by Philadelphia artist Peter Frederick Rothermel. The painting became an immediate sensation. It traveled the country on exhibition for over a decade—including a stint in the US Capitol—and cemented Henry's legacy into the 19th century and beyond. Today, Rothermel's *Patrick Henry* is on permanent display at Red Hill.

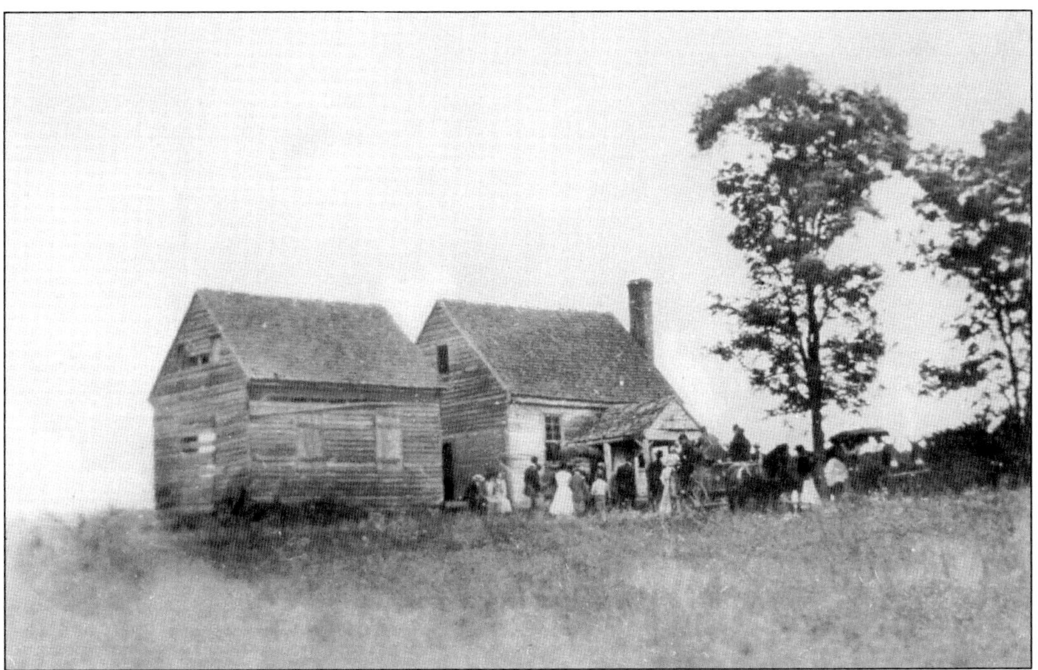

Roundabout Plantation, c. 1905. Located in Louisa County, Virginia, Roundabout plantation was the home of the Henrys from 1765 through 1770. It was here that Patrick Henry's wife first began to show signs of mental illness. The modest 18-foot-by-20-foot story-and-a-half wood structure was the only one of Henry's homes built for him. The house survived until the 1920s.

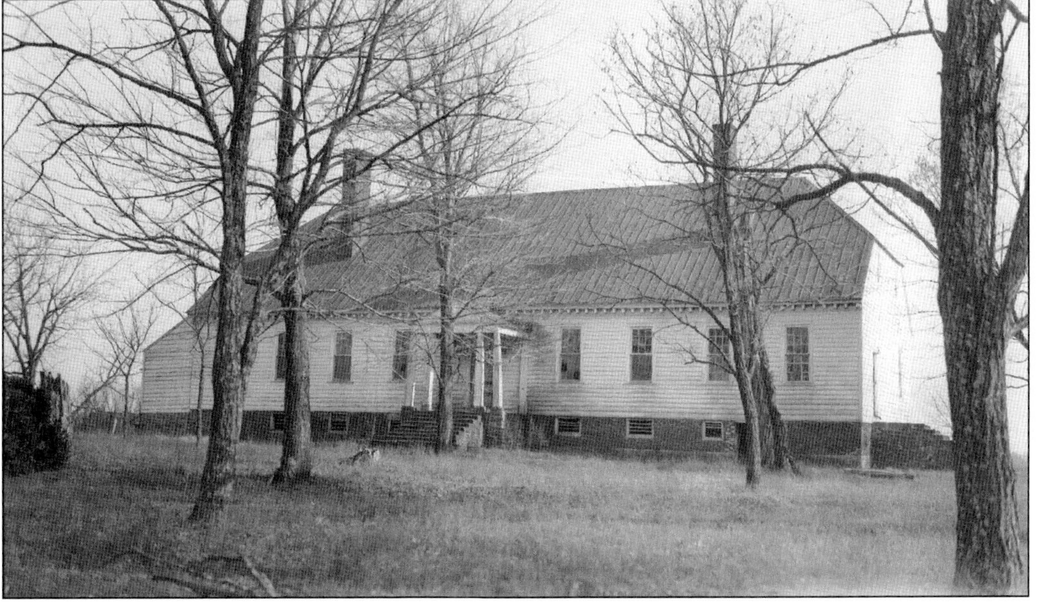

Scotch Town Plantation, 1936. Patrick Henry purchased Scotch Town in 1770 "with the fond hope of improving his wife's waning health." Still standing today, contemporary Baron Von Closen described Scotch Town as one of the most "spacious and handsome" homes in all of Virginia. Henry traveled from this property to attend the First and Second Continental Congresses as well as the Second Virginia Convention in Richmond. (LOC.)

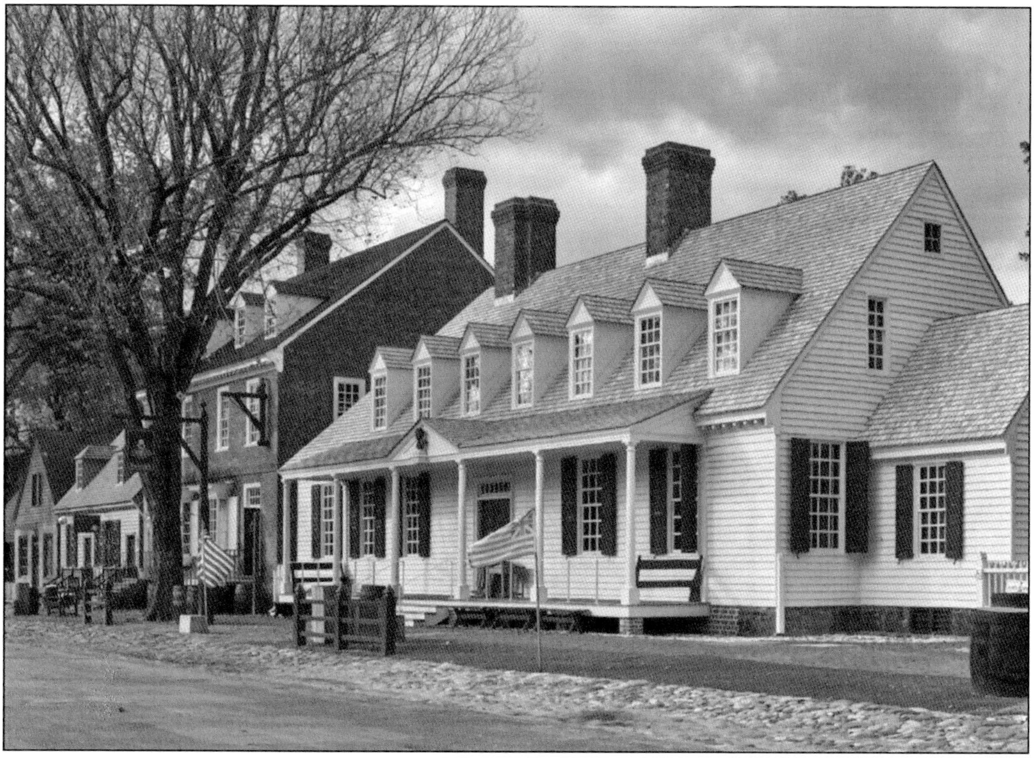

Raleigh Tavern, Williamsburg, 2019. Described as "the Town Meetinghouse of the South," the Raleigh Tavern was a meeting place for Virginia's leading patriots. Here, in 1773, Patrick Henry and Thomas Jefferson met to develop an intercolonial Committee of Correspondence. In 1774, after being dissolved by Governor Dunmore, the burgesses met here to draw up a nonimportation of British goods and to call for the meeting of a Continental Congress. (LOC.)

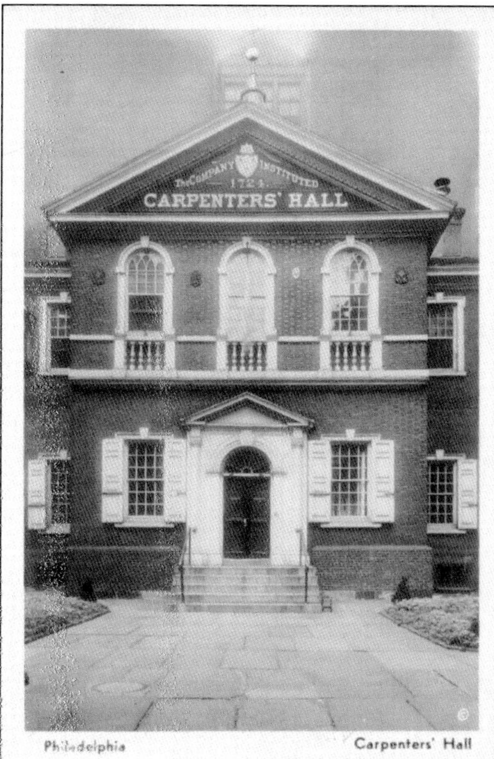

Carpenters' Hall, Philadelphia, 1936. Built by and for the Carpenters' Guild of Philadelphia, Carpenters' Hall was the meeting place for the First Continental Congress from September 5 to September 26, 1774. On September 6, Patrick Henry (one of seven delegates from Virginia) delivered his "I am not a Virginian, but an American!" speech before Congress to unify the colonies against Parliamentary oppression. (LOC.)

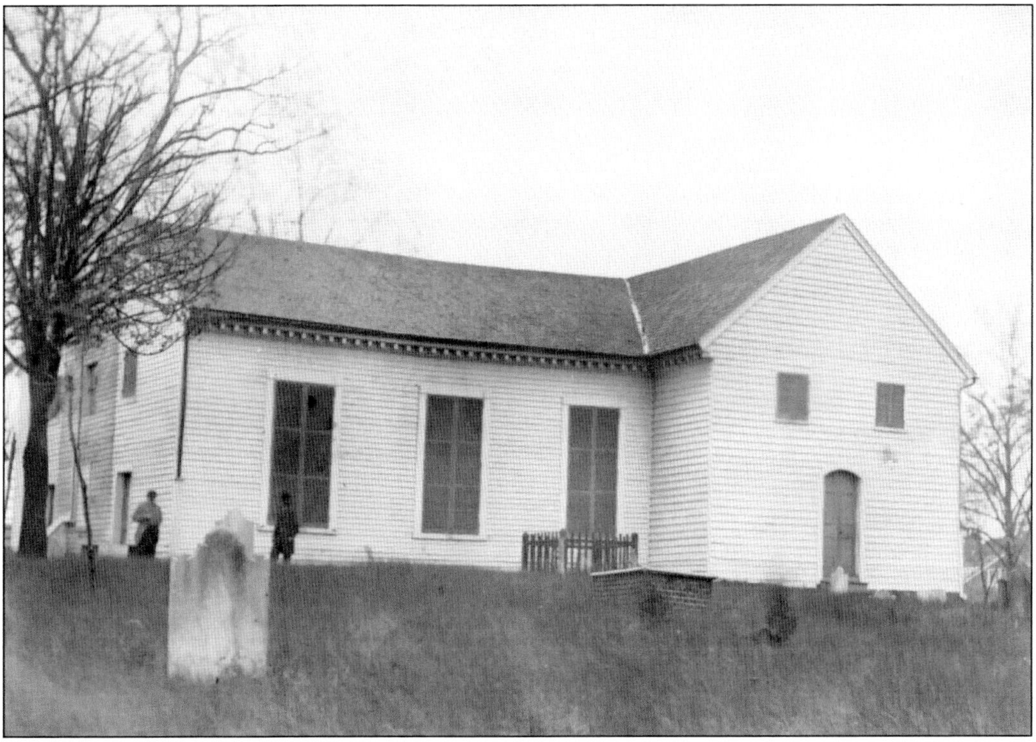

St. John's Episcopal Church, c. 1863. From March 20 to 27, 1775, over 120 delegates of the Second Virginia Convention crowded into this building, then known as Henrico Parish Church, in Richmond. On the fourth day of proceedings, Patrick Henry gave his immortal cry of "Give me liberty or give me death!" to encourage the raising of independent militia companies throughout Virginia in case war with England became necessary. (LOC.)

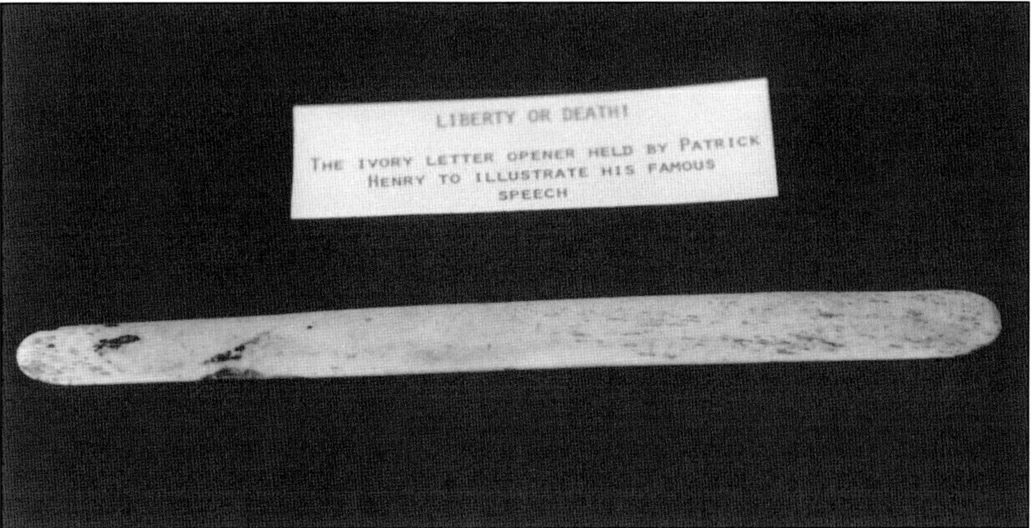

Patrick Henry's Paper Cutter, 1977. This whalebone paper cutter was said to have been held by Patrick Henry during his "Liberty or Death!" speech in 1775. At the end of his famous oration, the patriot thrust this paper cutter toward his breast like a dagger piercing his heart. The prized possession remained in the Henry family until 1976. It is now on display at Red Hill.

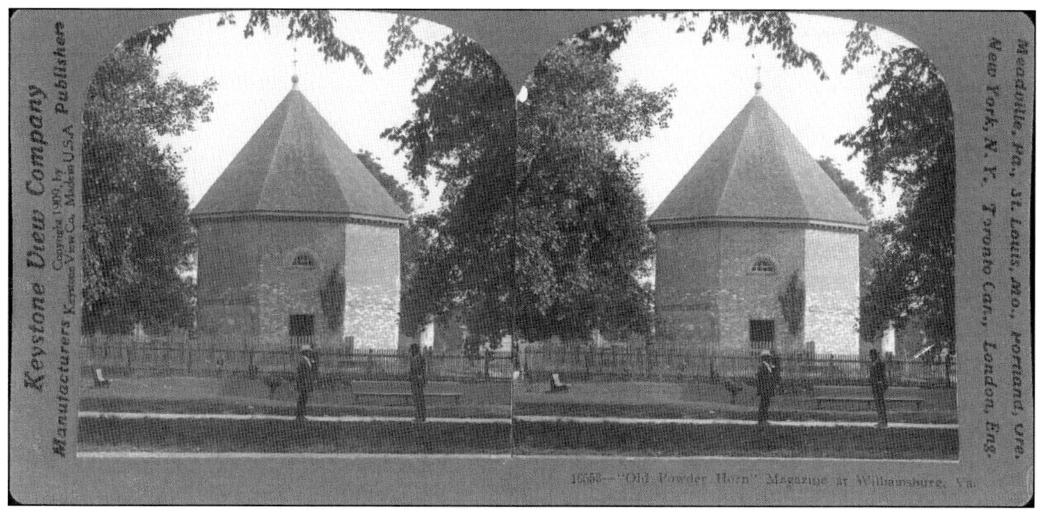

POWDER MAGAZINE, WILLIAMSBURG, 1909. On April 21, 1775, the royal governor of Virginia, Lord Dunmore, ordered the removal of the colony's gunpowder from the magazine in Williamsburg to a British warship. In response, Patrick Henry led an armed militia group toward the capital to demand the return or payment of the stolen gunpowder. This was "the first overt act of war in Virginia," recalled Thomas Jefferson. (LOC.)

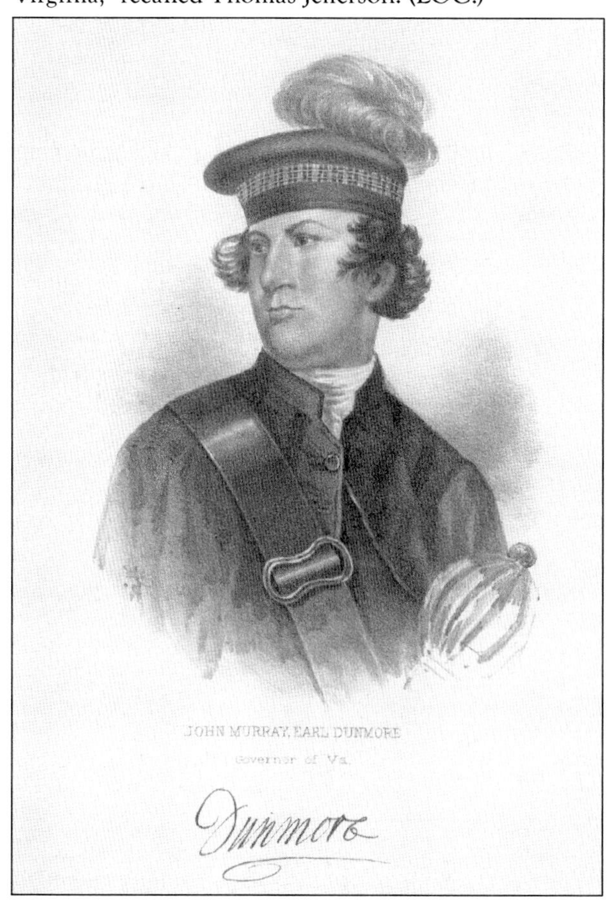

JOHN MURRAY, 4TH EARL OF DUNMORE, 1880. Scottish-born Murray became royal governor of the Colony of Virginia in 1771 and remained popular until the Gunpowder Incident of 1775. After Patrick Henry forced payment for powder removed from the Williamsburg Magazine, Dunmore issued a proclamation charging Henry with extortion and forbidding the citizenry to assist Henry in any way. This proclamation was not revoked until 1986. (NYPL.)

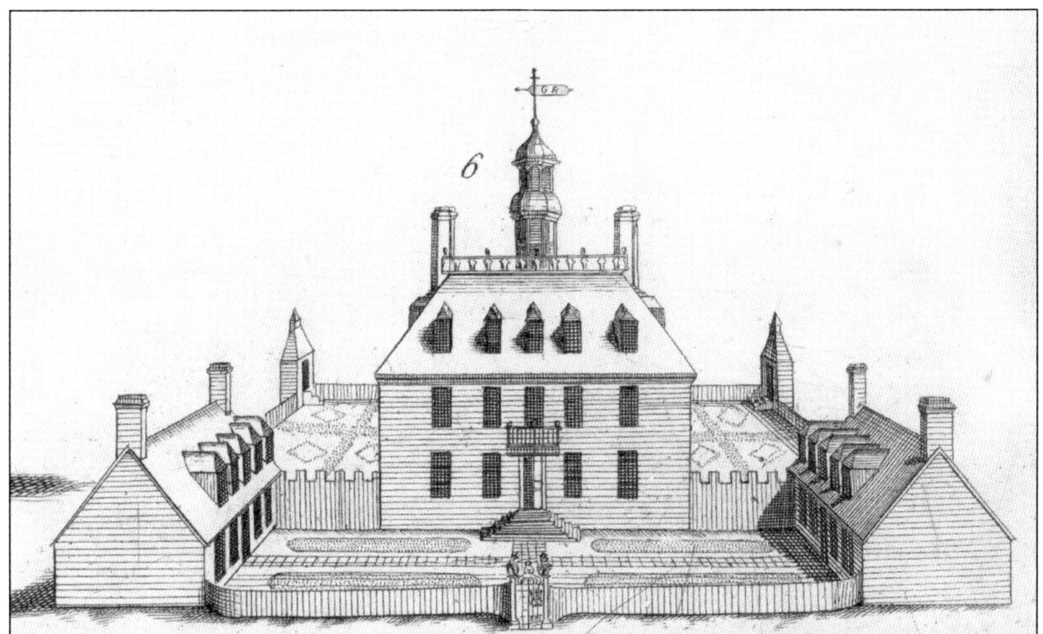

Governor's Palace, c. 1735. On June 29, 1776, the Fifth Virginia Convention elected Patrick Henry the first governor of the commonwealth. From 1776 to 1779, Henry resided at the Governor's Palace in Williamsburg, which had served as the official residence of seven royal governors before the revolution. During his second term, Henry married Dorothea Dandridge, the granddaughter of the first occupant of the palace, Lt. Gov. Alexander Spotswood. (LOC.)

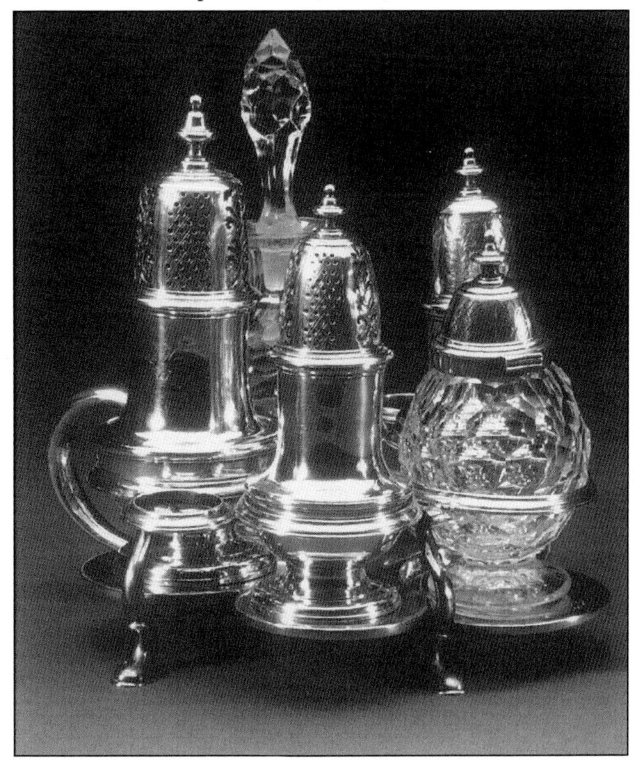

Patrick Henry's Caster Set, c. 1996. Patrick Henry purchased this caster set—made by London silversmith Thomas Rush—from the estate of Lord Dunmore in June 1776. Henry may have engraved each piece with "PH 1777" to celebrate his marriage to Dorothea Dandridge on October 9, 1777. The couple used it while living at the Governor's Palace. It features silver and glass cruets that hold sugar, pepper, vinegar, mustard, and other condiments.

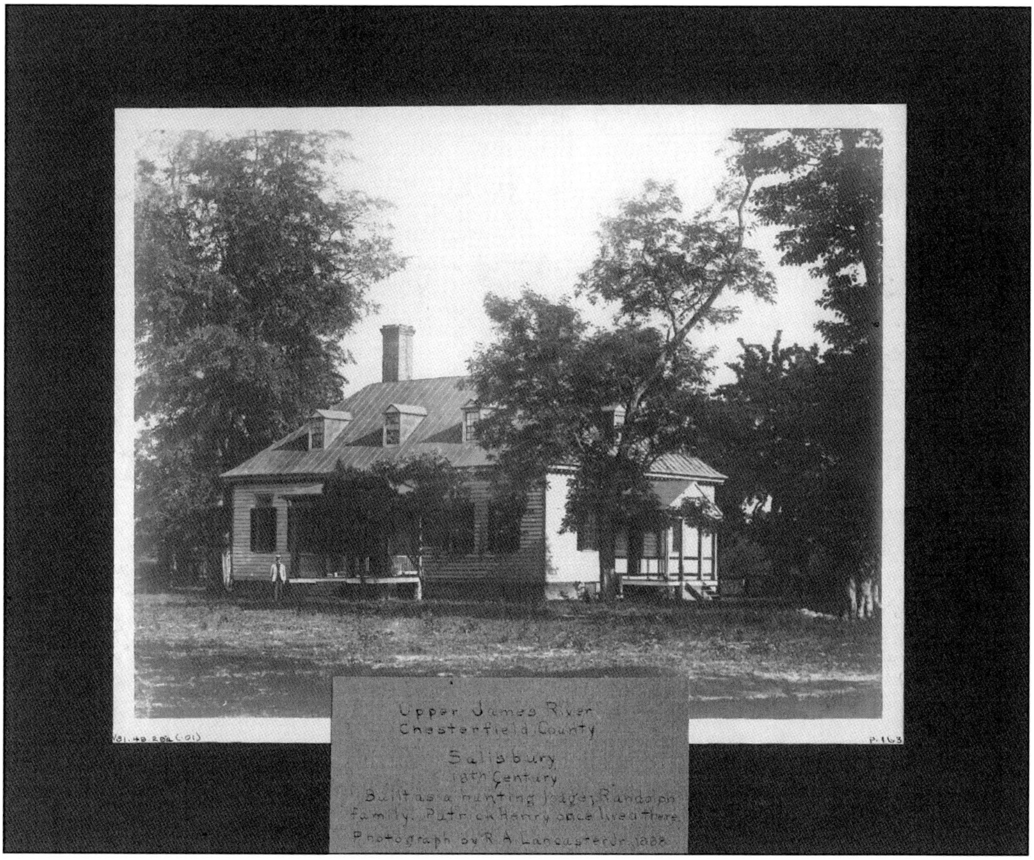

SALISBURY PLANTATION, 1888. Finding the governor's residence in Richmond too small to accommodate his large family, Patrick Henry rented Salisbury from Thomas Mann Randolph during his fourth and fifth terms as governor (1784–1786). The commodious house sat on a 1,500-acre plantation on the outskirts of Richmond, where Chesterfield Country Club stands today. Fire destroyed the house in 1923. (TV.)

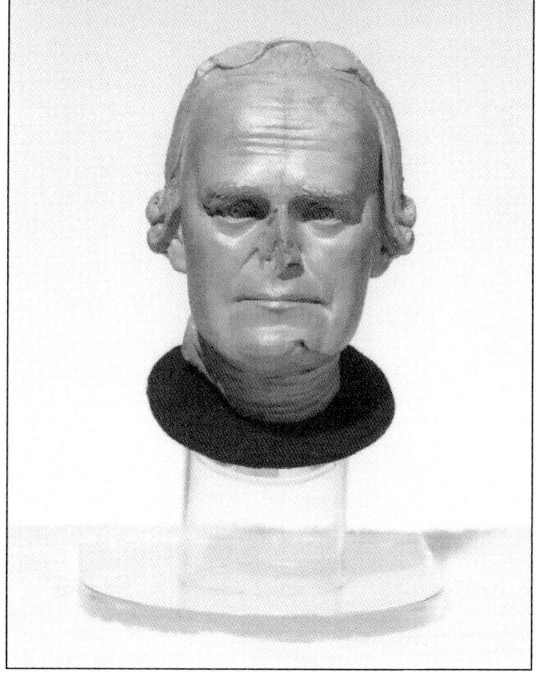

***PATRICK HENRY* BY UNKNOWN, 1996.** Described as a "perfect likeness" by his family, this terra-cotta bust is the only sculpture of Patrick Henry executed from life. Made by an unknown Italian artist, Henry sat for it at the request of his friends while attending the Virginia Ratifying Convention in Richmond in 1788. Originally a three-quarter-length bust, the entire piece from the neck down was destroyed some time in the 20th century.

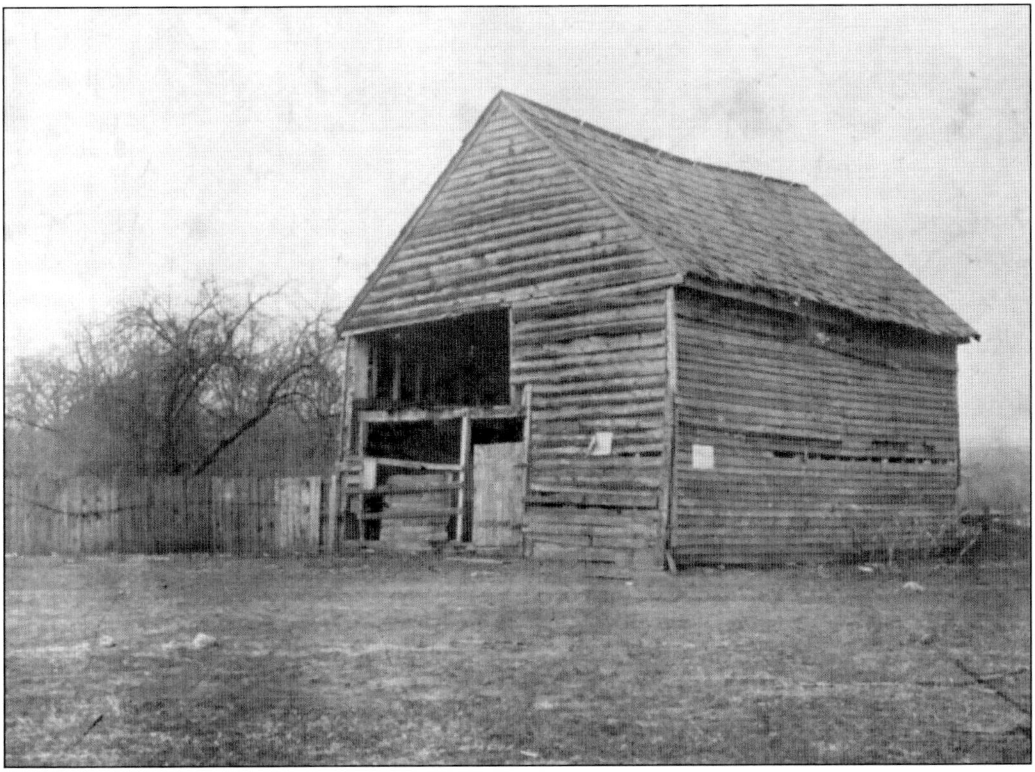

Old Charlotte Courthouse, c. 1890. Constructed in 1785 and painted patriotic red, white, and blue, this wooden courthouse was replaced by a larger brick courthouse in 1823. The building was then used as a stable until its demolition around 1920. Patrick Henry gave his last political speech, opposing the Virginia-Kentucky Resolutions, at Charlotte Courthouse on March 4, 1799.

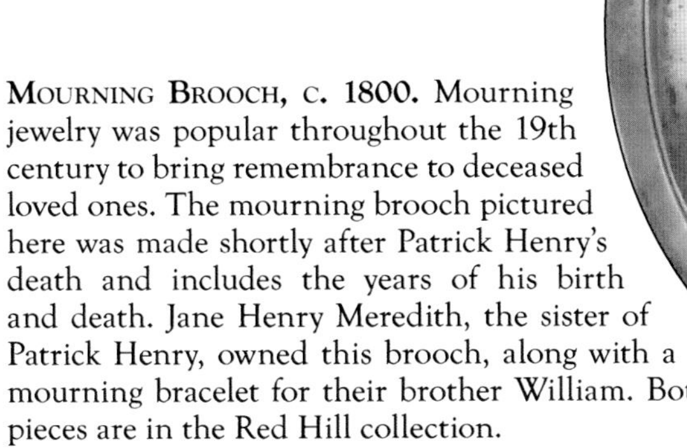

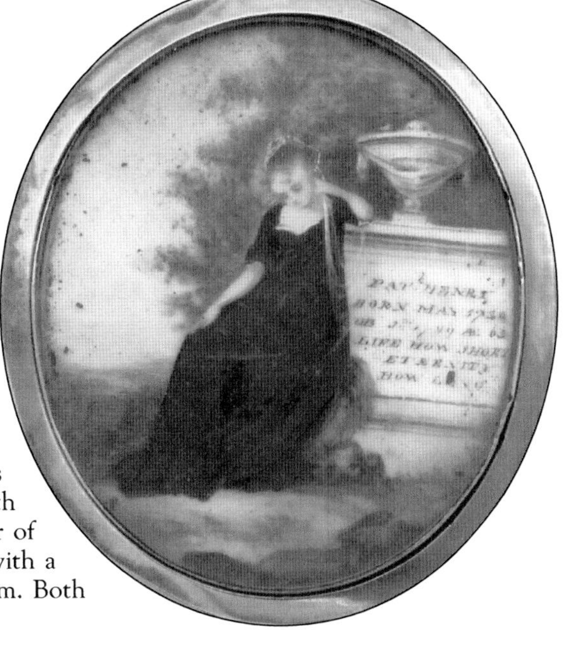

Mourning Brooch, c. 1800. Mourning jewelry was popular throughout the 19th century to bring remembrance to deceased loved ones. The mourning brooch pictured here was made shortly after Patrick Henry's death and includes the years of his birth and death. Jane Henry Meredith, the sister of Patrick Henry, owned this brooch, along with a mourning bracelet for their brother William. Both pieces are in the Red Hill collection.

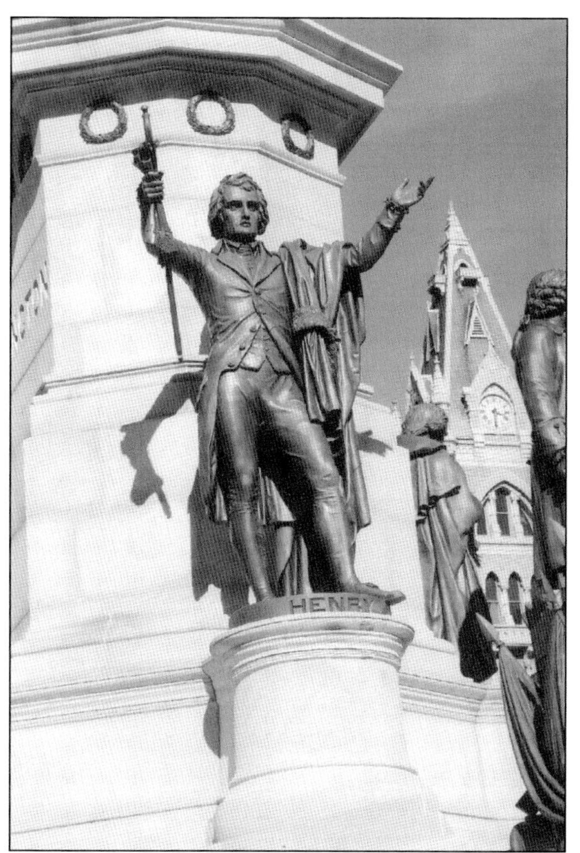

VIRGINIA WASHINGTON MONUMENT, C. 2005. Located on Capital Square in Richmond, Virginia, George Washington sits atop his horse with six other Virginians from the American Revolution around the base. Designed by sculptor Thomas Crawford and completed in 1869, the monument stands 21 feet tall. It features full-body figures of Patrick Henry, Thomas Jefferson, John Marshall, George Mason, Andrew Lewis, and Thomas Nelson Jr.

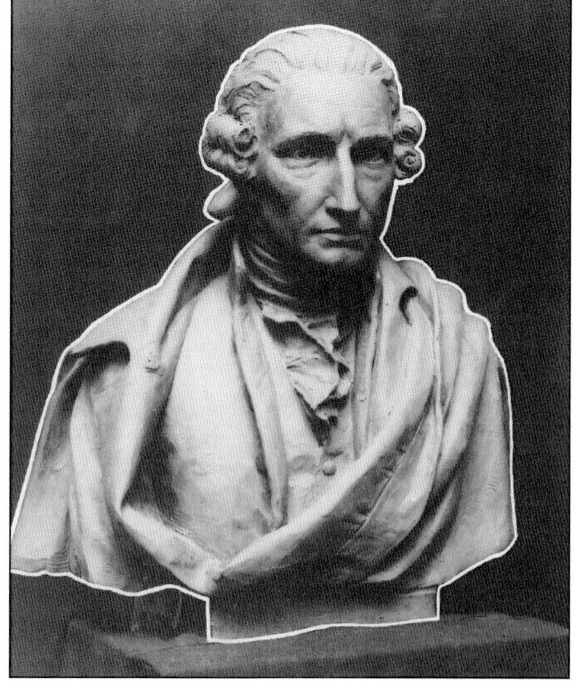

PATRICK HENRY BY CHARLES KECK, C. 1931. Noted American artist Charles Keck sculpted this bronze bust of Patrick Henry in 1930 for the Hall of Fame for Great Americans at New York University, now the campus of Bronx Community College. Keck based his sculpture on Thomas Sully's famous 1815 portrait of the patriot. Henry's bust stands today with 95 other honorees in a loggia designed by architect Stanford White.

Two

Garden Spot of the World 1600–1799

While Red Hill is most closely associated with the American patriot Patrick Henry, the property was a domicile long before he bought the land in 1794. Through the centuries before Henry, Indigenous communities lived along the banks of the Staunton River, including the Saponi tribe. In 1714, Virginia's acting governor, Alexander Spotswood (grandfather of Patrick Henry's wife Dorothea Dandridge), established a reservation at Fort Christanna in Brunswick County for these and other tribes to live in safety. Archaeology performed at Red Hill suggests a Saponi settlement was in place until the early 1700s, when Indigenous people were likely responsible for planting an extant Osage orange tree on the property. Tradition says one of the tribesmen lived in a nearby cave and fathered an enslaved coachman of the Henry family.

Richard Booker owned swathes of land along the Staunton River, and his son Richard Marot Booker inherited the 700-acre Red Hill Tract by 1772. Red Hill is believed to have been established as a plantation in the 1770s and was the home of Booker and his family until its purchase by Patrick Henry on March 14, 1794.

When Henry purchased Red Hill, bordered on the southwest by the Staunton River, he and his family lived at Long Island plantation, located 13 miles upstream. The Henrys split their time between the two plantations before moving full-time to Red Hill in 1796. The plantation had a single story-and-a-half frame house and a detached kitchen and office. Enslaved communities lived in quarters on the western portion of the estate. This area, known as Quarter Place, contains a cemetery where over 147 African Americans have been laid to rest.

At Patrick Henry's death in 1799, Red Hill had grown to 2,965 acres. The most profitable of his plantations, Red Hill produced around 20,000 pounds of tobacco leaf a year through the labor of his enslaved workers. It was to an enslaved person that Henry referred to Red Hill as "one of the garden spots of the world."

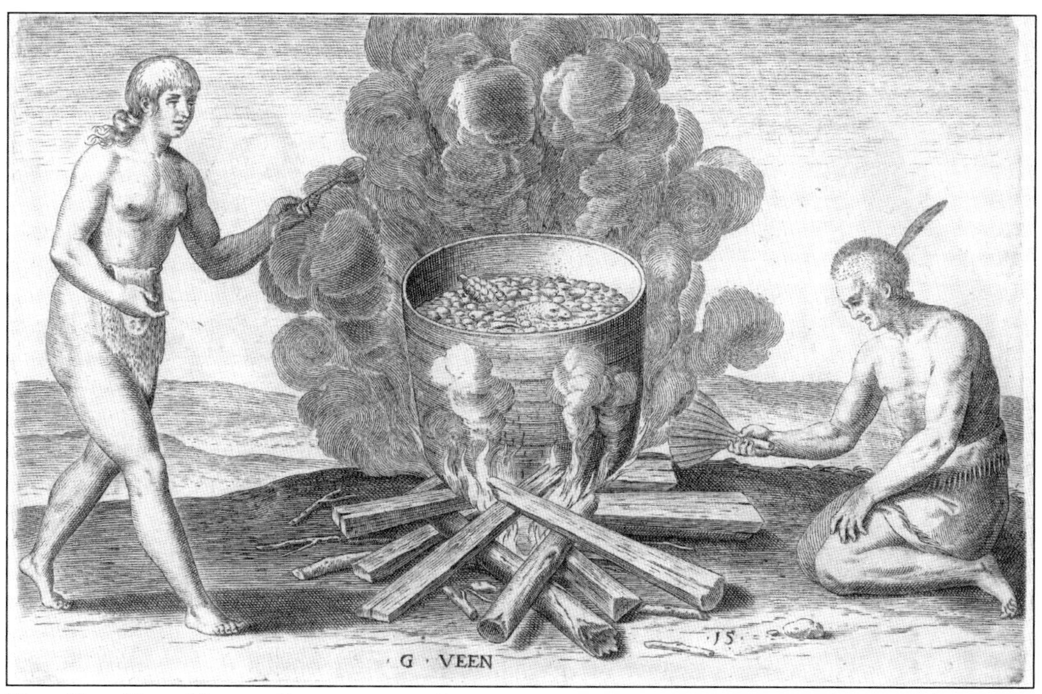

HOW THEY BOIL MEAT IN EARTHENWARE POTS BY THEODORE DE BRY, 1590. Before Patrick Henry's arrival at Red Hill, groups of Siouan-speaking Indigenous peoples called the land their home. They built a village and resided here year-round, constructing homes and hunting seasonal game. Images of Virginia tribes engaging in hunting and food preparation, such as the one seen here, were published for de Bry's America book series. (LVA.)

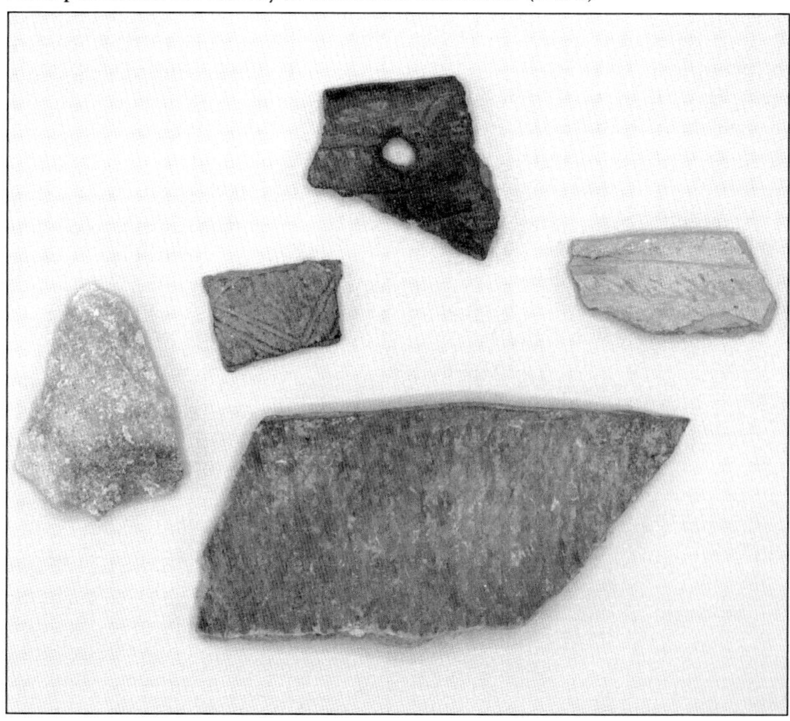

CERAMIC SHERDS, 2024. Archaeologists uncovered these ceramic sherds and projectile points at an Indigenous American site along the Staunton River in 1965. Most of these ceramics are Dan River Ware, linked to Indigenous groups in the Southern Piedmont from 1300 to 1725 CE. Artisans crafted these vessels, which were used for cooking, drinking, and storage, from clay mixed with sand or quartz.

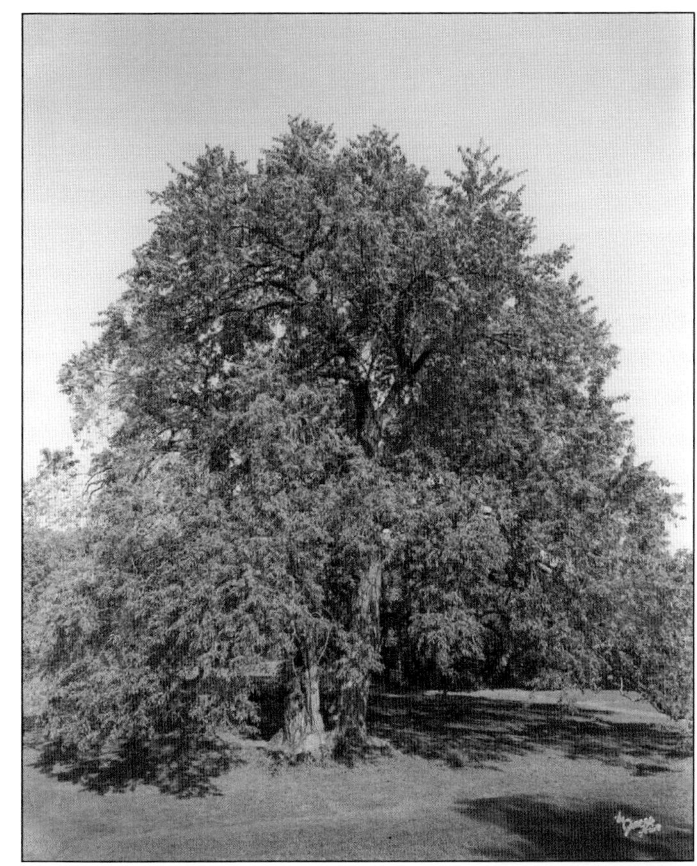

Osage Orange Tree, c. 1960. This Osage orange tree (*Maclura pomifera*) near Patrick Henry's house at Red Hill is the largest of its species in North America and has been estimated at nearly 350 years old. Not indigenous to the region, it is believed that the tree cutting was passed along the North Indian trade network to the Saponi Indians who once lived in the area.

Staunton River, c. 1948. The Roanoke River becomes the Staunton River in the middle of its path through Virginia. The Staunton has been a source of food, water, and transportation for early Indigenous tribes, followed by white explorers and settlers. By his death in 1799, Patrick Henry owned close to 8,000 acres along the Staunton River.

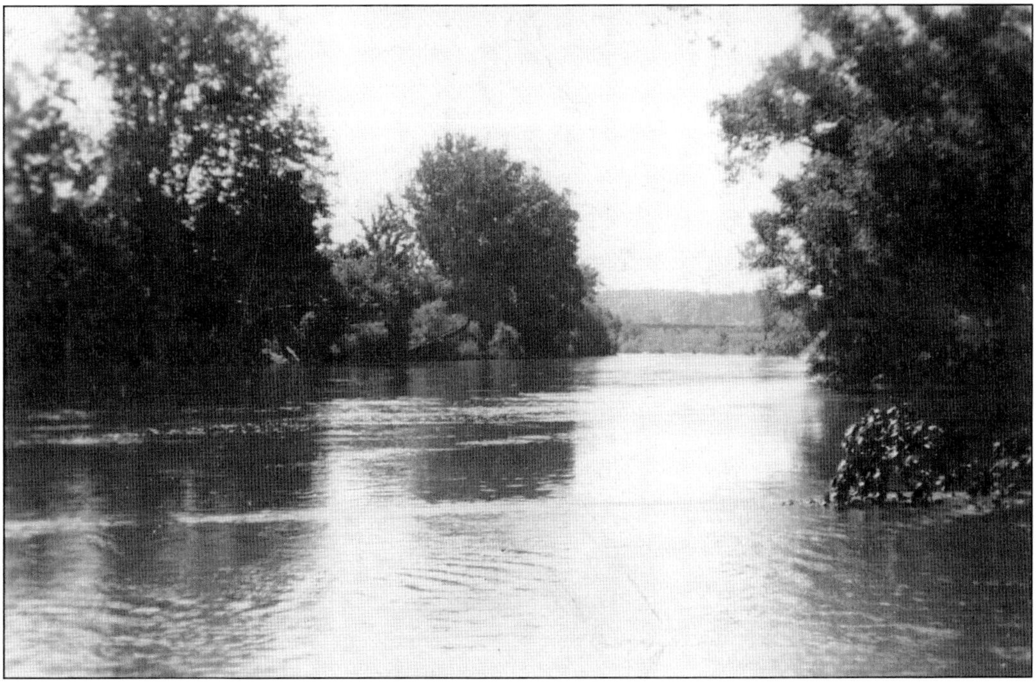

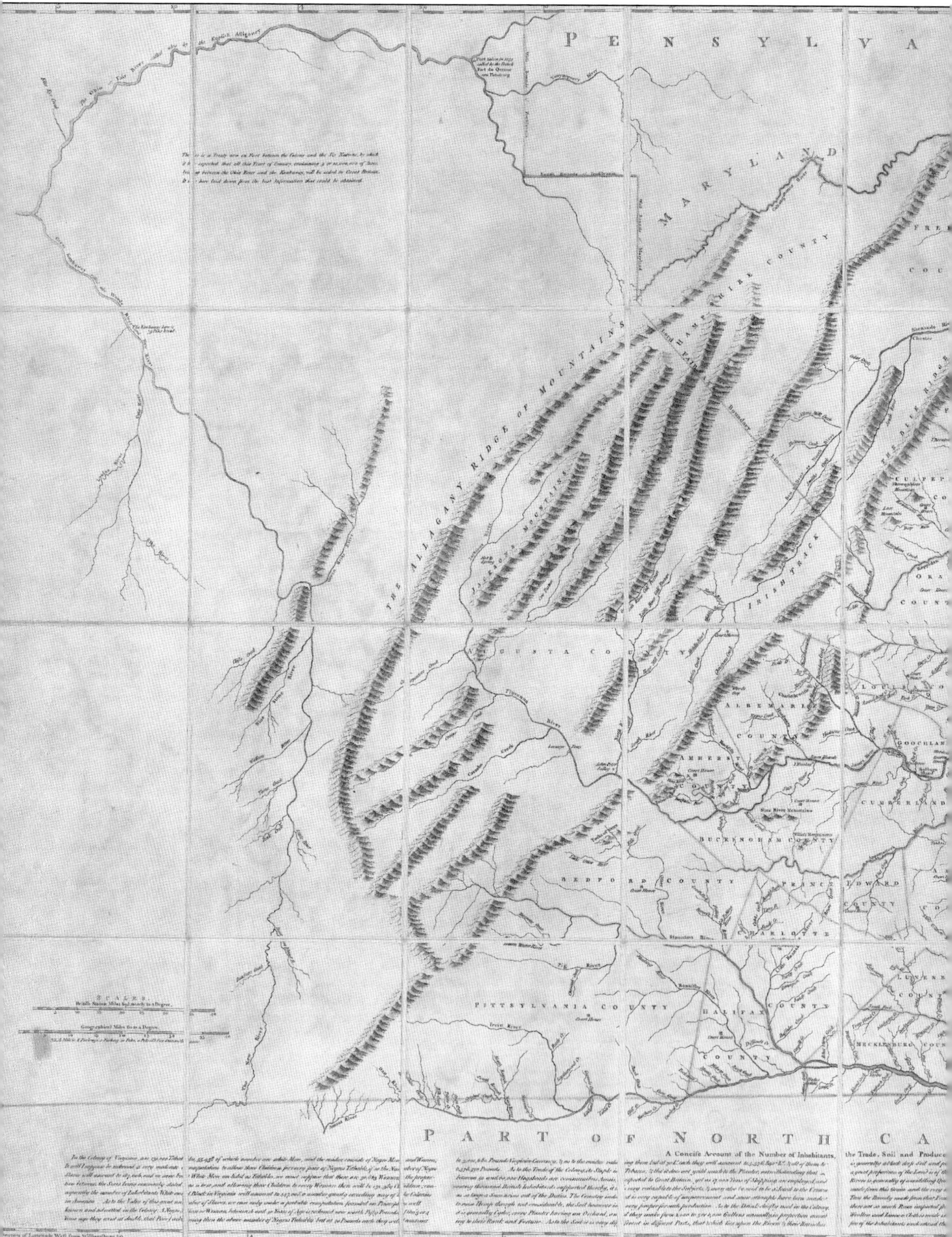
P E N S Y L V A
M A R Y L A N D
THE ALLAGANY RIDGE OF MOUNTAINS
IRISH TRACK
AUGUSTA COUNTY
ALBEMARLE
COUNTY
AMHERST
COUNTY
GOOCHLAND
CUMBERLAND
BUCKINGHAM COUNTY
BEDFORD COUNTY
PRINCE EDWARD
COUNTY
PITTSYLVANIA COUNTY
HALIFAX COUNTY
MECKLENBURG COUN
SCALES
P A R T O F N O R T H C A
A Concise Account of the Number of Inhabitants,
the Trade, Soil and Produce

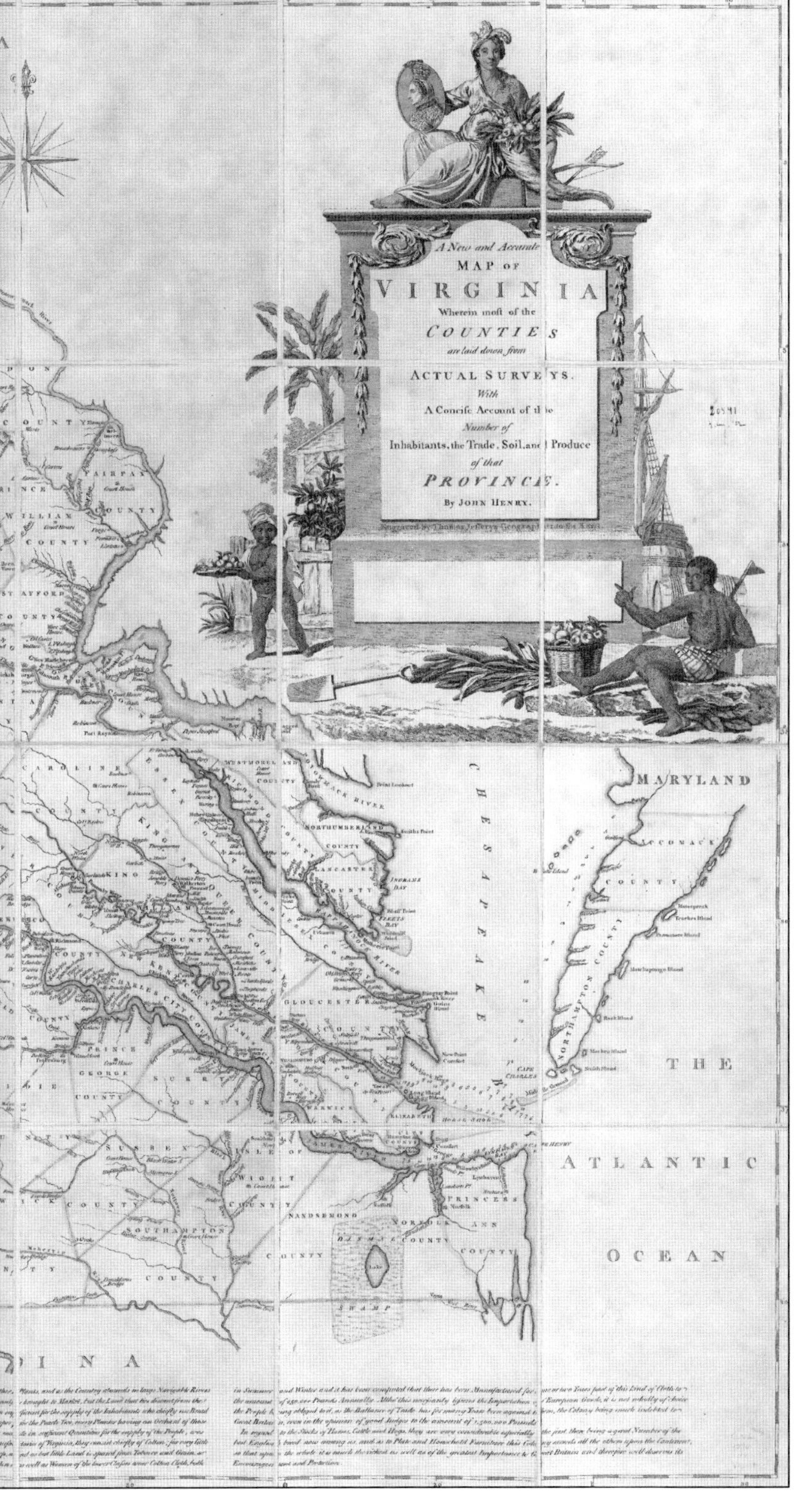

A *New and Accurate Map of Virginia*, 1770. In the 1760s, John Henry set out to create "a new and accurate map of Virginia." Unable to obtain financial support for his project from the legislature, Henry sold his publication rights to his son Patrick in 1770. Although considered inferior to the Fry-Jefferson Map (1753), Henry's map was the first to lay out county boundary lines and locations of county courthouses. Subscribers to the map's publication had their residences labeled on the map. Patrick Henry's Roundabout plantation can be seen as well as John Henry's Mount Brilliant seat. Lord Botetourt purchased one of John Henry's maps for the Governor's Palace and hung it in the dining room. Visitors to Red Hill can view a full-size copy of the map and often marvel at its accuracy as they find familiar landmarks. (LOC.)

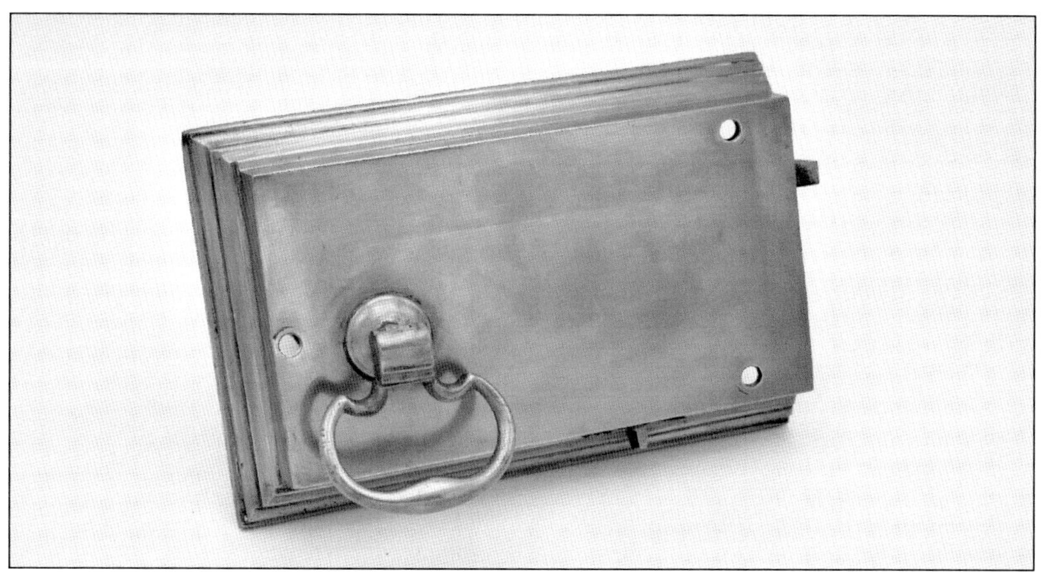

Door Lock, 2023. In 1793, Richard Randolph was brought before the Cumberland County Court's April session charged with infanticide. Randolph hired Patrick Henry and John Marshall as his defense attorneys, and after a dramatic trial, he was acquitted. According to family tradition, Patrick Henry purchased seven brass door locks for his home from his attorney fees. Only one of these locks survives and is in the Red Hill collection.

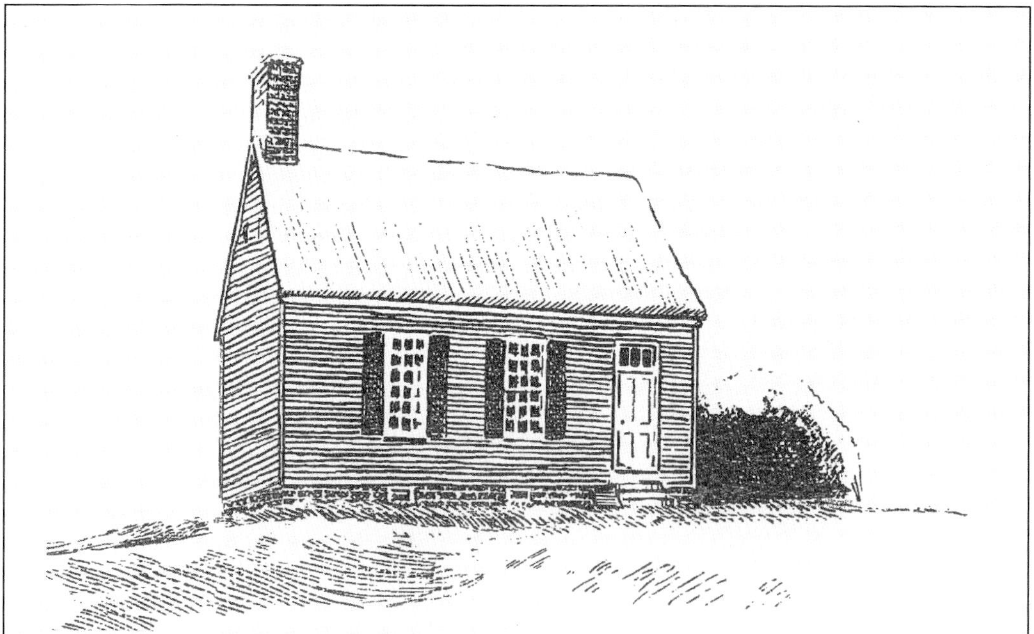

Patrick Henry House, c. 1794. Built for Richard Booker around 1772, this humble dwelling remained unchanged during Patrick Henry's residency. This simple 20-foot-by-30-foot building was where Henry raised his family and spent his last years. Unlike the grand additions made by Washington and Jefferson to their homes, Henry made no such alterations to his final residence.

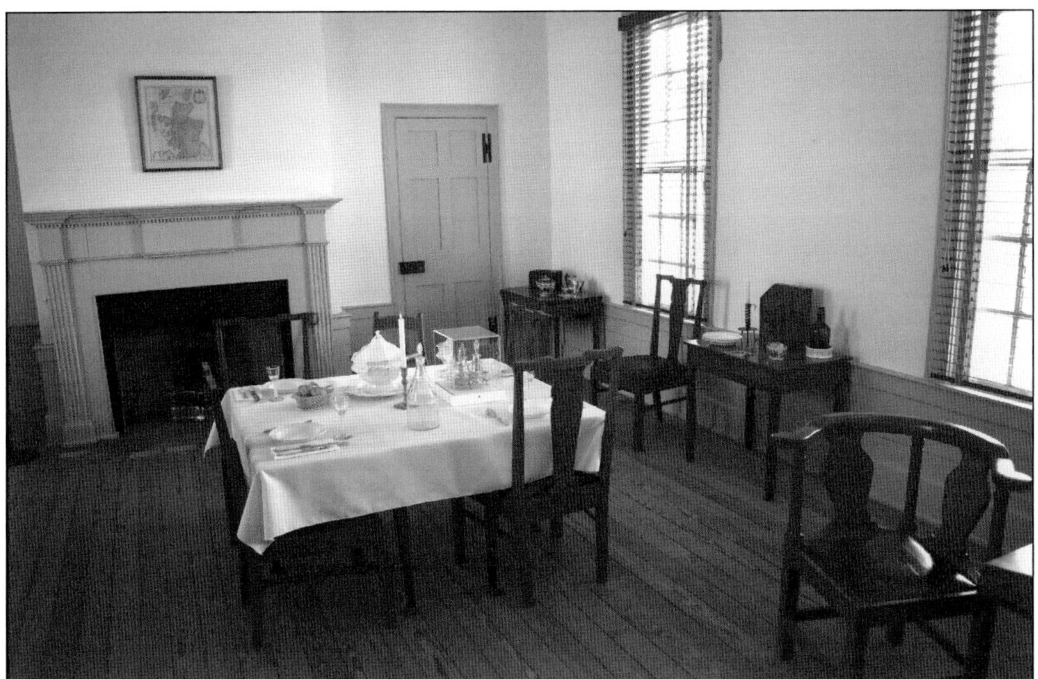

Henry House Parlor, 2024. This interior view of Patrick Henry's reconstructed home depicts the elder statesman's plain and simple lifestyle. The Henrys dined, socialized, and entertained in this one room, and enslaved domestics saw to their every need. The furnishings are based on the estate inventory taken after Henry's death. Many of them belonged to Patrick Henry.

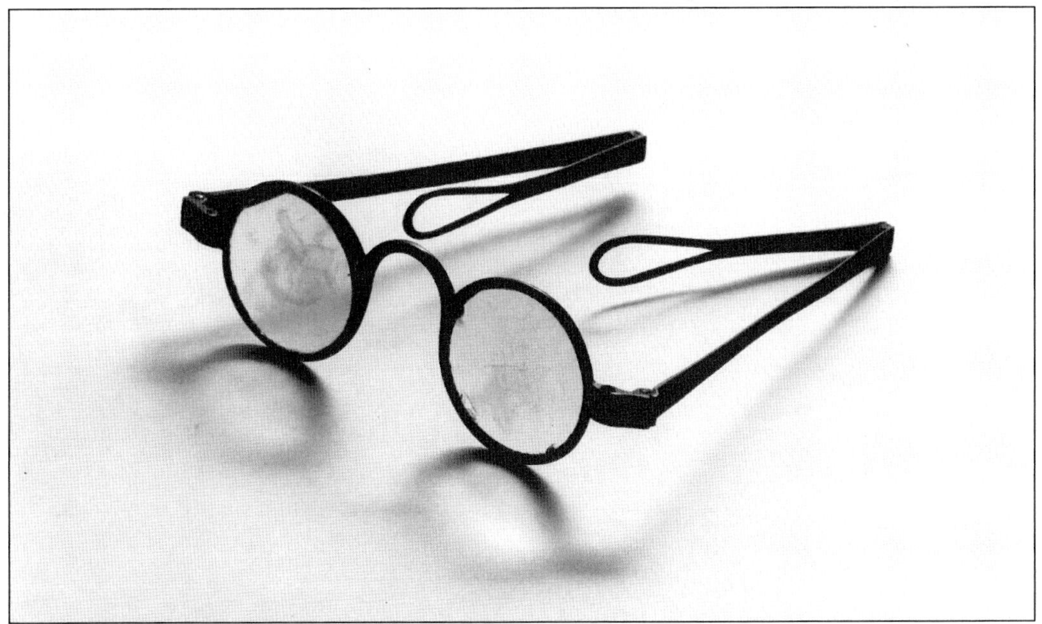

Patrick Henry's Spectacles, c. 1995. According to contemporary Hardin Burnley, "If Mr. Henry's answer was to be brief, he would make it without removing his spectacles from his nose. But if he was ever seen to give his spectacles a cant to the top of his wig, it was a declaration of war, and his adversaries must stand clear." The Virginia Historical Society now owns the spectacles. (VMHC.)

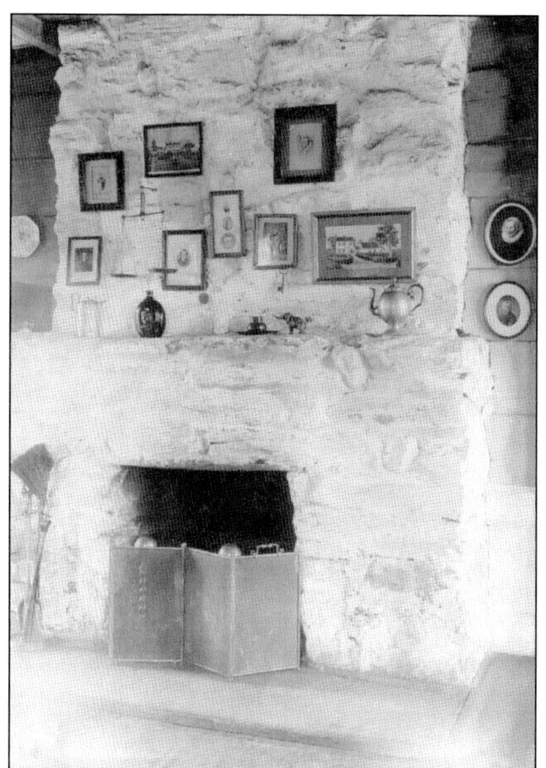

Interior of Patrick Henry's Law Office, c. 1930. This massive stone fireplace occupied Patrick Henry's law office before the building's restoration. It is seen here during the residency of Lucy Henry Harrison, who renovated the office as living quarters around 1910. Several artifacts, such as the hanging brass scales and iron key, belonged to Patrick Henry.

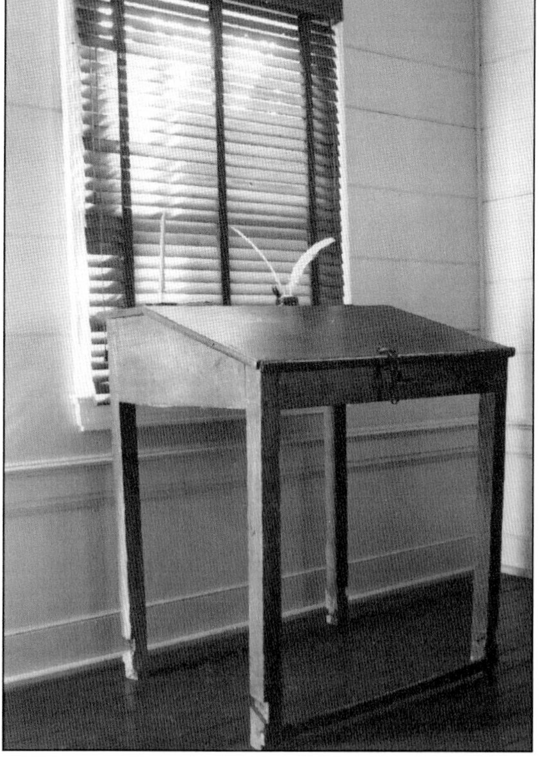

Patrick Henry's Standing Desk, 1989. While standing desks are experiencing a resurgence in popularity, the concept is not a new one. Patrick Henry used this desk, as did his son John after his father's death. Likely crafted by a local carpenter, the desk features a hinged top that covers a shelf and three drawers. The simple design reflects Henry's modest tastes.

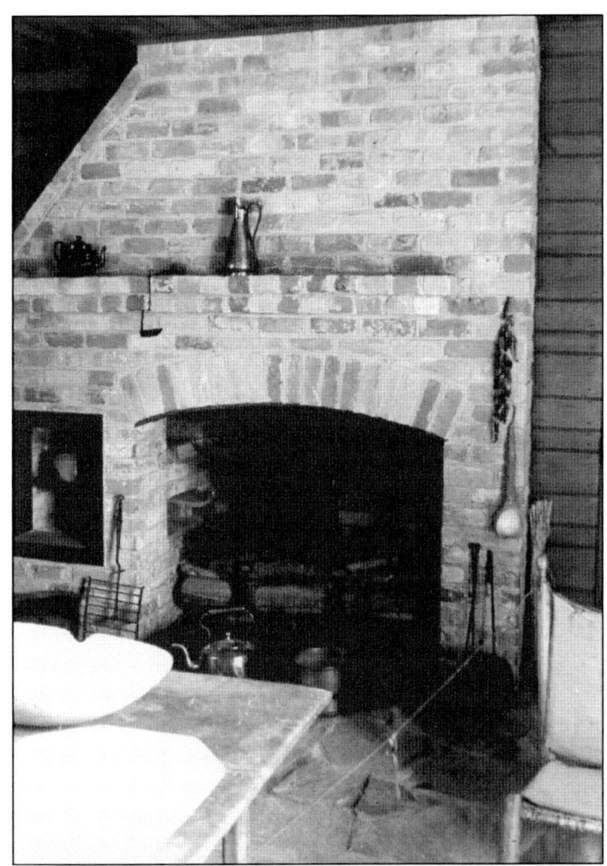

KITCHEN, 1977. The detached frame kitchen at Red Hill was reconstructed by architect Stanhope Johnson in 1957. Patrick Henry was known to prefer simple meals made from food grown on the plantation. Among the kitchen items listed in the 1799 estate inventory, which the enslaved cook used to prepare the meals, were three Dutch ovens, two iron pots and skillets, iron spits, and a gridiron used for grilling.

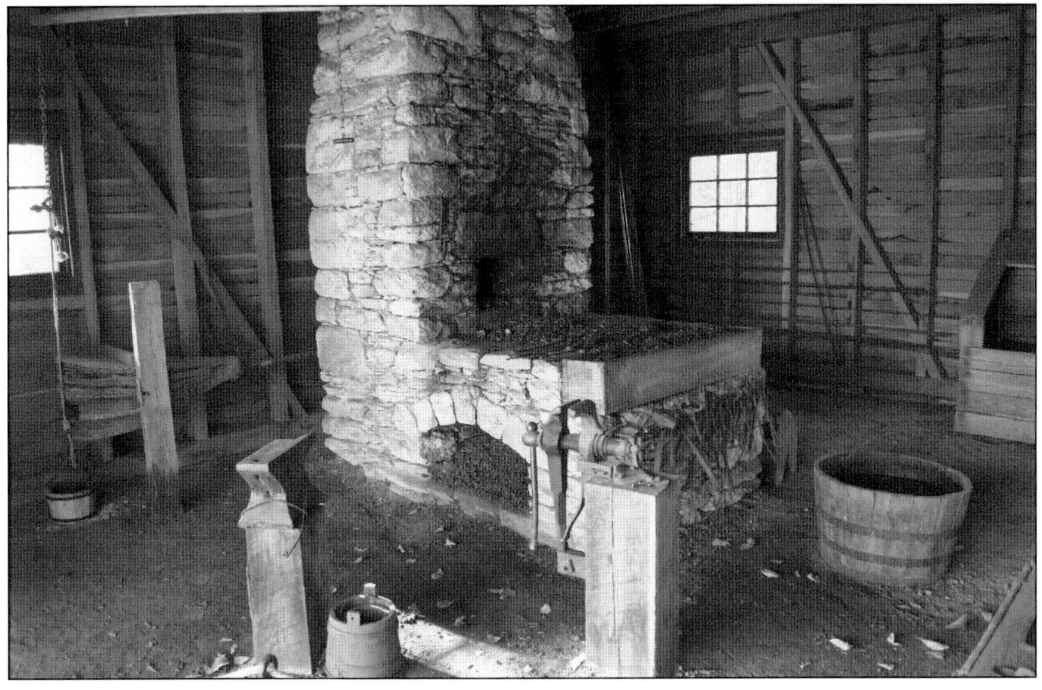

BLACKSMITH SHOP, 2024. One of the most valuable workers on an 18th-century plantation was the blacksmith, who crafted and repaired tools and other metal items for use on the plantation. Blacksmiths worked in a shop, like this one reconstructed at Red Hill, using a forge to heat iron stock, making it pliable for shaping. An enslaved man named Jessee was possibly the blacksmith during Patrick Henry's time.

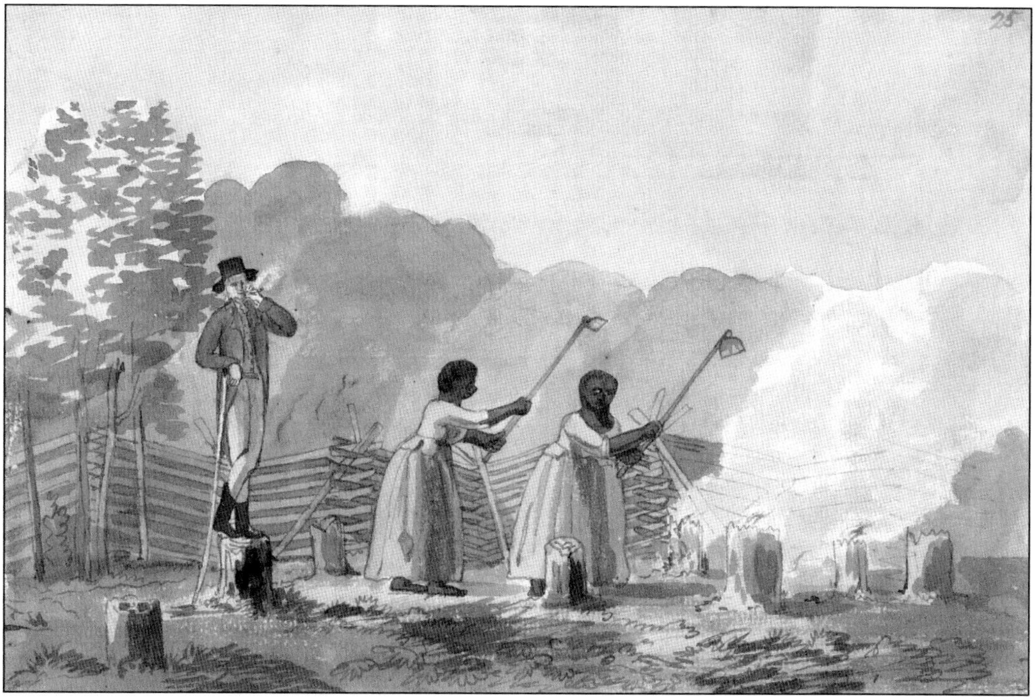

AN OVERSEER DOING HIS DUTY NEAR FREDERICKSBURG, VIRGINIA BY BENJAMIN LATROBE, C. 1798. This watercolor of an overseer supervising two enslaved women at work depicts plantation life in Virginia in the 1790s. Patrick Henry had 67 enslaved African Americans on his plantation in 1799 who tended to the crops, livestock, distillery, and domestic duties. Through their forced labor, Red Hill became a profitable and largely self-sustaining plantation. (MCHC.)

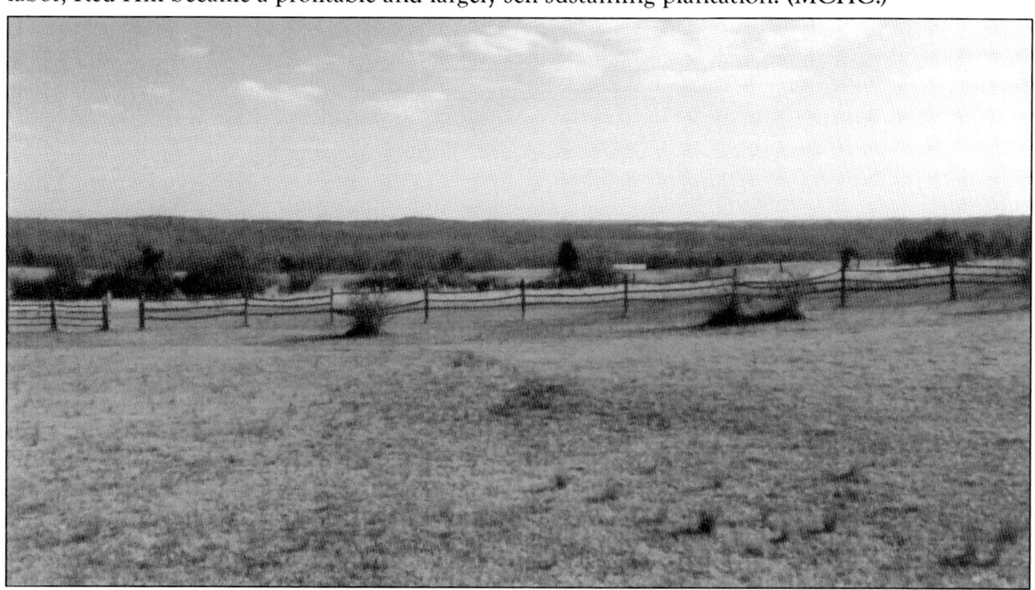

LOW GROUNDS OF RED HILL, C. 1985. Patrick Henry's home stood upon an eminence overlooking the Staunton River valley to the south. According to his grandson, Henry often stood in his yard and gave orders and directions to his enslaved laborers working in the low grounds a half-mile distant from him. Henry grew corn, wheat, flax, rye, cotton, and tobacco at Red Hill.

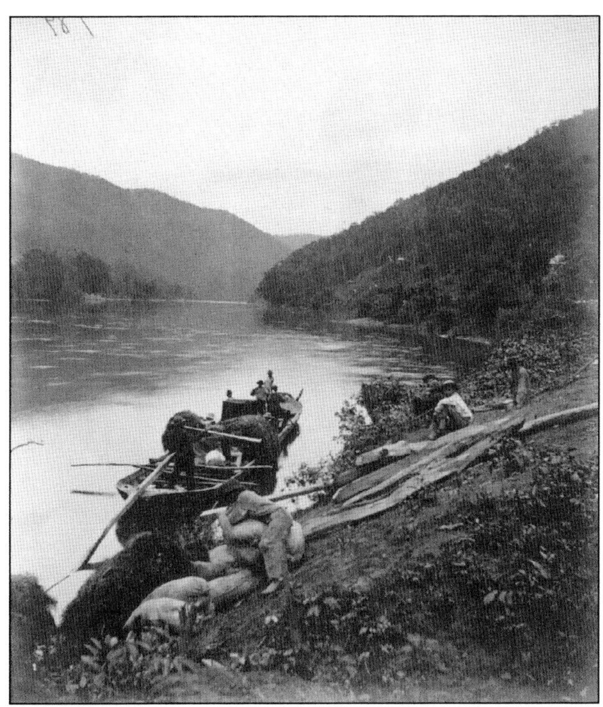

Bateau on the New River, June 1872. This shallow-draft, flat-bottomed boat, known as a bateau, was used extensively across North America during the 18th and 19th centuries to transport tobacco and other cargo. During Patrick Henry's residency, bateaux could travel up the Staunton River as far as present-day Brookneal, thus adding to Red Hill's value for commerce and trading purposes. (LOC.)

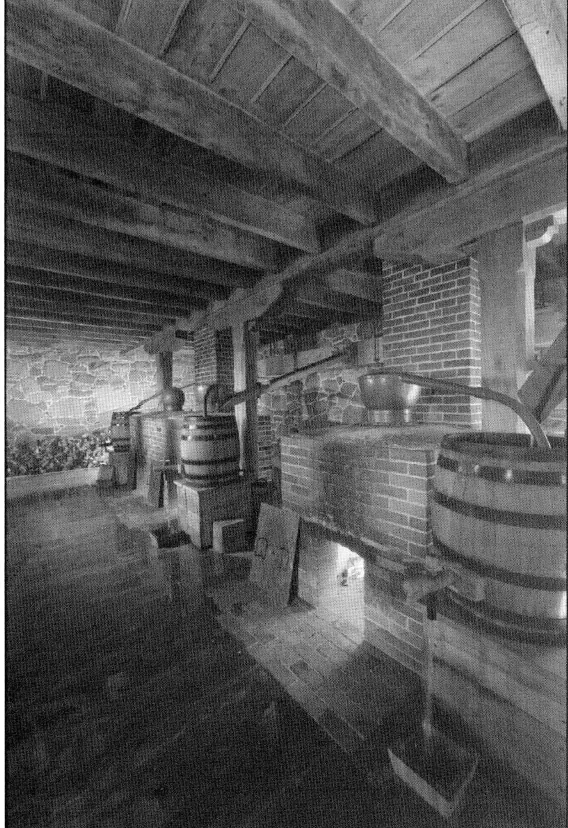

Distillery Stills, 2011. By 1795, Patrick Henry began operating a licensed whiskey distillery at Red Hill to diversify his income. Entries in Henry's account book indicate he was selling the whiskey to neighbors, merchants, and local tavern owners at around six shillings per gallon. The rye, corn, and barley used to make the whiskey mash were all grown on his Staunton River plantations. (MVLA.)

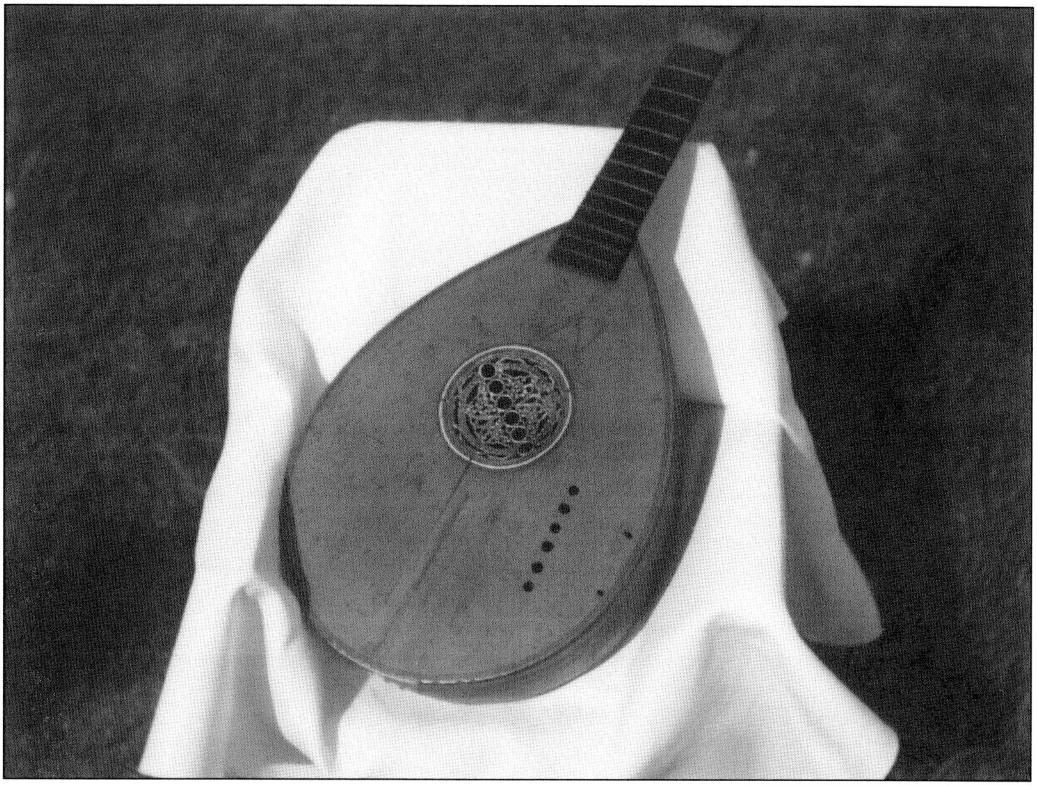

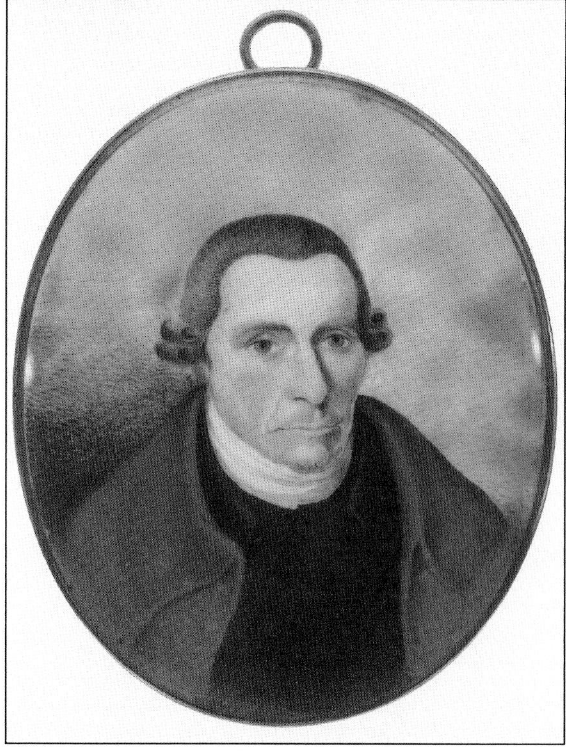

DOROTHEA HENRY'S GUITAR, C. 1976. With Patrick Henry on the violin, his wife Dorothea on this guitar, and perhaps one of their daughters playing pianoforte, music filled the Red Hill home. German piano builder Christian Claus crafted this instrument in New York after he fled British creditors in 1789. Passed down through the family of Patrick's sister, Jane Meredith, the guitar is now in the Red Hill collection.

***PATRICK HENRY* BY LAWRENCE SULLY, 1795.** Lawrence Sully (1769–1803) painted this portrait of Patrick Henry from life in 1795, one year after Henry purchased Red Hill. The 59-year-old orator is dressed in a black suit, a scarlet cloak over his shoulders, and a brown bob wig. The miniature was passed down through Henry's half-brother's family until 1910, when it was sold at auction. (AC.)

MRS. PATRICK HENRY (DOROTHEA DANDRIDGE) BY ASAHEL POWERS, 1826. This oil painting of an elderly Dorothea Henry is attributed to a New England artist who likely never saw his subject. Even in her old age, Dorothea was known for her vivaciousness and pleasant demeanor. In 1831, Dorothea died at her daughter's home in Halifax County at the age of 73, and she was later buried at Red Hill. (MFA.)

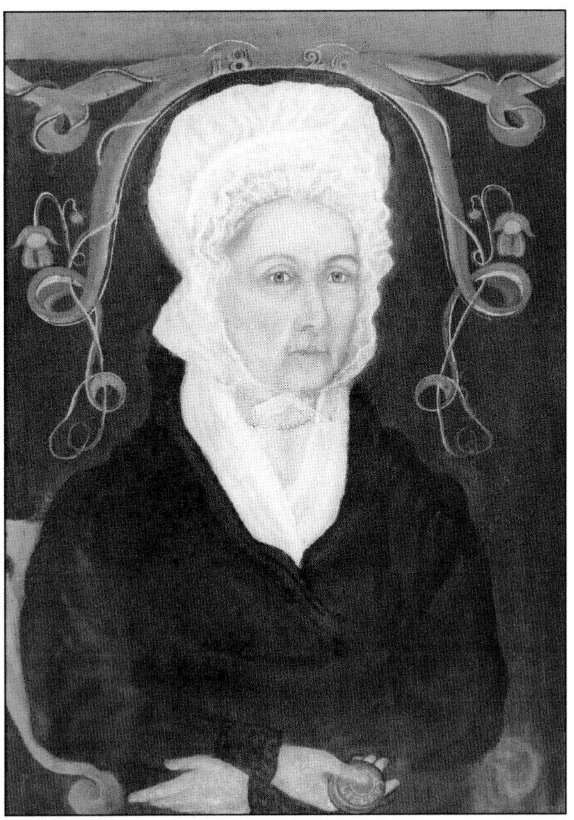

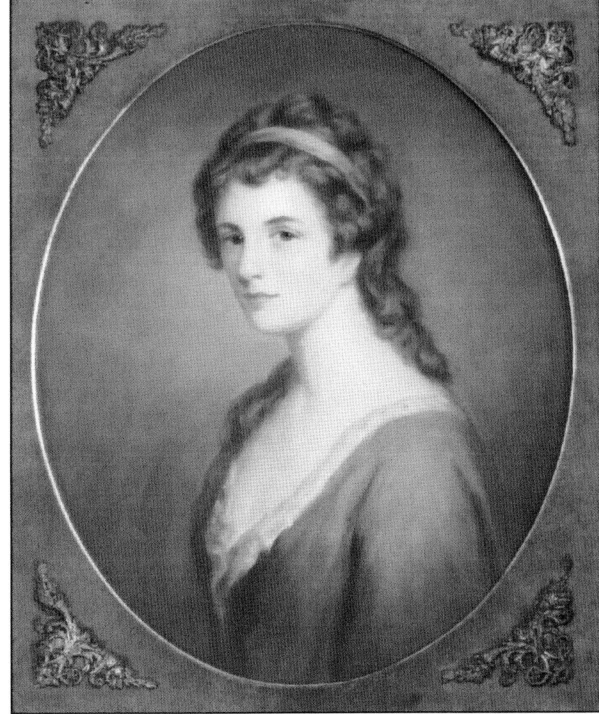

MISS HENRY, DAUGHTER OF PATRICK HENRY BY JAMES SHARPLES THE ELDER, C. 1796. Born at the Governor's Palace in Williamsburg in 1778, Dorothea Spotswood was the first of 11 children born to Patrick and Dorothea Henry. At the age of 17, Dorothea married her cousin George Winston at Red Hill. Her beauty is seen in this portrait painted of her at the age of 18 by the English artist James Sharples.

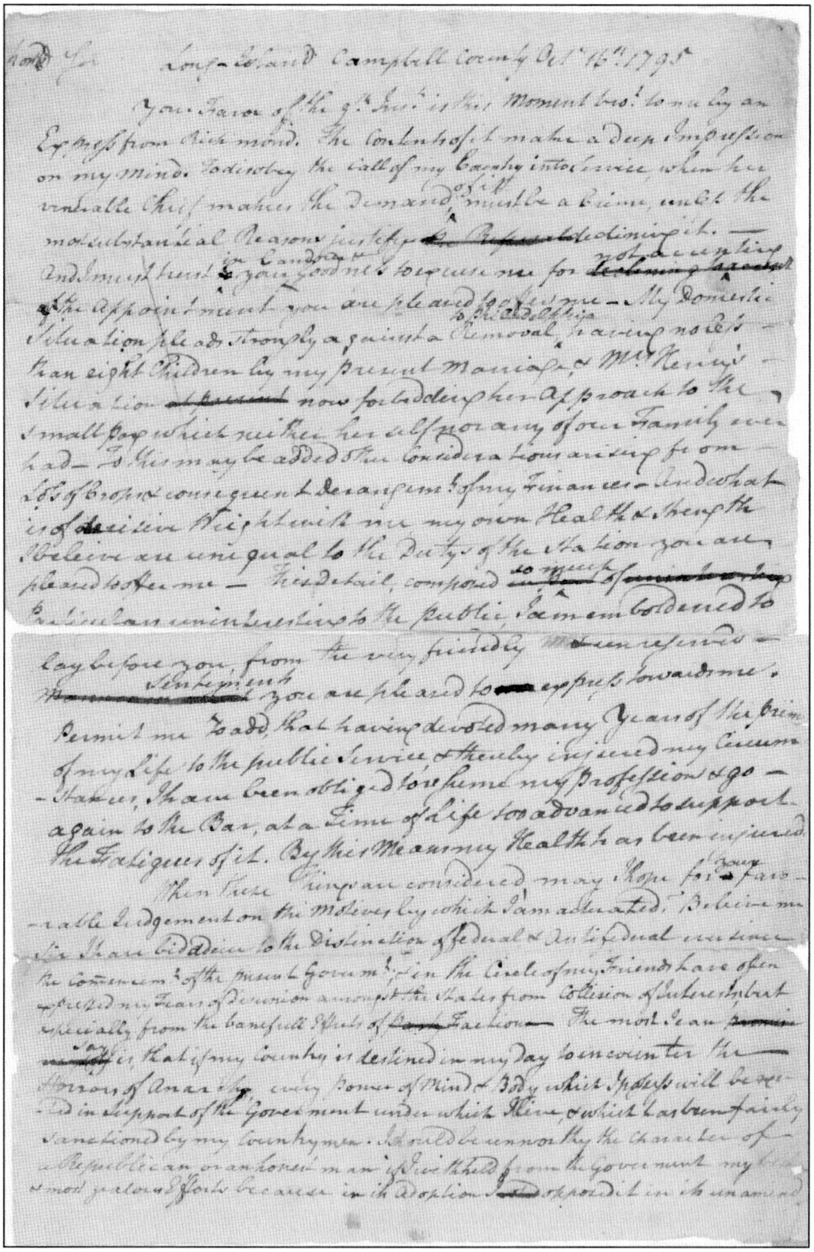

Patrick Henry to George Washington, 1795. During his retirement years, Patrick Henry declined several positions within the federal government. Positions such as the filling of a vacant senate seat, ambassadorships to France and Spain, and a seat on the Supreme Court were all declined by Henry as he focused on his health, his family, and Red Hill. In 1796, he even circulated a letter asking not to be nominated as a presidential candidate in the upcoming election. In 1795, recognizing Henry's continuing influence, George Washington offered Patrick Henry the position of secretary of state. Henry's copy of his reply to the president (seen here) is in the Red Hill collection. In it, the aging statesman writes he is "unequal to the dutys of the station you are pleased to offer me," particularly as he cares for "no less than eight children by my present marriage."

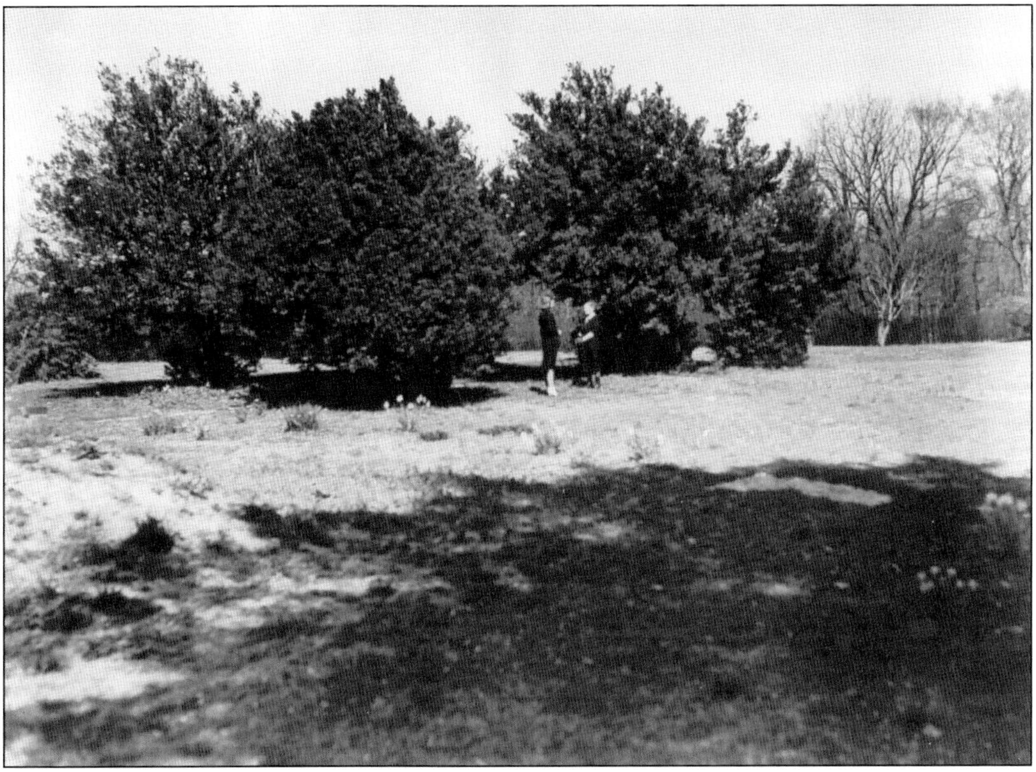

Boxwood Rows, c. 1958. These boxwoods date to the 18th century, possibly predating Patrick Henry's ownership of Red Hill. They stand at an intersection of paths that lead from the house to the law office. The path then extends toward the Henry family cemetery. Although now trimmed, the boxwoods still stand today, and visitors often marvel at their trunk size.

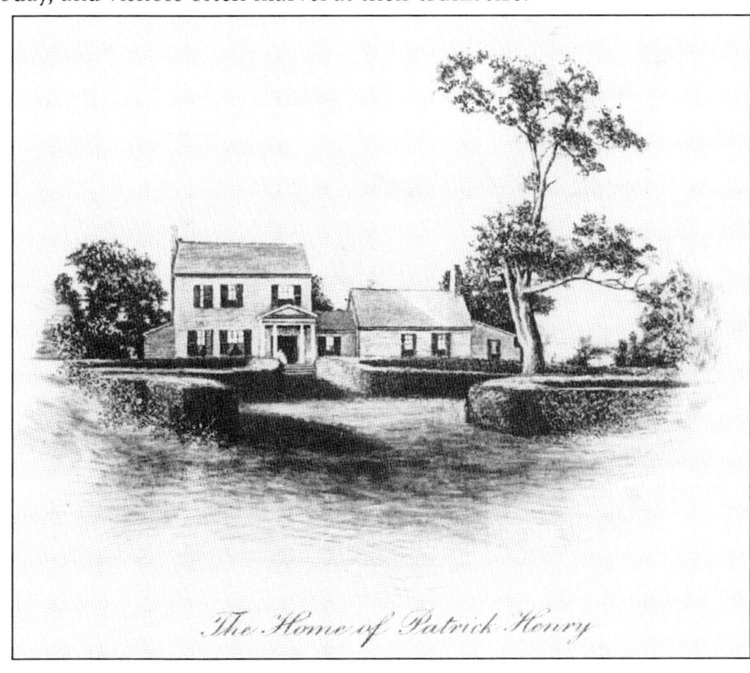

Patrick Henry's Locust Tree, 1889. This photograph shows the Henry house and surrounding gardens in the late Victorian era. The tall tree in the foreground was known as "Patrick's locust." According to historian Henry Howe, "Patrick Henry was accustomed in pleasant weather to sit mornings and evenings, with his chair leaning against the trunk, and a can of spring-water by his side." The tree stood until the early 1900s.

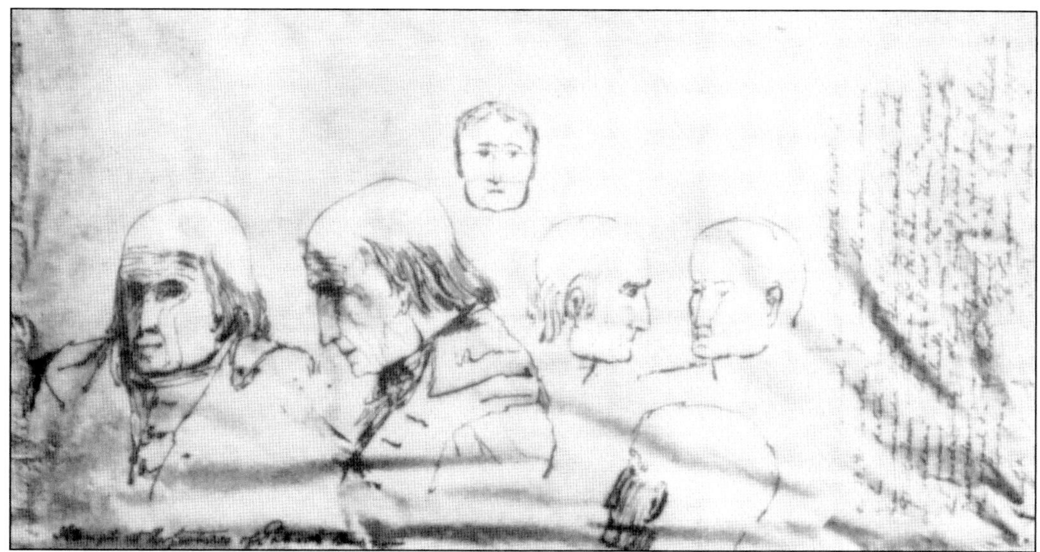

Latrobe Sketches, c. 1797. The famed architect Benjamin Henry Latrobe (1764–1820) executed a series of quick sketches of Patrick Henry in the late 1790s while the latter attended court in Richmond. The sketches comprise six male heads set down in Latrobe's notebook on a single page bearing the notation "Attempts at the features of Patrick Henry." (MCHC.)

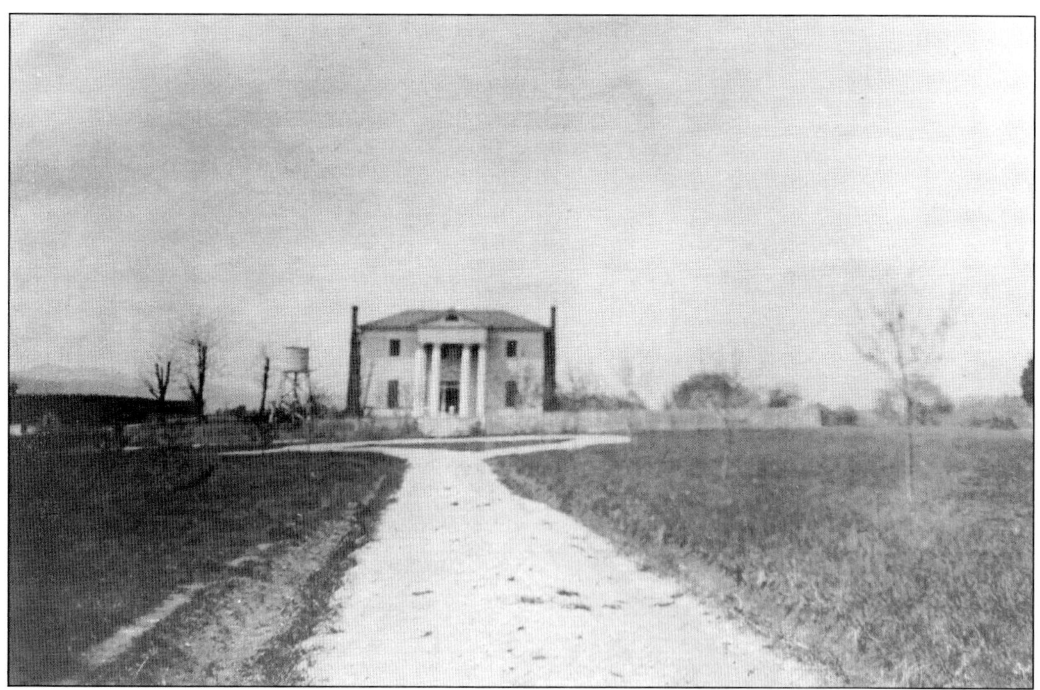

Winton, 1914. In Amherst County, near present-day Clifford, is Winton, a late-Georgian two-story frame house once owned by Patrick Henry's sister Jane and her husband, Col. Samuel Meredith. It was in this home that Patrick Henry's mother, Sarah Winston, spent the last four years of her life and where she died in 1784. Sarah was laid to rest 200 yards west of the manor house.

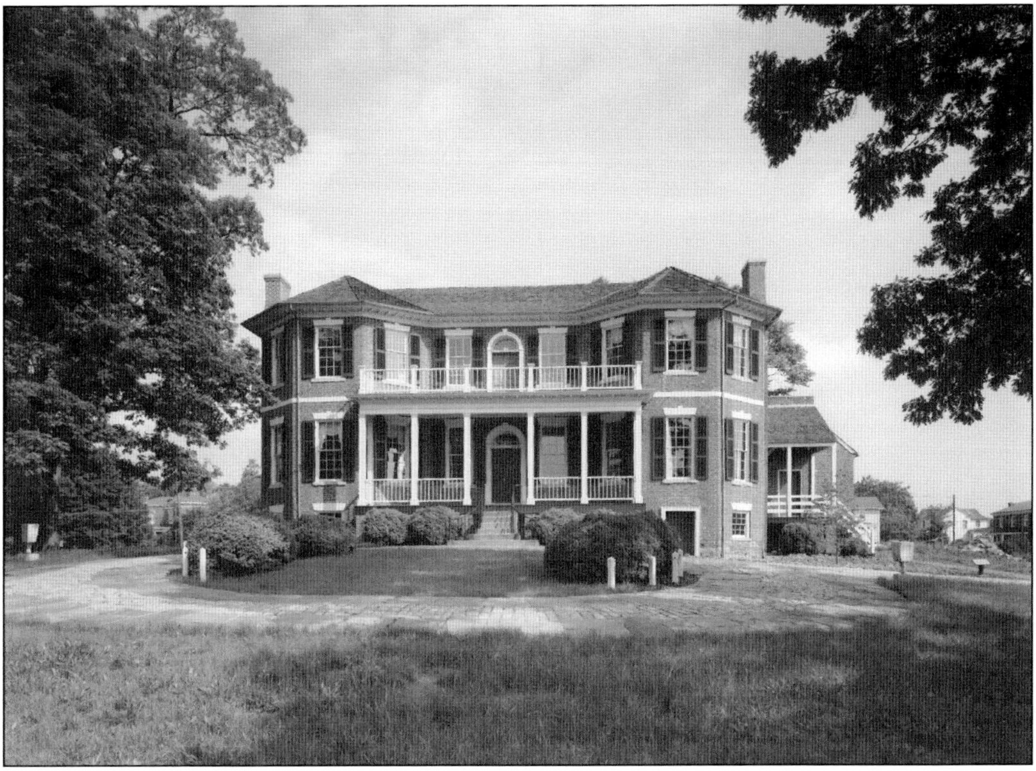

POINT OF HONOR, 1976. Completed in 1815, Point of Honor was the home of Dr. George Cabell, friend and physician of Patrick Henry. In 1818, Judge Edmund Winston, George Cabell's father-in-law and second husband of Dorothea Dandridge Henry, died while visiting Point of Honor. The home, once a sprawling plantation, is now located in downtown Lynchburg as a city museum. (LOC.)

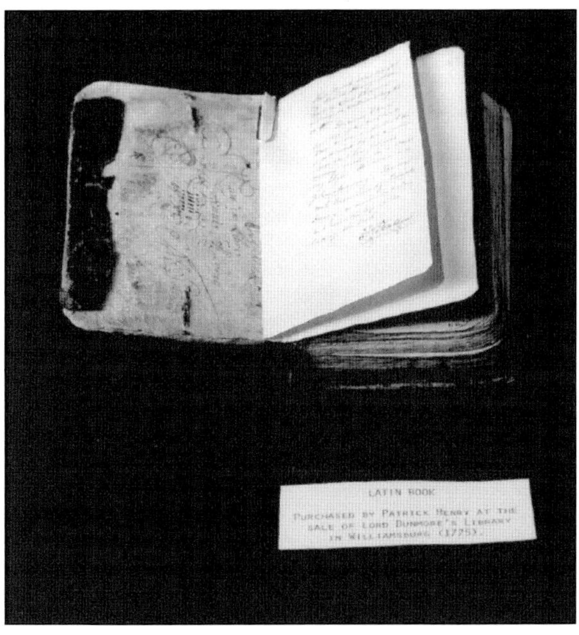

***D. JUNII JUVENALIS ET AULI PERSII FLACCI SATYRAE*, 1977.** John Murray, 4th Earl of Dunmore, owned this 1669 Latin book. Patrick Henry purchased the book in 1776 at a public auction of Lord Dunmore's possessions following the governor's flight from Williamsburg. Both Henry and Dunmore signed the inside cover. Henry owned this book at the time of his death in 1799, and it was listed in his estate inventory.

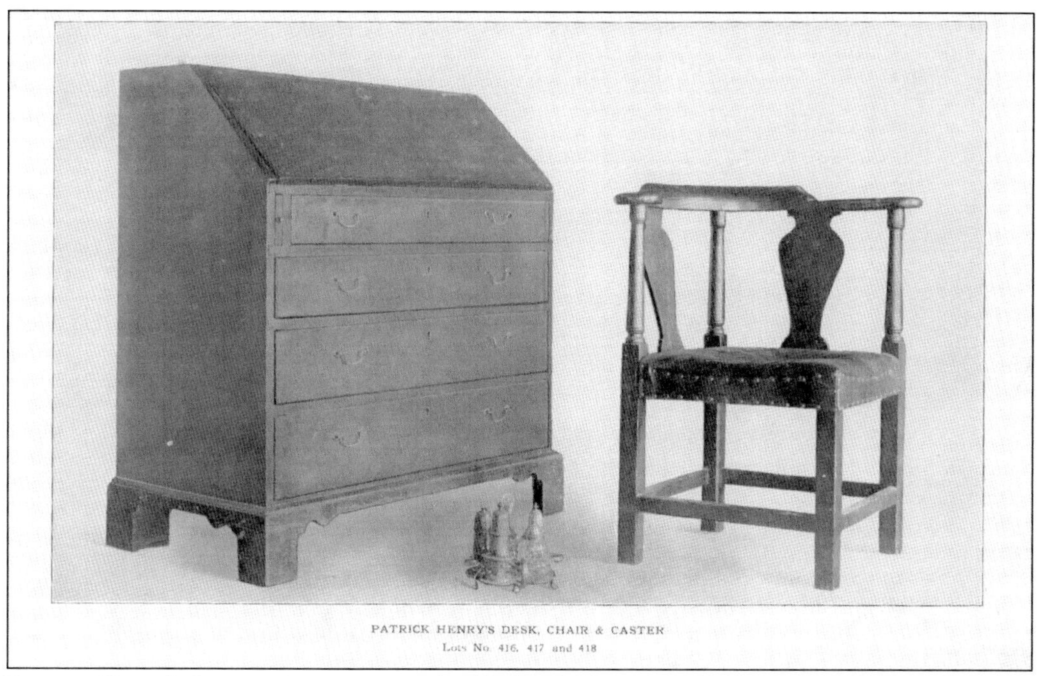

PATRICK HENRY'S CORNER CHAIR, 1910. This black walnut corner chair, which boasts a unique over-the-rail upholstery, was made around 1770. According to family tradition, Patrick Henry sat in this chair when he died from an intestinal blockage on June 6, 1799. The chair remained at Red Hill until 1910, when it was auctioned. It is currently owned by the Colonial Williamsburg Foundation.

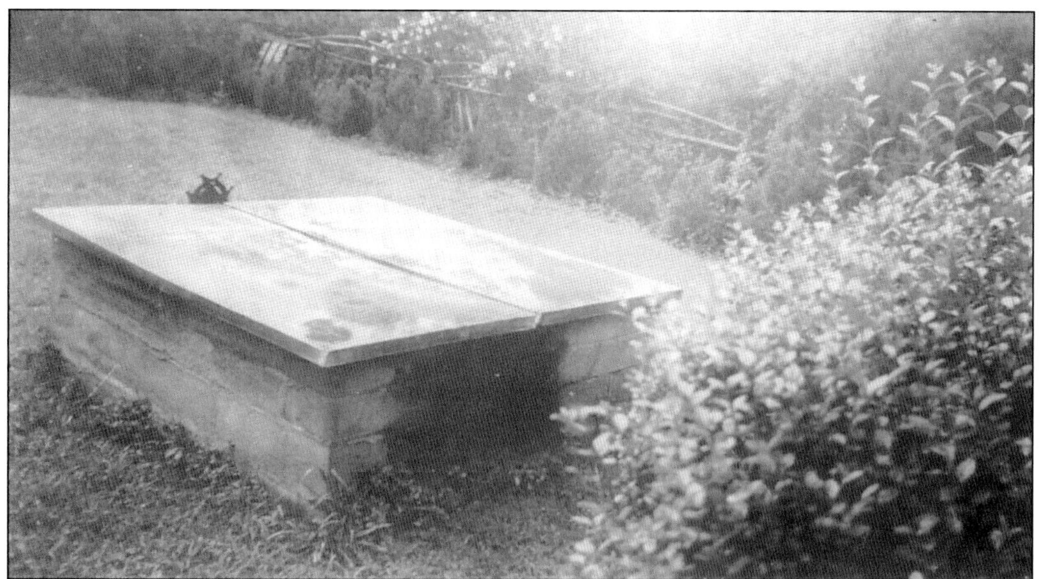

GRAVES OF PATRICK AND DOROTHEA HENRY, 1941. Patrick Henry died in 1799 and his wife Dorothea in 1831. It was not until 1858 that the youngest son, John, permanently marked the final resting place of his parents in the family cemetery at Red Hill. As a testimony to the patriot's contributions to history, John included an inscription on the marble slab over Patrick Henry that reads, "His fame his best epitaph."

Three

Passing the Torch 1800–1875

On June 6, 1799, Patrick Henry died at Red Hill aged 63. In his will, he left his Red Hill estate to his wife, stipulating that at her death, the property would be divided between two sons of her choosing. Three years after Henry's death, his widow married Judge Edmund Winston, Henry's executor and first cousin. Upon their marriage, Dorothea and her children moved into Winston's home, Huntingtour, located on the outskirts of Lynchburg, Virginia.

By 1810, John and Edward Winston (Dorothea's two youngest sons by Patrick Henry) moved back to Red Hill. They were joined by their mother three years later, after the death of Judge Winston. In 1814, the brothers divided the property between them. John received the home tract and 1,706 acres of land. The balance was deeded to his brother Edward Winston, who named his half Windstone.

In 1832, John Henry contracted with a builder to remodel and enlarge his father's home. The new house consisted of a two-story addition connected to the old house by a hyphen and a one-room addition to the east described as the "nursery." At this time, John's wife, Elvira McClelland, ordered extensive improvements to the grounds, including the creation of a boxwood garden fronting their home. As with other Southern plantations, the Civil War had a profound impact on Red Hill's economy and upon the lives of the 54 recently freed enslaved African Americans. While many of John Henry's formerly enslaved workers left the plantation, some remained as sharecroppers. When John died in 1868, he left the estate to his wife, who continued to reside at Red Hill until her death in 1875.

Upon Elvira Henry's death, the property passed to her eldest son, William Wirt Henry, a distinguished lawyer and historian. Because of his workplace demands, Wirt Henry moved to Richmond, leaving his brother to care for his Charlotte County estate. Wirt Henry died in 1900, and in 1905, his daughter Lucy Gray Henry Harrison purchased the interest of her mother and siblings in Red Hill for $20,000.

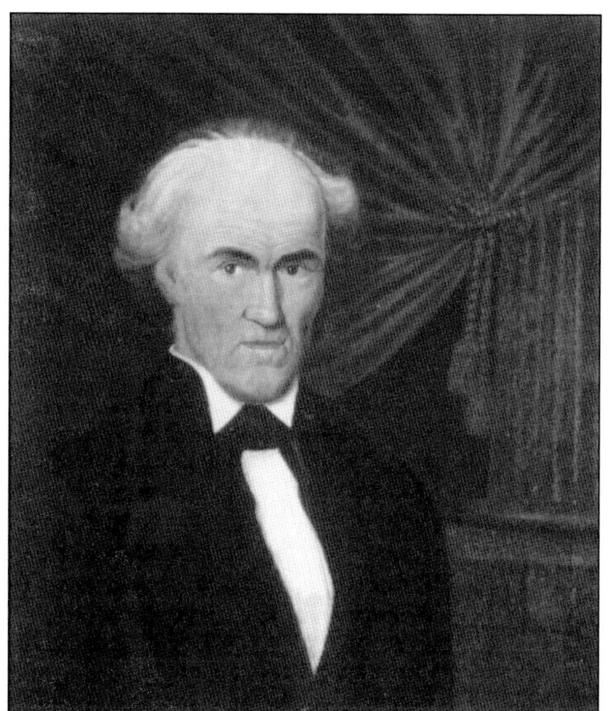

Patrick Henry Fontaine by Edward Fontaine, 1845. According to Patrick Henry Fontaine, who witnessed his grandfather's passing, the old orator was seated in his favorite armchair, speaking words of comfort and love to his family. He then turned to his doctor, who was a religious skeptic, and asked him to witness the truth of the Christian religion, which allowed him to die without fear.

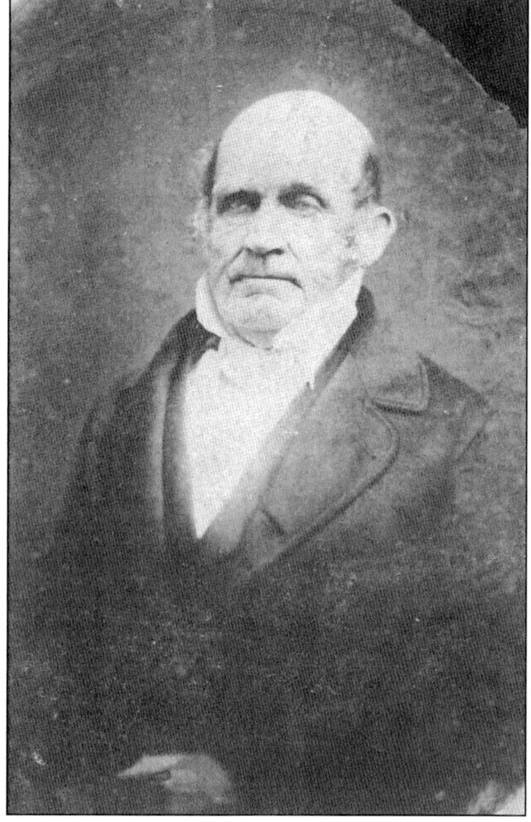

John Henry, c. 1860. Born in 1796, John Henry was the youngest son of Patrick and Dorothea Henry. Only three years old when his father died, John would grow up and inherit the family seat at Red Hill. His occupation was the running of the plantation and its enslaved workers, and his enjoyments were his family, good books, and cats. The latter he did not want to be publicly known.

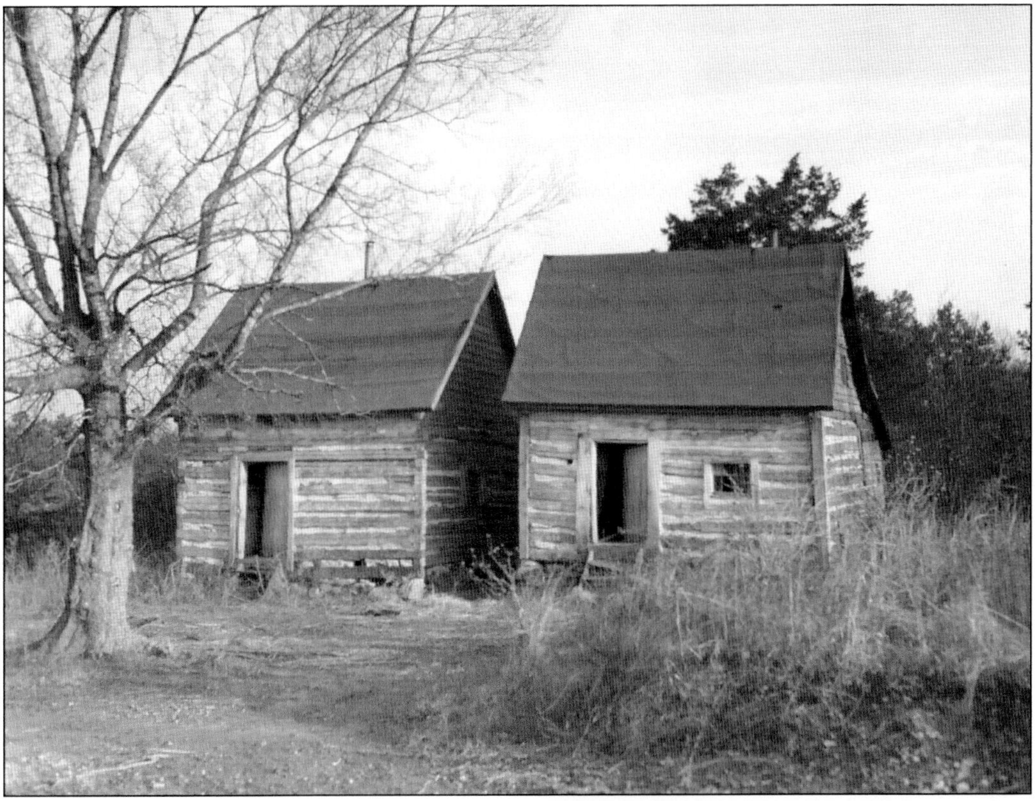

SLAVE QUARTERS AND BARN, C. 1950. These two log buildings, dating to the mid-19th century, stood on a ridge northwest of the Henry home in an area known as Quarter Place. The structure on the right served as living quarters for the enslaved, while the one on the left was originally used as a work shed or storage barn. Only the stone foundations of the two structures survive today.

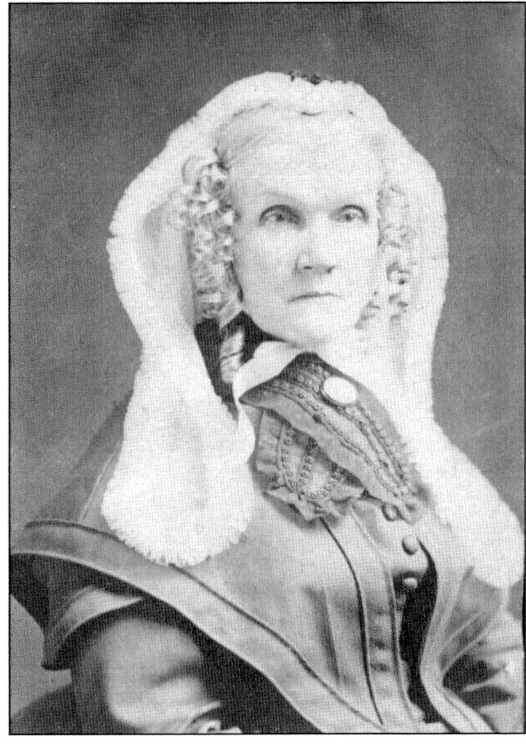

ELVIRA MCCLELLAND HENRY, C. 1860. Born in 1808 into the prestigious Cabell family of Virginia, Elvira was described by her granddaughter as "lovely, both in person and character." She and her husband, John, spent their married life at Red Hill. In late 1875, after an extended bout with cancer, Elvira "gradually faded away, suffering no pain." She was laid to rest next to her husband in the family cemetery.

William Wirt by Anson Dickinson, 1828. William Wirt authored the first biography of Patrick Henry, published in 1817. While not the most accurate, it certainly ranks in importance historically. Among other things, Wirt re-created the "Liberty or Death" speech for posterity. He also became US attorney general in 1817 and served for 12 years under presidents James Monroe and John Quincy Adams.

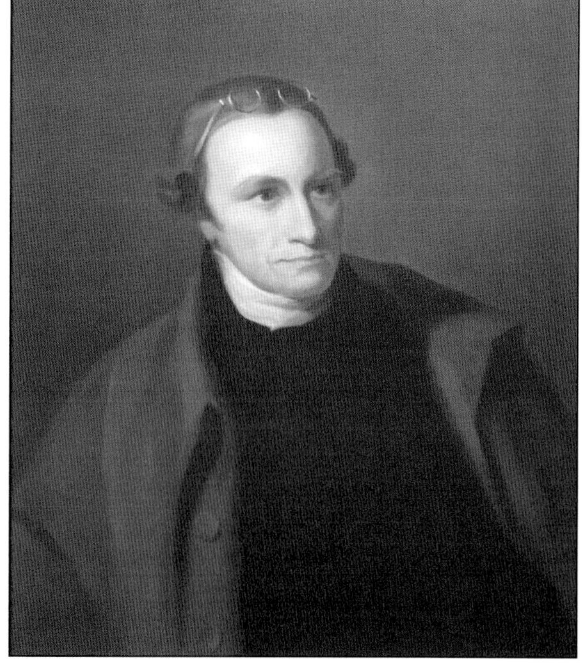

Patrick Henry by Thomas Sully, 1815. Sully painted this oil portrait for Patrick Henry's first biographer, William Wirt, in 1815. Sully based the portrait on a miniature of Henry painted by his half-brother Lawrence Sully in 1795. Wirt presented the finished portrait to Henry's family, who declared the painting "the best likeness they ever saw" of him. The portrait remained at Red Hill until it was sold in 1910.

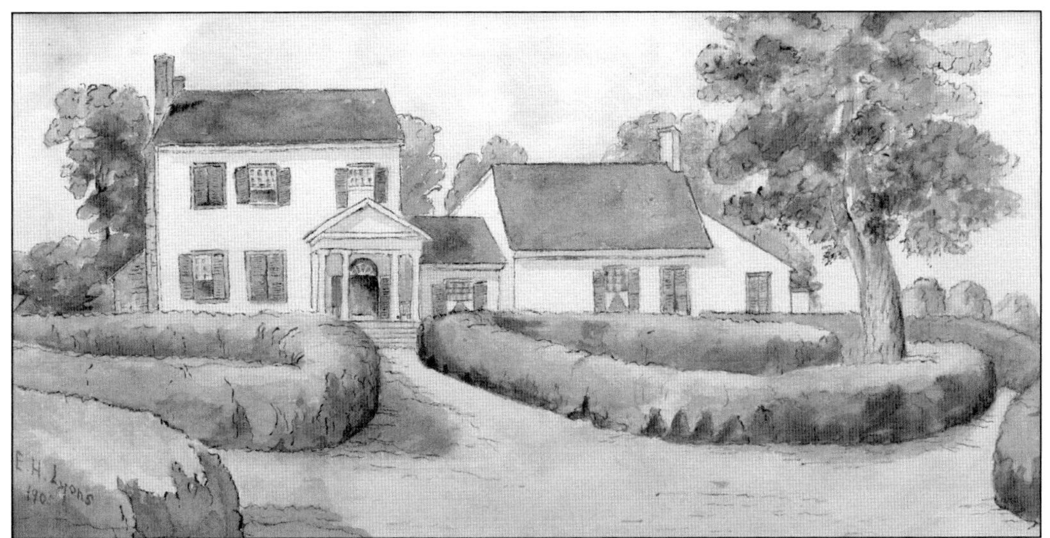

The Henry House by Elizabeth Henry Lyons, 1905. In 1832, John Henry hired builders to construct a two-story addition, passageway, and nursery room to his father's simple story-and-a-half home. John Henry's granddaughter Elizabeth Henry Lyons painted this watercolor with her great-grandfather's favorite locust tree (seen at right) in a boxwood garden.

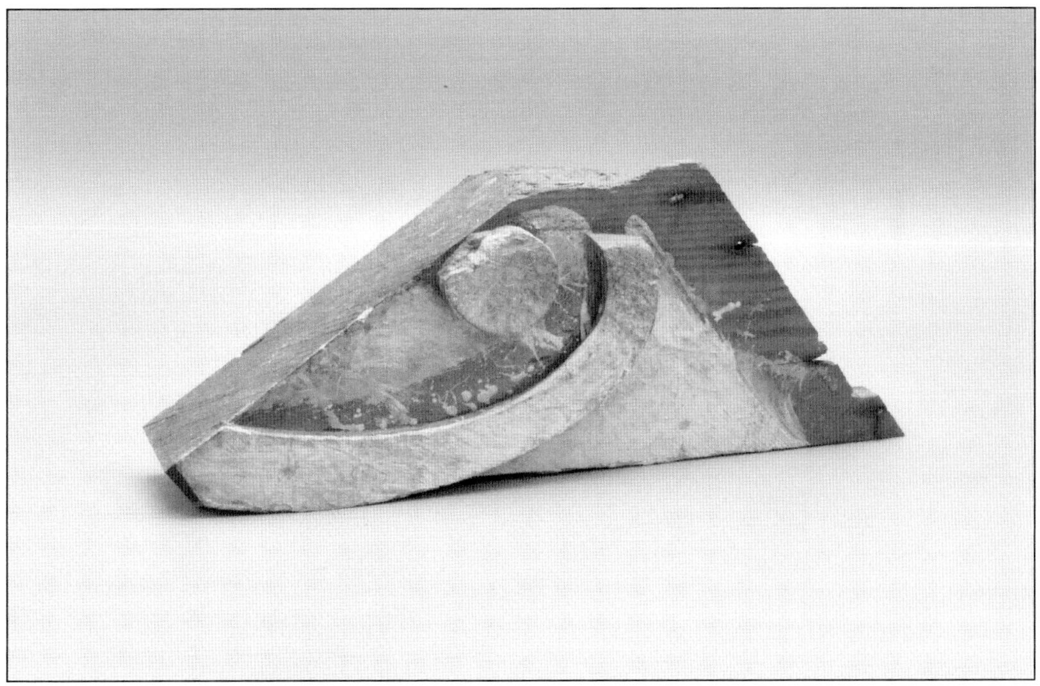

Staircase Fragment, 2023. This piece of a staircase stringer is all that remains of John Henry's staircase, constructed in 1832 as an addition to the Henry home. The staircase was moved to the law office when Lucy Henry Harrison had it enlarged around 1910. Restoration work forced the removal of the stairs in 1961. Foundation staff discovered this fragment in 2022.

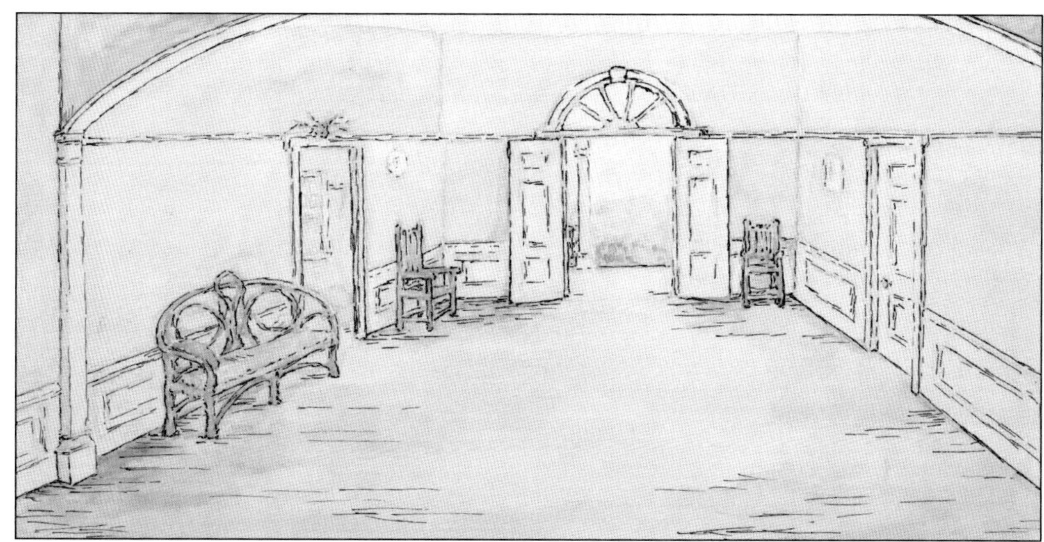

NORTH HALLWAY AT *RED HILL* BY SUSAN ALRICH LOW, 1904. Additions to the Henry home under John's ownership included this entrance hall with French doors and fine wood paneling. Susan Low, a cousin of the Henry family, painted this work as part of a series of watercolors while visiting Red Hill. The hall remained largely unchanged since its construction 72 years earlier.

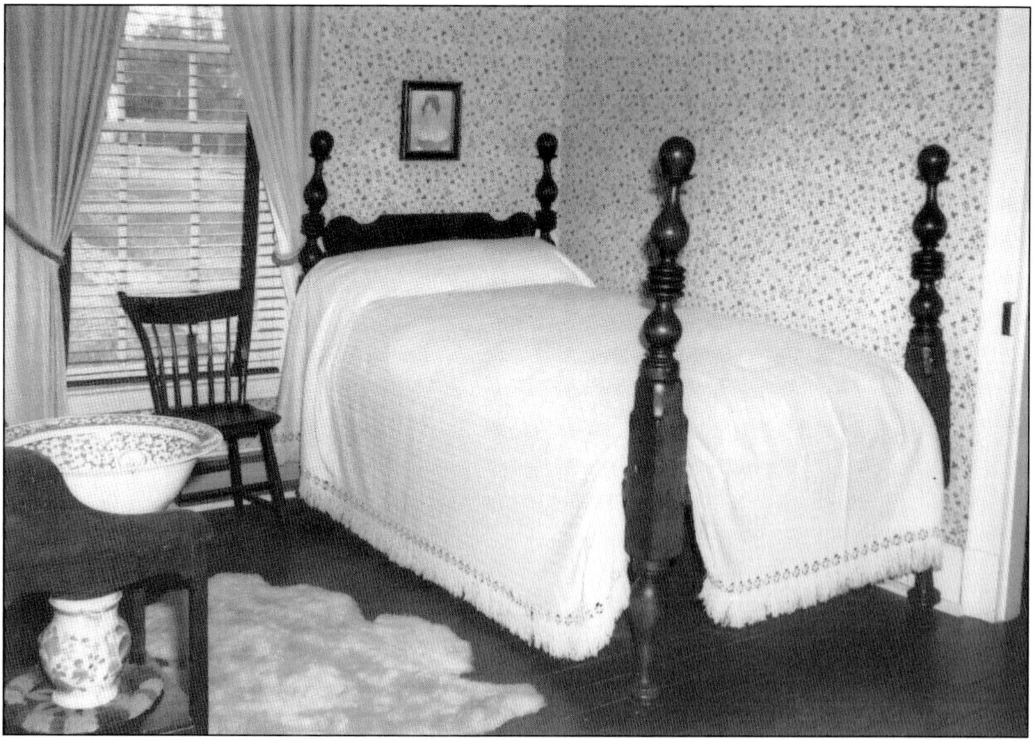

JOHN HENRY'S BED, 1980. This mid-19th-century mahogany cannonball bed belonged to John Henry. It likely appeared in John's estate inventory, which was taken at Red Hill after his death in 1868. Located in the over parlor, it was listed as "1 Cottage bedstead" and valued at $3. A bedstead refers to the framework of a bed on which the mattress is placed.

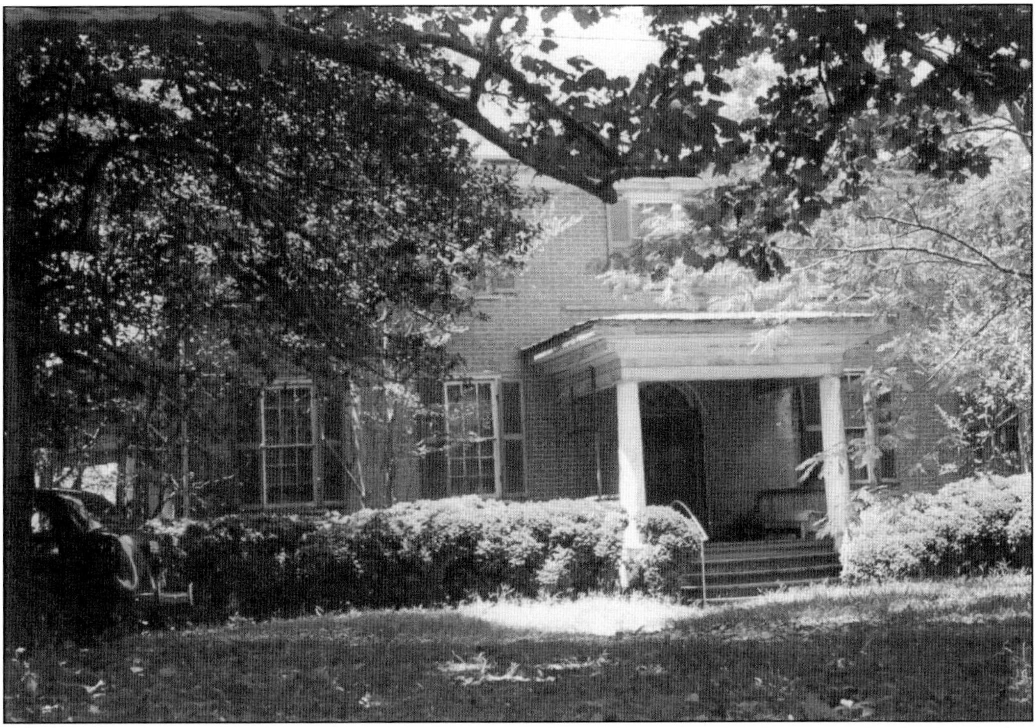

WINDSTONE, C. 1945. In 1814, the Red Hill estate was divided between Dorothea's sons John and Edward. Edward received the southeastern portion of the property, where he built a brick mansion known as Windstone. Edward died at Windstone at the age of 78 in 1872. The last family owner of the estate was Dandridge Yuille Henry, grandson of Edward. Fire destroyed the mansion on February 24, 1951.

STAFFORDSHIRE TUREEN, 1994. Edward Winston Henry owned this English-made Staffordshire tureen. Edward married Jane Yuille in 1817, and family tradition suggests it may have been part of the couple's wedding china. It depicts a body of water with a large temple in the background. This piece passed through the family and has been part of the Red Hill collection since 1950.

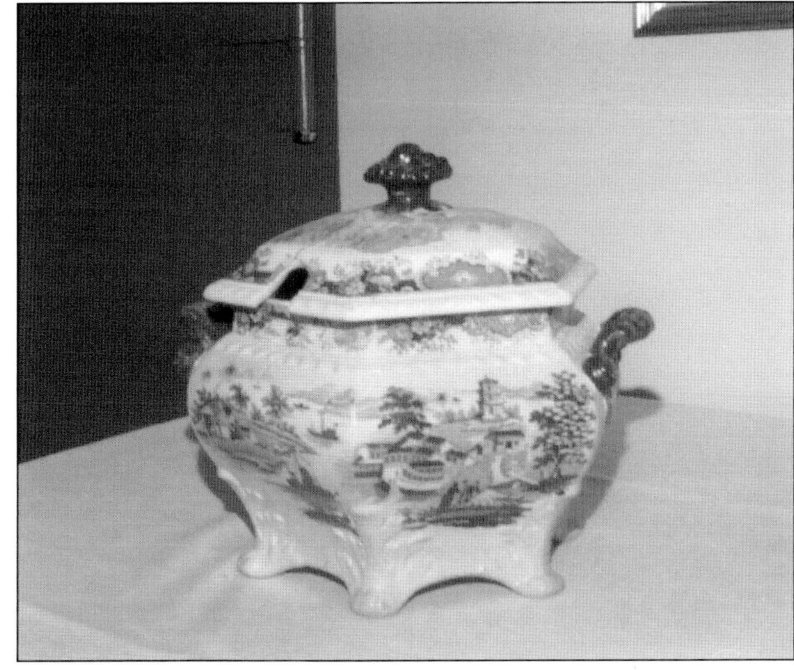

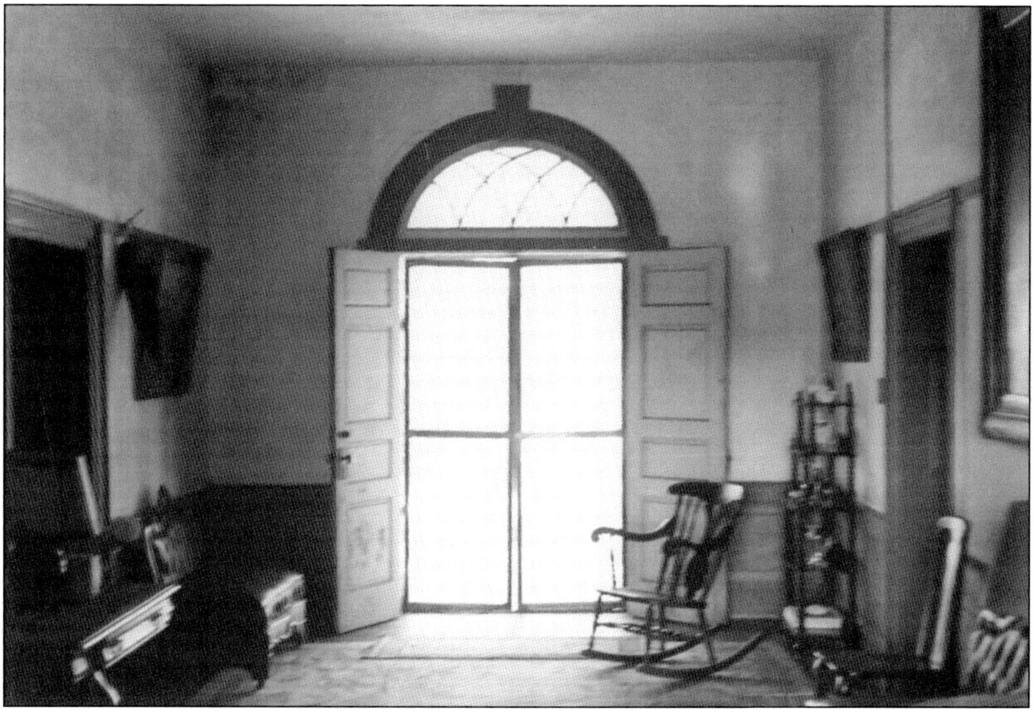

WINDSTONE INTERIORS, C. 1945. These two interior shots of Windstone were taken shortly before fire destroyed the Henry family home in 1951. The above photograph is of the east hall. The lunette window above the door resembles that found in John Henry's addition at Red Hill. Below is the living room. Photographs of various family members fill the desk and mantel.

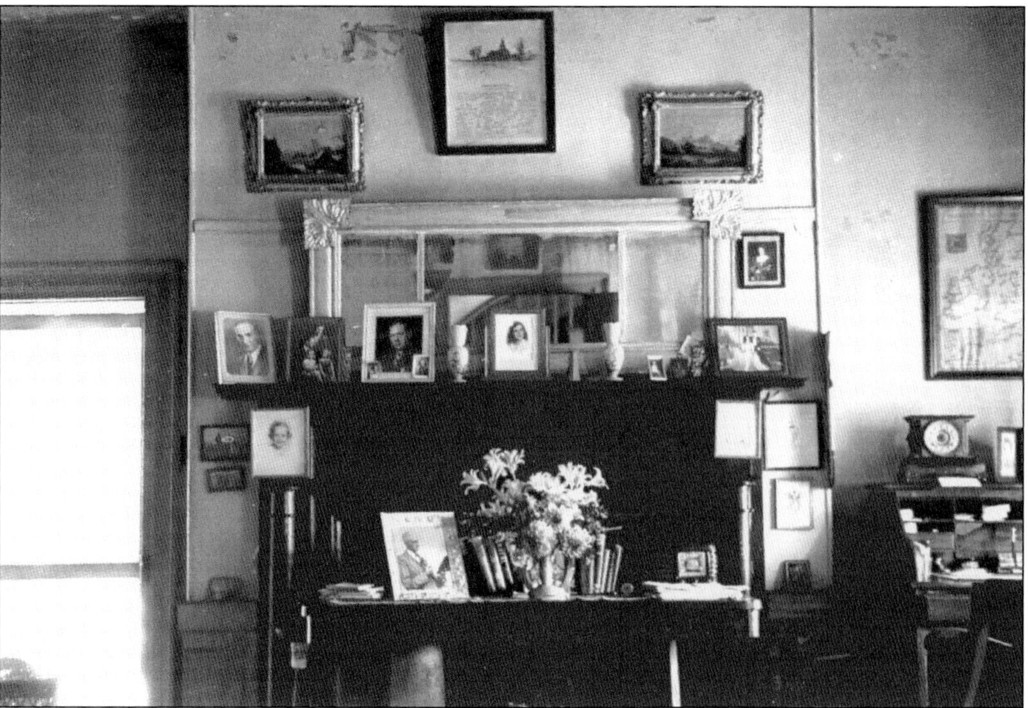

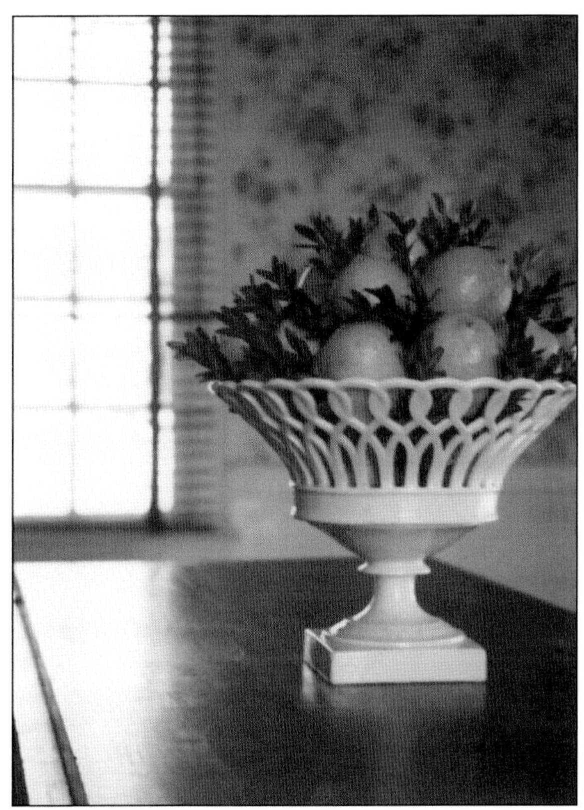

Reticulated Compote, c. 1980. This is one of two reticulated compote bowls purchased by Elvira McClelland Henry with proceeds earned from selling lemons grown in her orangery at Red Hill. The matching bowl is now lost. Unlike a standard compote bowl, which was designed to hold syrupy liquids, this style, with its reticulated or open latticework design, was designed to display fresh fruit or flowers.

Elvira Henry's Cooking Book, 2024. Family anecdotes tell of Elvira McClelland Henry's love of cooking. John and Elvira Henry lived their entire married life at Red Hill, and during this time, she created this cookbook, filled with over 230 handwritten and printed recipes. The book is titled by hand on the front, "Elvira Henry Cooking Book," and is a cherished heirloom in the Red Hill collection.

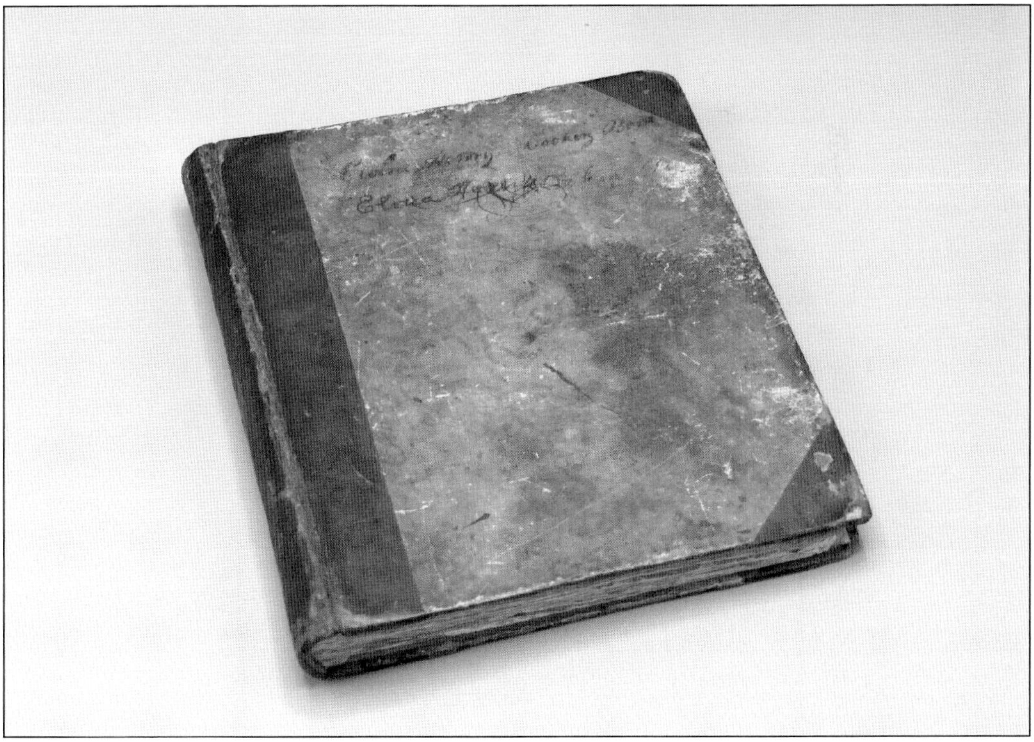

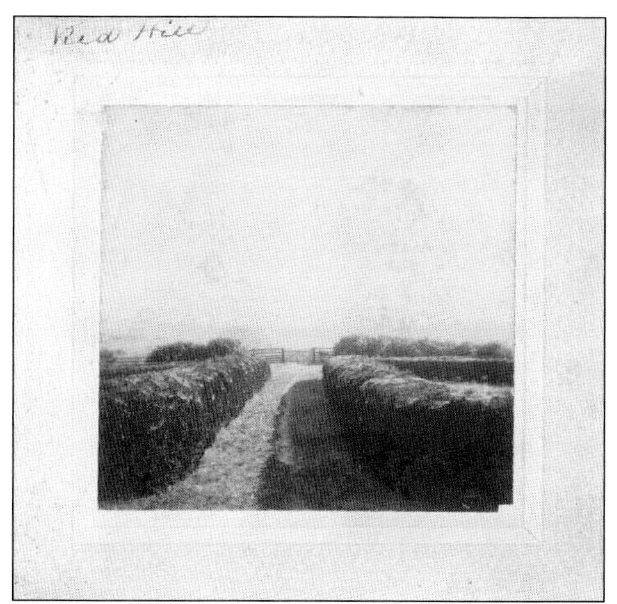

Boxwood Garden, c. 1895. After John Henry inherited Red Hill, his wife began beautifying the grounds. Along with having an orangery built and fruit trees and shrubs planted, Elvira designed a D-shaped boxwood garden in front of the house, reportedly patterned on the boxwoods at her childhood home, Union Hill. The American boxwood planted for Elvira Henry by enslaved gardeners can still be seen today.

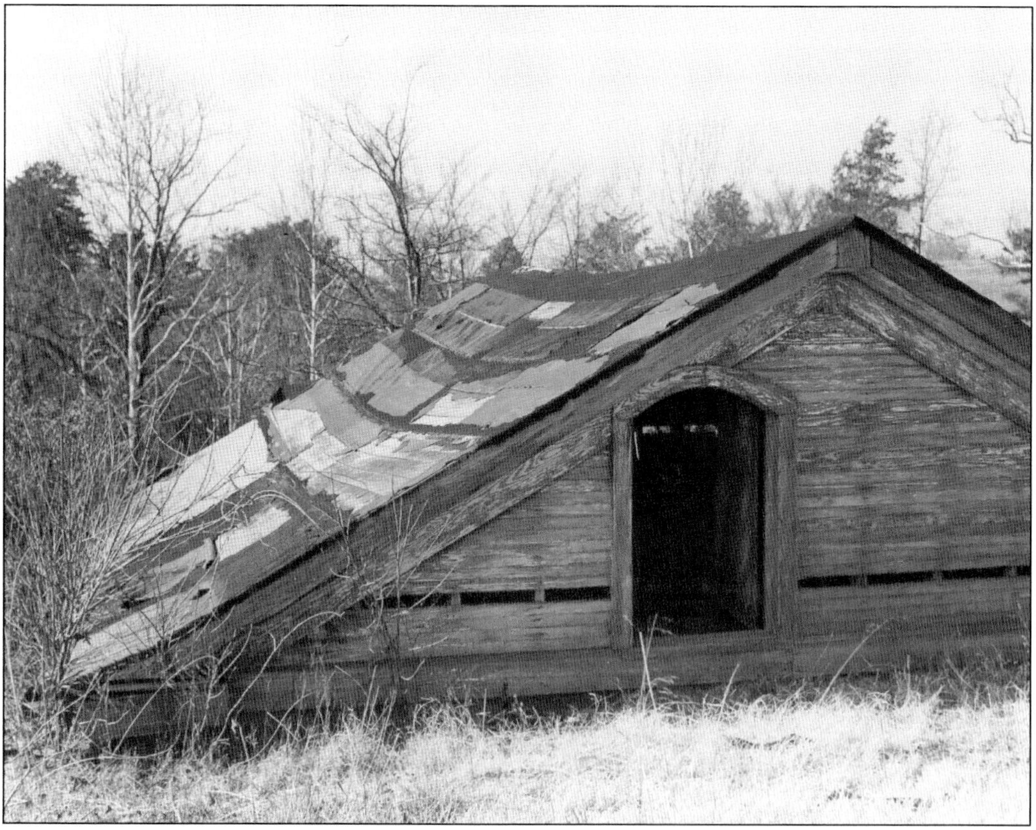

Icehouse, c. 1950. Before the advent of refrigeration, deep pits dug into the ground stored ice year-round. This photograph shows the ruins of the old icehouse, taken a few years after Lucy Harrison's death in 1944. To the right of the icehouse stood a dilapidated servant's house, constructed around 1930, and a small garden shed.

Tobacco Barn, c. 1950. Once a common sight at Red Hill, tobacco barns, like this one standing on Quarter Place, were used to dry and cure tobacco leaves before being pressed in barrels and sent to market. After the plant was cut from the ground, the stalks were split up the center and hung over wooden sticks inside the barns for four to six weeks over a smoldering fire.

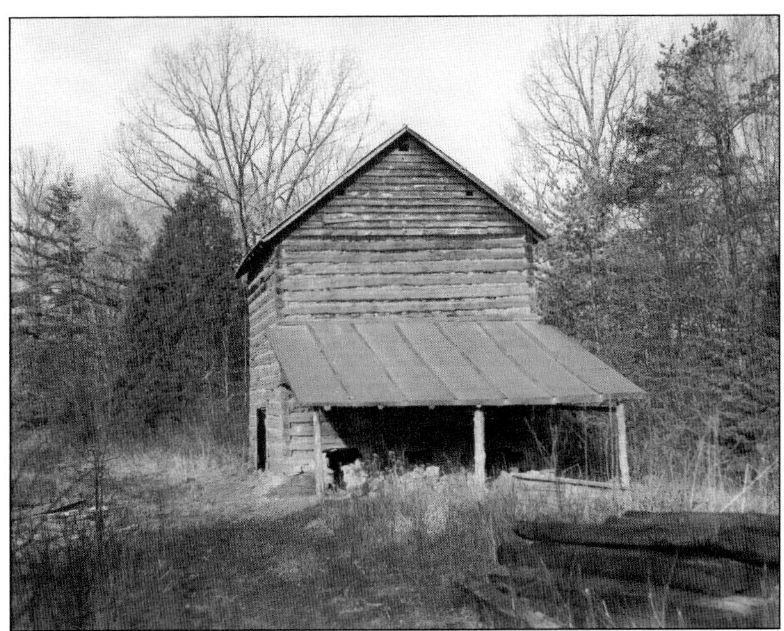

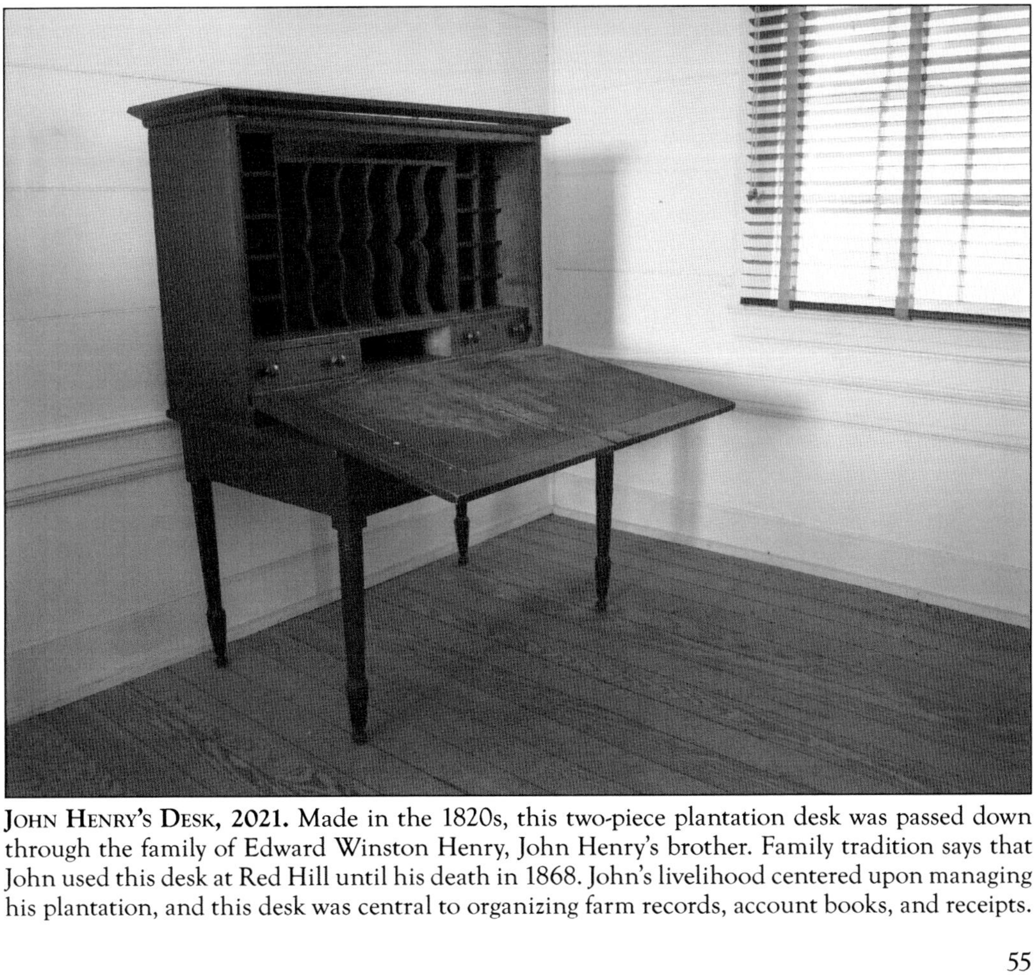

John Henry's Desk, 2021. Made in the 1820s, this two-piece plantation desk was passed down through the family of Edward Winston Henry, John Henry's brother. Family tradition says that John used this desk at Red Hill until his death in 1868. John's livelihood centered upon managing his plantation, and this desk was central to organizing farm records, account books, and receipts.

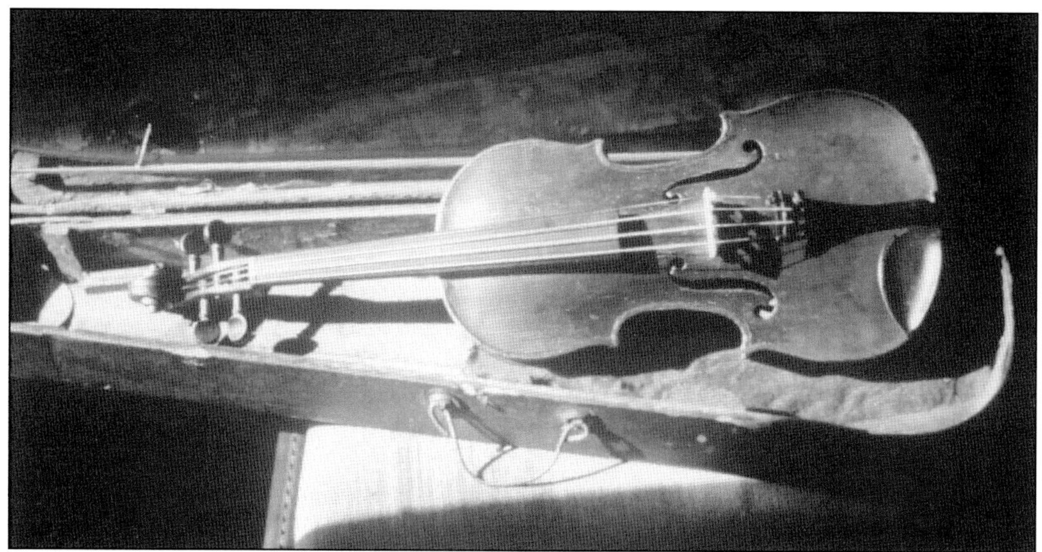

John Henry's Violin, 1988. In his youth, Patrick Henry learned to play fiddle and flute, and family tradition tells of him playing in his later years at Red Hill. Dorothea played the pianoforte and the English guitar. The enjoyment of music passed through the family as several children played musical instruments. This violin was purchased from the estate of a Henry family member.

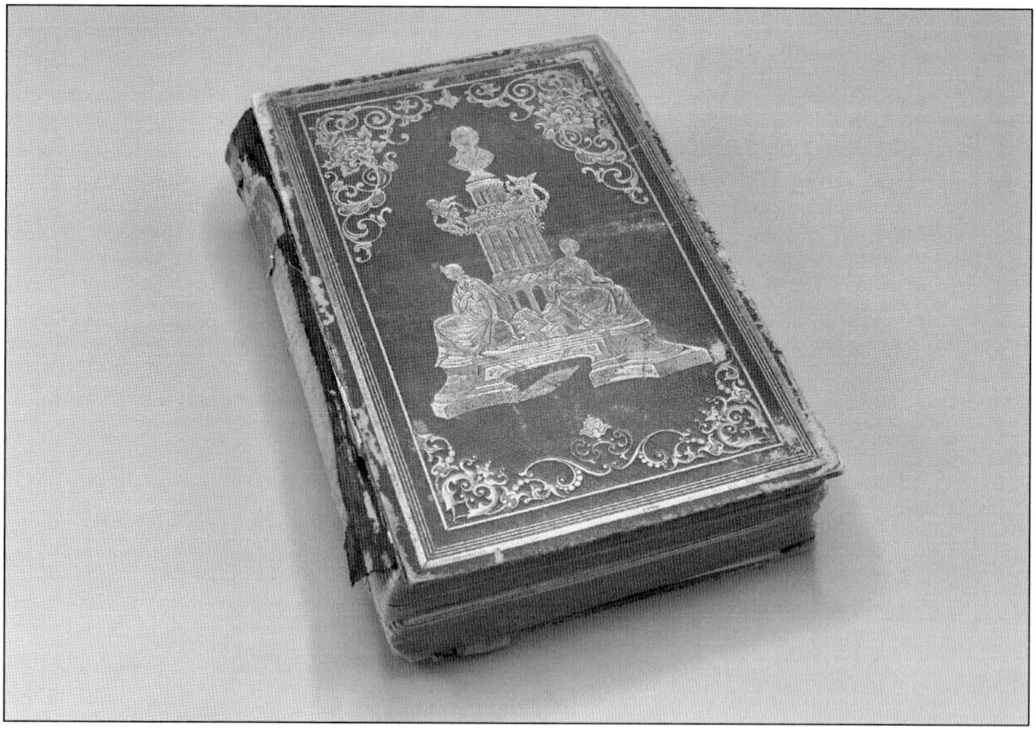

***The Complete Works of Robert Burns*, 2024.** Emma Henry Ferguson gave this 1860 edition of Robert Burns to her father, John Henry. Often referred to as the "National Poet of Scotland," Burns remains popular today. His works have inspired 20th-century writers like John Steinbeck and J.D. Salinger and musicians like Bob Dylan and Ian Anderson. His importance is often compared to that of William Shakespeare.

Margaret Henry Miller, c. 1855. Born at Red Hill in 1827 to John and Elvira Henry, Margaret married William Alexander Miller in 1849. The couple spent much of their young married life at Red Hill and would go on to have 12 children of their own. The Miller family seat, Sharswood, still stands in nearby Pittsylvania County.

William Wirt Henry, c. 1895. The eldest son of John and Elvira Henry, William Henry was born at Red Hill in 1831. After graduating from the University of Virginia in 1850, he pursued a career in law. While serving as the commonwealth's attorney for Charlotte County, the Civil War began, and William enlisted in the Staunton Hill Artillery. William returned to Red Hill and used it as his summer home.

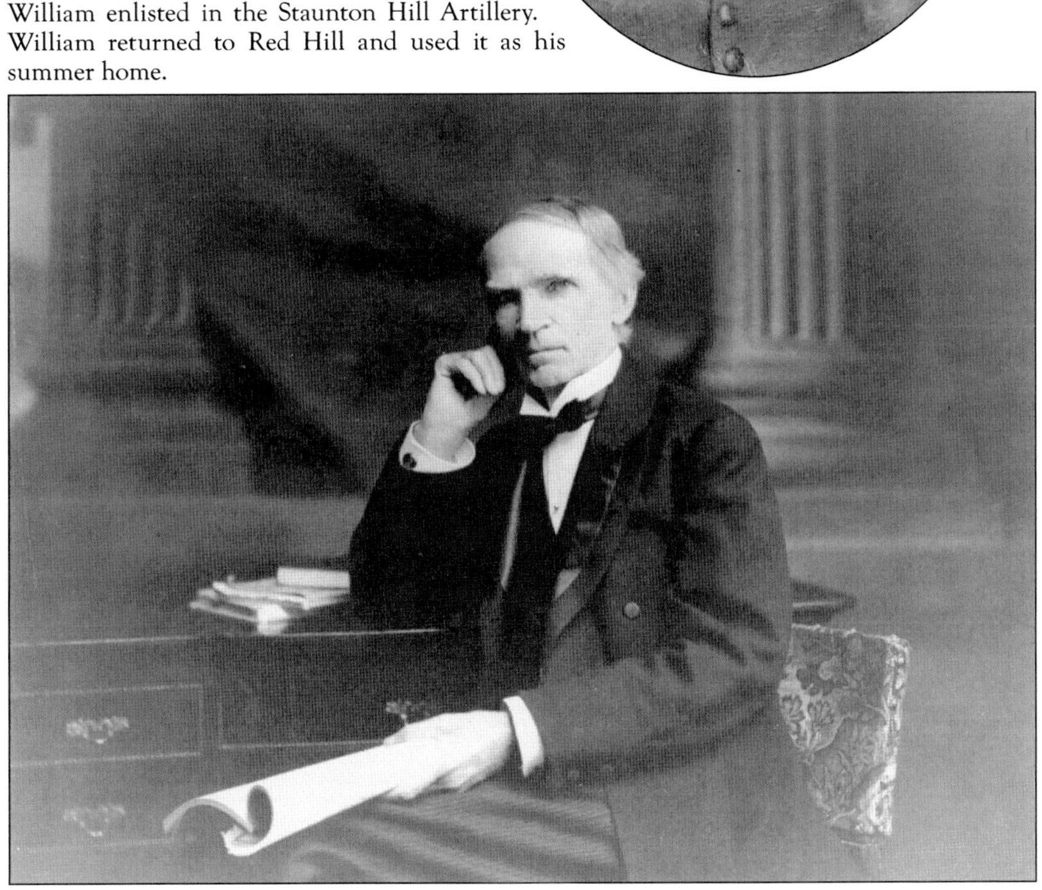

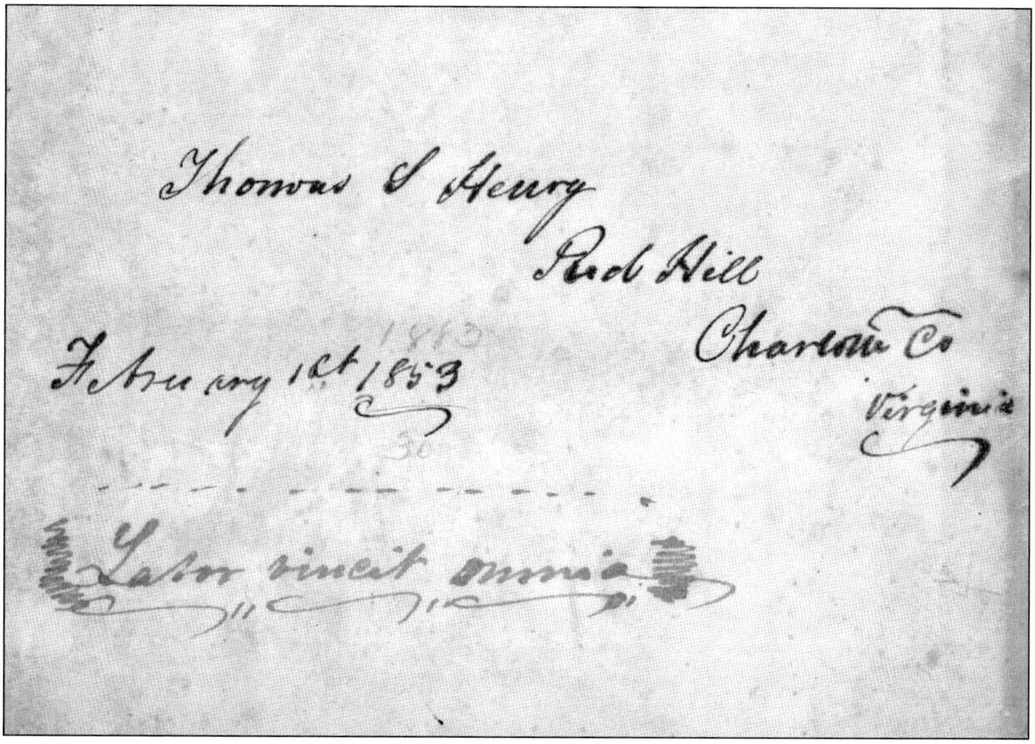

Thomas S Henry
Red Hill
Charlotte Co
Virginia
February 1st 1853

Labor vincit omnia

Thomas Stanhope Henry's Signature, 1853. Born in 1832 to John and Elvira Henry, Thomas took over the operation of Red Hill when his brother William moved to Richmond in 1873. The last surviving grandson of Patrick Henry, Thomas died at Red Hill in 1912 and was buried at Charlotte Court House next to his wife, Mary Gaines.

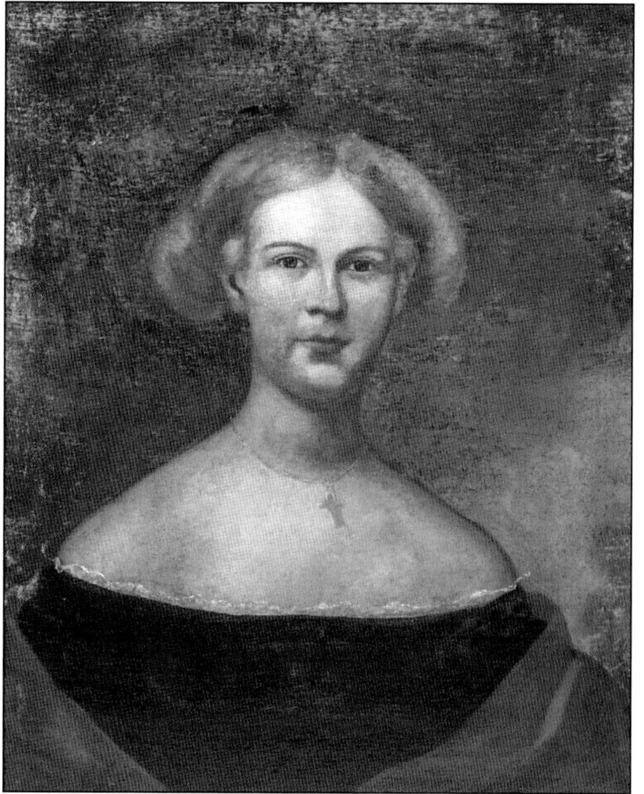

***Laura Helen Henry Carter* by J.W. King, 1863.** Laura Helen, the fifth child of John and Elvira Henry, was born at Red Hill on March 15, 1836. In 1855, Laura married Dr. James Carter, but she tragically died from tuberculosis two years later at the age of 20. Following her burial at Red Hill, Laura's sister commissioned artist J.W. King to paint this portrait after a photograph of her.

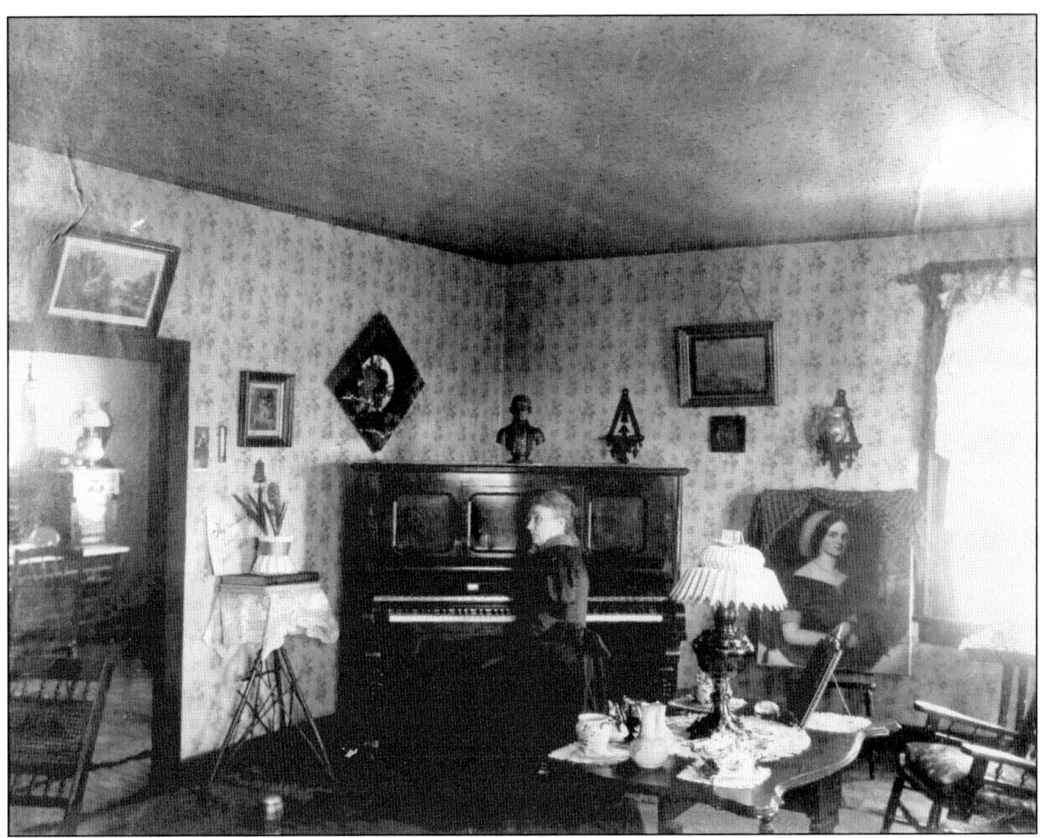

EMMA CABELL FERGUSON, C. 1896. Born at Red Hill in 1845, Emma Cabell was the daughter of John and Elvira Henry. She married Maj. James Boswell Ferguson, a blockade runner for the Confederacy, and moved to LaValle in Goochland County, Virginia, where she died in 1905. Like many members of the Henry family, Emma had a gift for music and played piano. She is seen sitting in her Lynchburg residence.

ELVIRA BRUCE HENRY, C. 1915. The second child of John and Elvira Henry, Elvira Bruce appears a sophisticated and wealthy woman in this portrait. She married twice, first to Jessie Higginbotham in May 1848 and secondly to Alexander F. Taylor in November 1851. This photograph of the work is all that remains, as the original painting was destroyed when the Henry mansion caught fire in 1919.

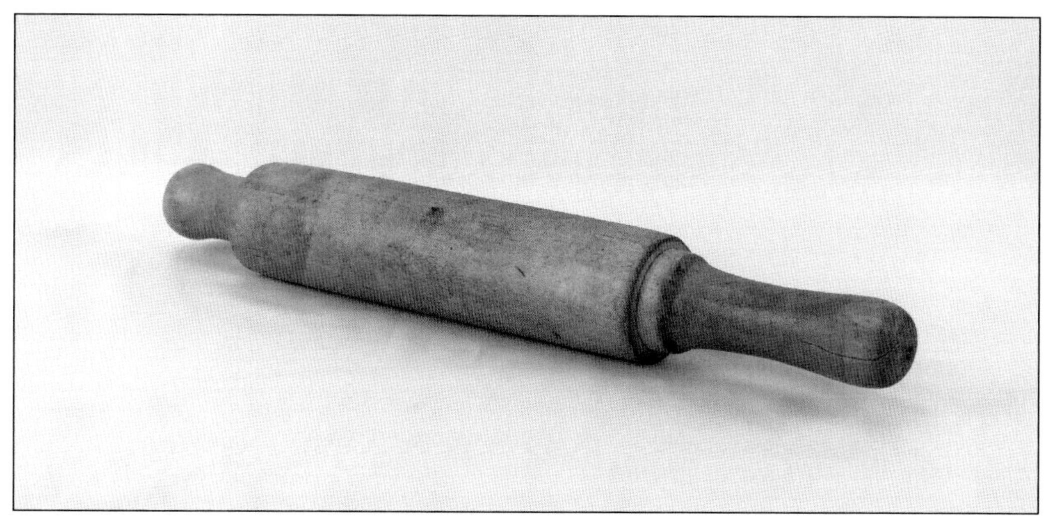

ROLLING PIN, 2023. An enslaved carpenter at Red Hill made this wooden rolling pin in the early 19th century. Enslaved cooks used it to prepare meals at Edward Winston Henry's plantation, Windstone. Cooks were considered some of the most important enslaved domestics, and they were highly educated and skilled in food science.

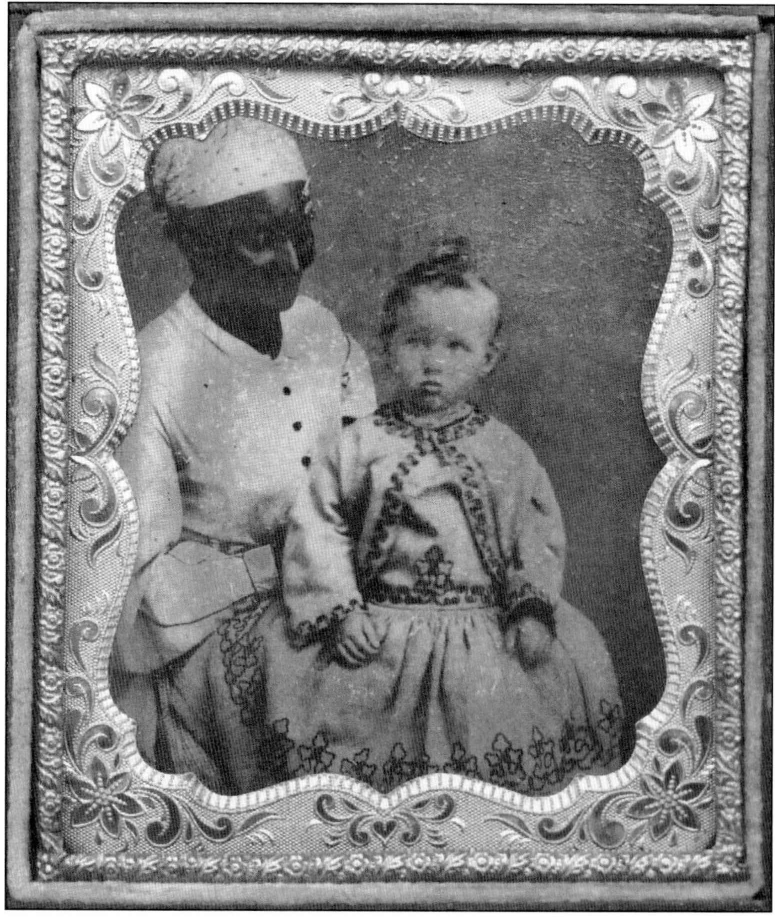

NANNY WITH CHILD, C. 1870. Images of enslaved persons are scarce. This tintype photograph of a freed nanny and her ward demonstrates the relationship between white children and their Black caretakers amid strained power dynamics. Although both sitters are unidentified, the nanny was likely enslaved at Windstone or Red Hill, and the child could be a Henry descendant.

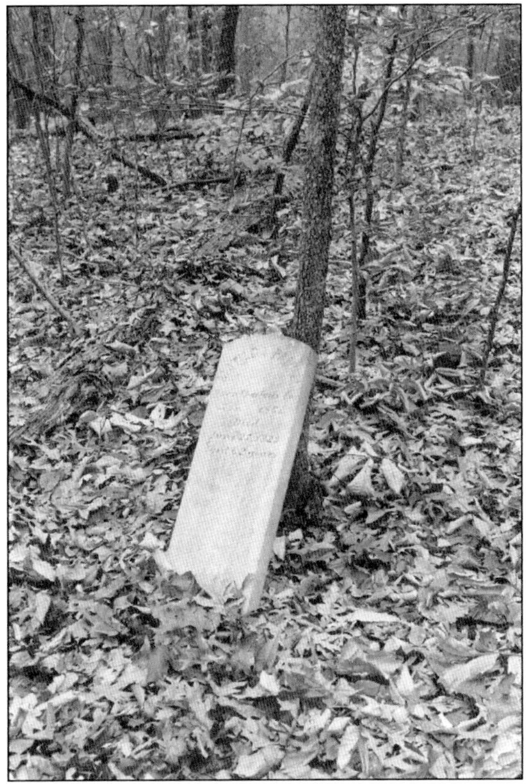

Grave of Matilda Pannell, c. 2005. Of the 147 known graves in Quarter Place Cemetery, only one is inscribed with a name. Matilda Pannell was born enslaved in 1861 at Red Hill and married Harry Pannell in 1880. She died free in 1923 and is buried here with her ancestors. Patrick Henry enslaved Matilda's great-grandmother Vilet, who appears on the 1799 estate inventory as a child.

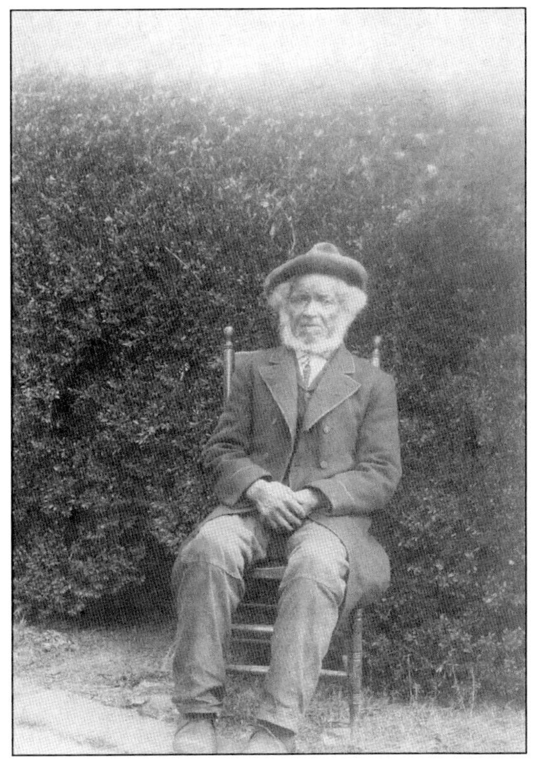

Harrison Henry, c. 1890. This cabinet card of Harrison Henry was taken at Red Hill among the boxwood gardens. Born into slavery around 1798, Harrison Henry carried Dorothea Henry's knitting basket and keys, and in later years, he served as the family's enslaved coachman. Harrison lived to around 108 and was buried in Quarter Place Cemetery. By one account, "He was an old time gentleman in manner and character."

List of Enslaved Persons, April 1865. Following the defeat of the Confederate army at Appomattox Court House on April 9, 1865, Virginia enslavers manumitted their enslaved workforce under the 13th Amendment to the US Constitution. In 1865, John Henry had 54 enslaved people at Red Hill. While most formerly enslaved left the plantation, some remained as sharecroppers or domestic servants. (VMHC.)

HARRISON AND MILLY HENRY, C. 1885. Harrison and his wife, Milly Henry, are seen as freedpeople in front of their home at Red Hill. Little is known about Milly except that she may have been purchased by John Henry from his brother Alexander Spotswood and the Dabney brothers in 1839. An advertisement in the *Lynchburg Virginian* lists 19 enslaved people for sale, one of which was a woman named Milly.

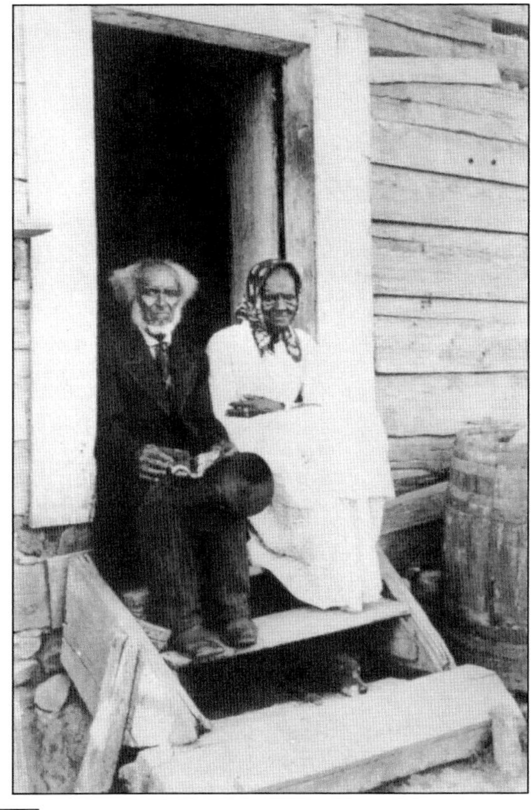

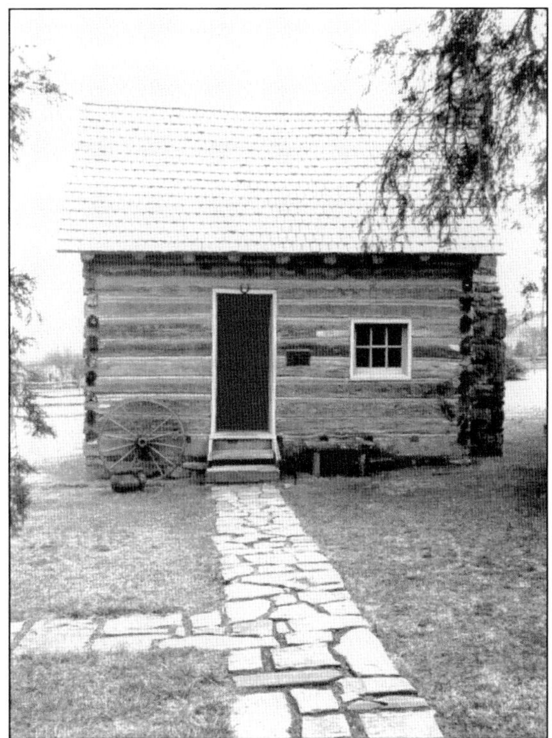

HARRISON'S CABIN, 1980. Built as slave quarters in the mid-19th century, this cabin was later given to Harrison Henry by William Wirt Henry after emancipation. Harrison lived here with his wife, Milly, until his death around 1906. The building was restored in 1961 using about a quarter of the original logs and is now furnished as a freedmen's cabin.

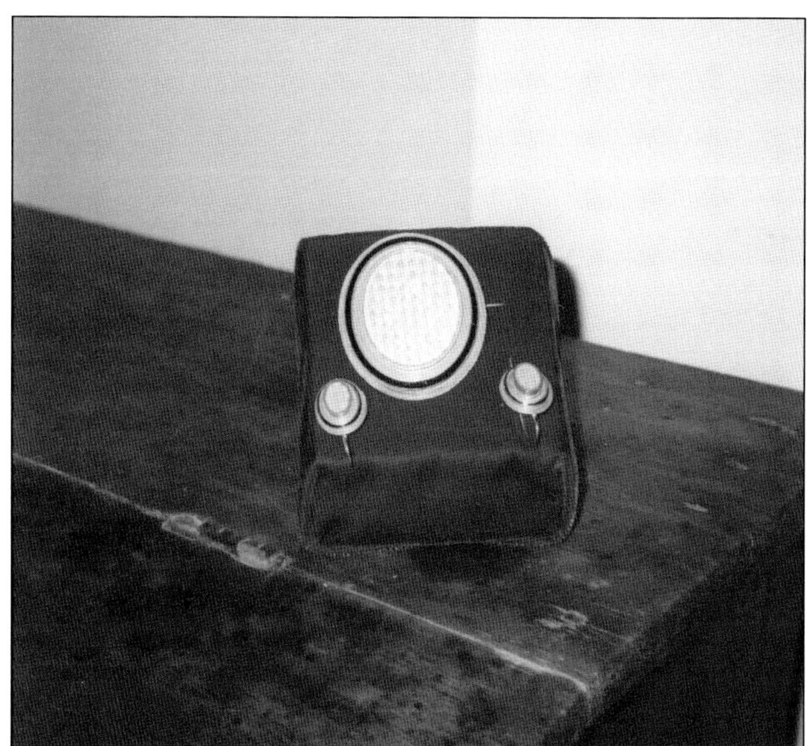

Hair Jewelry, 1996. Hairwork, like this brooch and earrings set, was popular for mourning jewelry from the 18th through the 19th centuries. Hair cut from the deceased was crafted into a keepsake for the family to wear during the period of mourning. This brooch bears the inscription, "Sacred to the memory of John Henry of Red Hill; Died January 7, 1868." These pieces contain John Henry's hair.

Graves of John and Elvira McClelland Henry, 1999. In 1875, Elvira Henry died at Red Hill, seven years after her husband. The couple was interred in the family cemetery just feet from John's illustrious parents. Rogers & Miller, a Richmond-based stonemason firm, carved and installed the marble slabs. The rough-cut stone walls were likely found on the property.

Four

Growth and Loss 1876–1944

The history of Red Hill in the Henry family continued beyond the deaths of John and Elvira Henry. William Wirt Henry, the grandson of Patrick Henry, and subsequently his daughter Lucy Gray Henry Harrison would perpetuate the family's 150-year legacy of ownership and residency.

William Wirt Henry, who enjoyed a distinguished legal career and served in both the House and Senate of the Virginia Legislature, retained ownership of Red Hill while residing primarily in Richmond. He delegated the plantation management to his brother Dr. Thomas Stanhope Henry. Sharecroppers residing on or near the property cultivated the estate's extensive tobacco and other crop fields.

Upon William Wirt Henry's death in December 1900, he bequeathed Red Hill to his wife and three of his four children. A widow since her husband's passing in 1892, Lucy Henry Harrison was left out of her father's will "not because I do not love her as much as my other children but because she already has a larger estate than what I estimate my estate at." In 1905, Lucy purchased Red Hill from her mother and siblings, initiating substantial modifications to the estate.

The property underwent significant transformations following Patrick Henry's death in 1799 and extending into the early 20th century. Under Lucy's direction, the residence was transformed into an impressive Colonial Revival mansion comprising over 20 rooms. Unfortunately, in February 1919, a devastating fire destroyed the mansion. Despite no injuries, the structure was lost. George Ed Britton, a Black teenage sharecropper, and other estate workers salvaged valuable items from the house. Although the mansion was never rebuilt, the Henry office was enlarged, and Lucy resided in the relatively modest wooden structure on the property until her death in 1944.

Subsequently, in 1945, the estate was sold to the newly established Patrick Henry Memorial Foundation, which sought to preserve the patriot's legacy and narrate the history of all those who lived and worked at Red Hill.

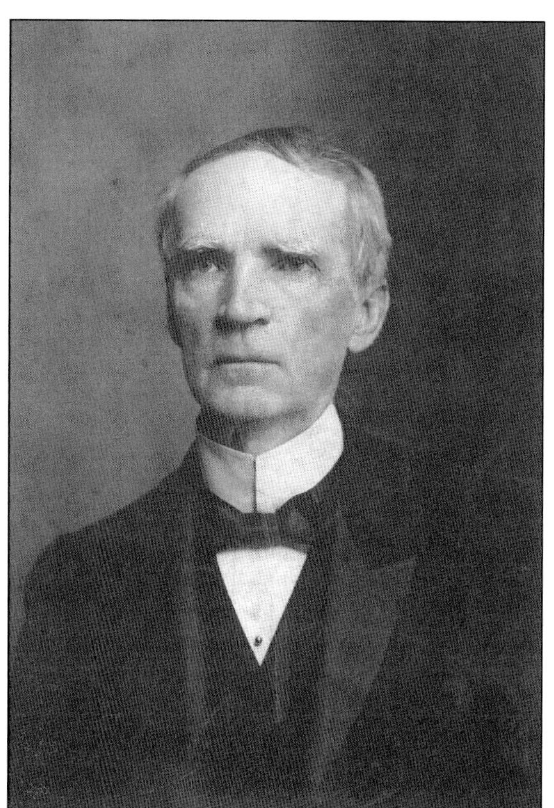

William Wirt Henry, 1890. In 1873, William moved to Richmond, leaving the operation of Red Hill in the hands of his younger brother Thomas Stanhope. During his time in the city, William served in the Virginia Legislature and later in the state senate. William died at his Richmond home in 1900. His three-volume work, *Patrick Henry: Life, Correspondence, and Speeches* (1891), is considered the preeminent biography of the patriot.

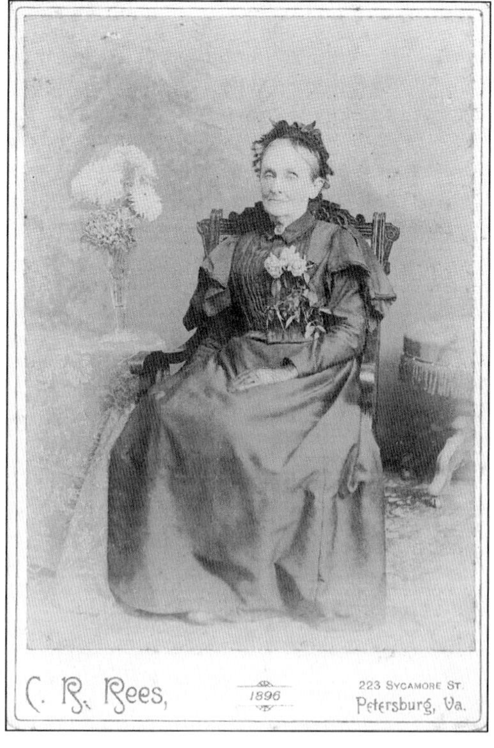

Lucy Gray Marshall Henry, 1896. The daughter of Col. James P. Marshall of Charlotte Court House, Virginia, Lucy Gray Marshall married William Wirt Henry in 1854. In 1891, she became the first regent of the Virginia Society Daughters of the American Revolution. Eminent Civil War–era photographer Charles R. Reese captured this image of Lucy in 1896 in his Petersburg, Virginia, studio.

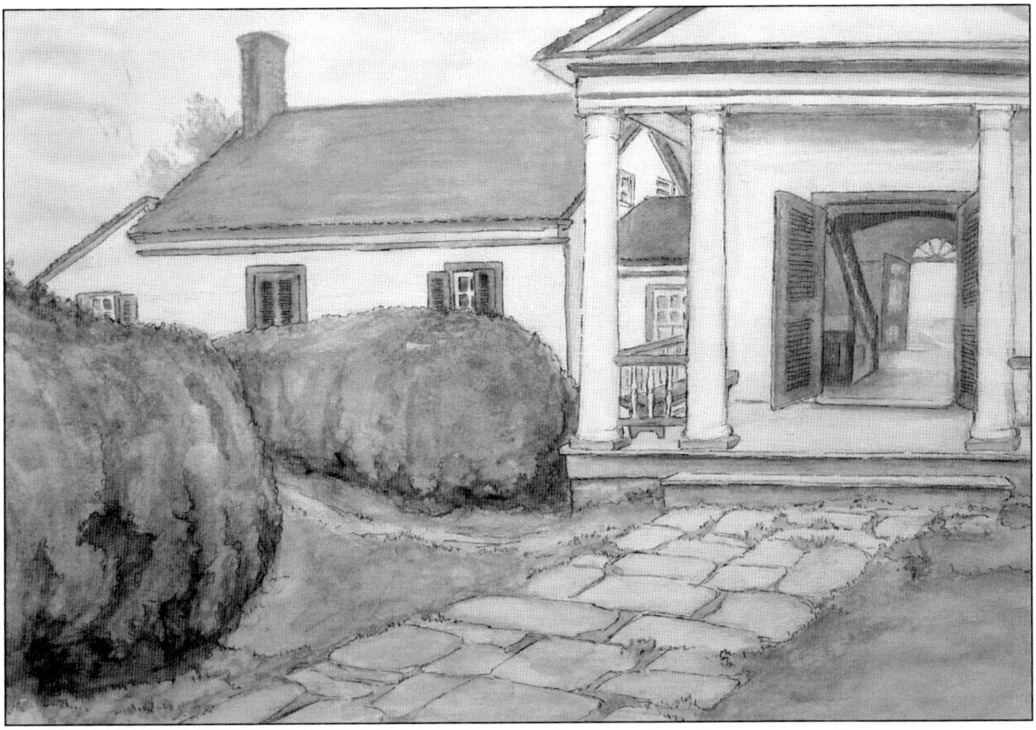

North Entrance at Red Hill by Susan Alrich Low, 1904. This watercolor provides a rare view of the north side of the Henry family home. The original portion lived in by Patrick Henry is seen on the left. The shuttered doors of the John Henry addition are open, allowing a view of the hallway and staircase. The rolling hills of Halifax County can be seen through the open south doors.

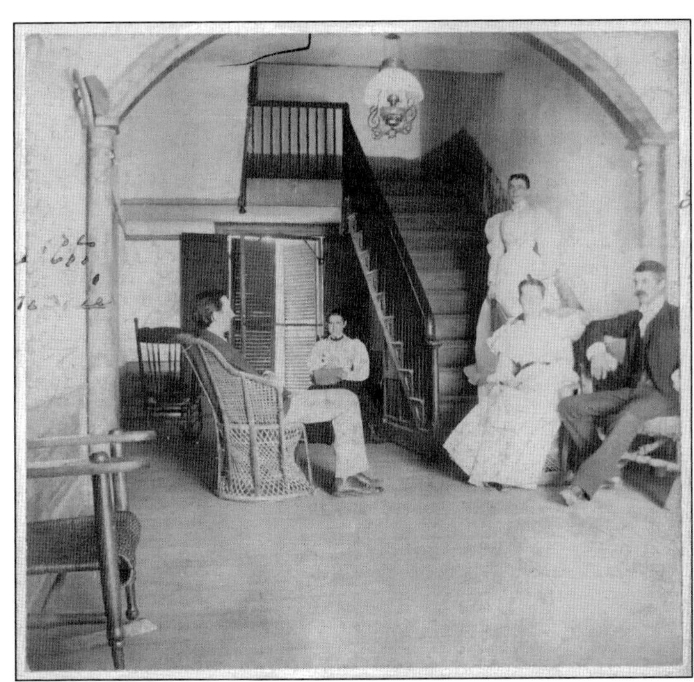

The Henry Family, c. 1900. This group photograph of Henry family members was taken in the entry hall of the main house at Red Hill. Three subjects—William Wirt Henry Jr. (far right), his sister Elizabeth Henry Lyons (second from right), and Lucy Gray Henry Harrison (second from left)—are great-grandchildren of Patrick Henry. A few years after this photograph was taken, Lucy would completely renovate this space.

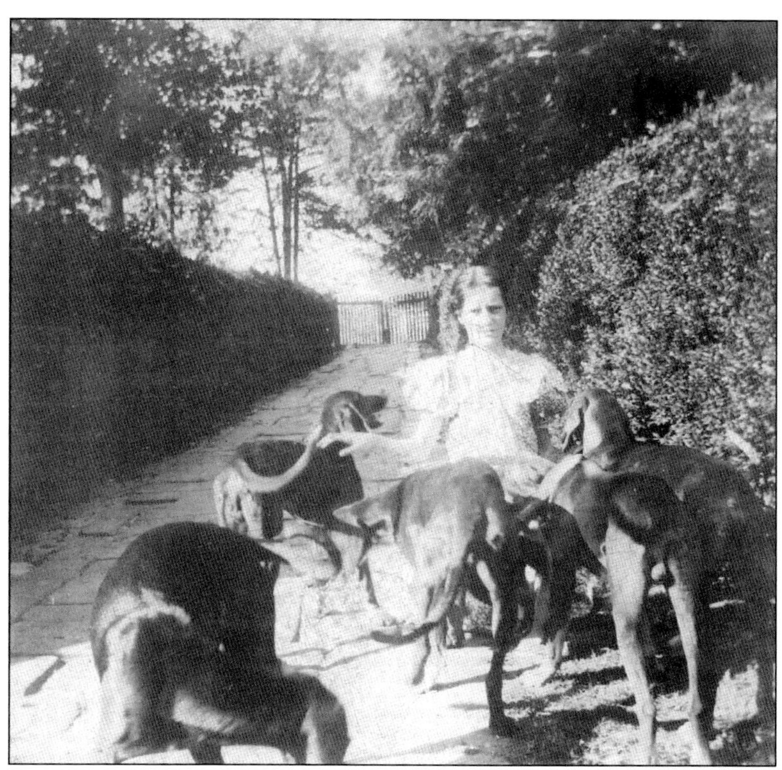

Henningham Lyons and Henry Hounds, c. 1900. Henningham Lyons, a great-great-granddaughter of Patrick Henry, sits on a walkway at Red Hill with her father's hunting dogs, known as the "Henry Hounds." Around 1838, her distant cousin Thomas Yuille Henry began breeding hounds from a direct offspring of a famous Irish hound called Mountain. Renowned for their speed and endurance, the Henry Hounds were much sought after by hunters.

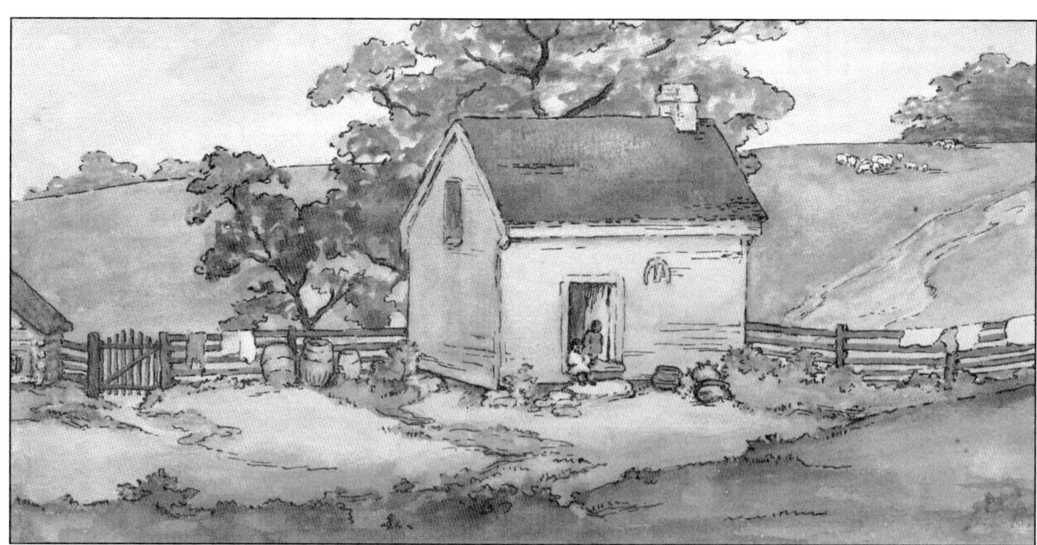

***Kitchen at Red Hill* by Susan Alrich Low, 1904.** This watercolor painting captures a glimpse of plantation life at Red Hill. Two African American children (likely the cook's children) are seen in the old kitchen doorway as laundry dries on the fence. In the distance, sheep graze on the hill where the visitor center stands today. Unfortunately, this building burned down in 1928.

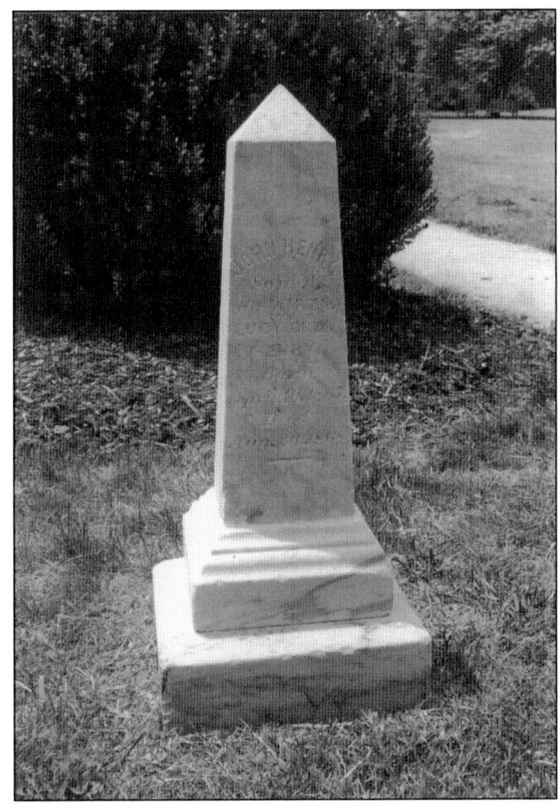

Grave of John Henry, 1999. On occasion, tragedy struck the Henry family. The youngest son of William Wirt and Lucy Marshall Henry, little John was born at Red Hill with his twin brother, James, in 1867. Unfortunately, only James would live to adulthood. Little John died of dysentery in August 1868 at just over a year old and was buried in the family cemetery under a small obelisk marker.

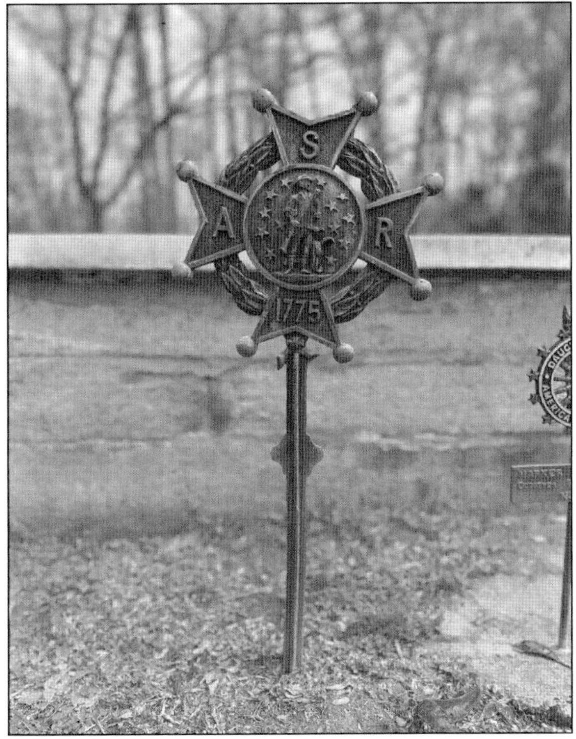

Sons of the American Revolution Grave Marker, 2023. The Sons of the American Revolution commemorate those who contributed to the Revolutionary War. One of its goals is to identify and mark the graves of these patriots. Placed in 1895 by the Massachusetts Society, this bronze marker was possibly installed with Henry's grandson, William Wirt Henry, who founded the Virginia Society and served as state president from 1890 to 1897.

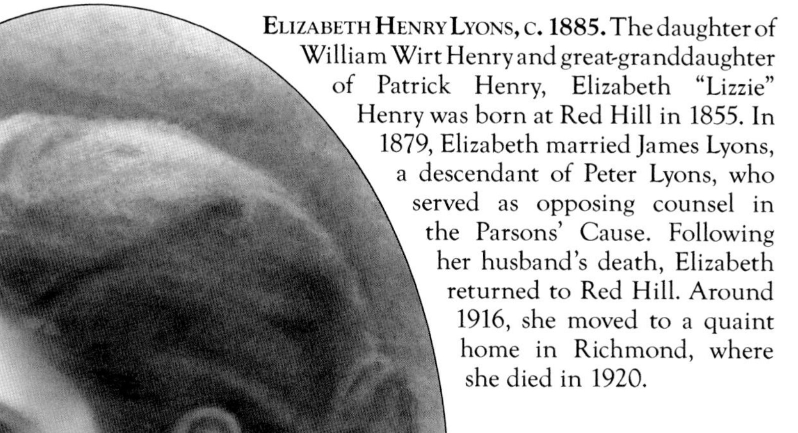

ELIZABETH HENRY LYONS, C. 1885. The daughter of William Wirt Henry and great-granddaughter of Patrick Henry, Elizabeth "Lizzie" Henry was born at Red Hill in 1855. In 1879, Elizabeth married James Lyons, a descendant of Peter Lyons, who served as opposing counsel in the Parsons' Cause. Following her husband's death, Elizabeth returned to Red Hill. Around 1916, she moved to a quaint home in Richmond, where she died in 1920.

HOME OF ELIZABETH HENRY LYONS, APRIL 1946. Lucy Harrison gave her sister this Colonial Revival home upon her return to Red Hill in 1914. The photograph was taken after the local Aspen School 4-H Club cleaned the grounds. Elizabeth lived here until returning to Richmond in 1916. Tenant farmers later lived here until a fire destroyed the house in 1977.

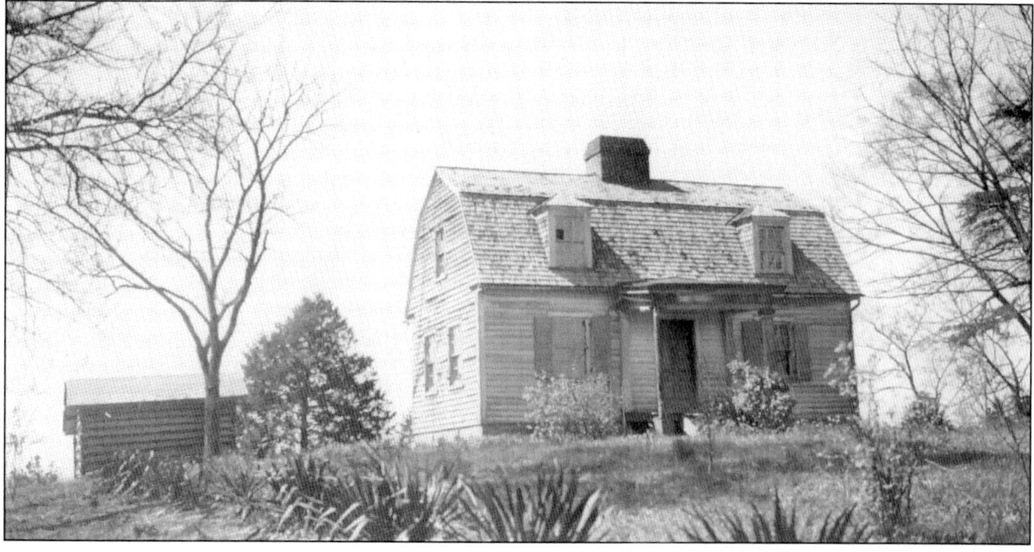

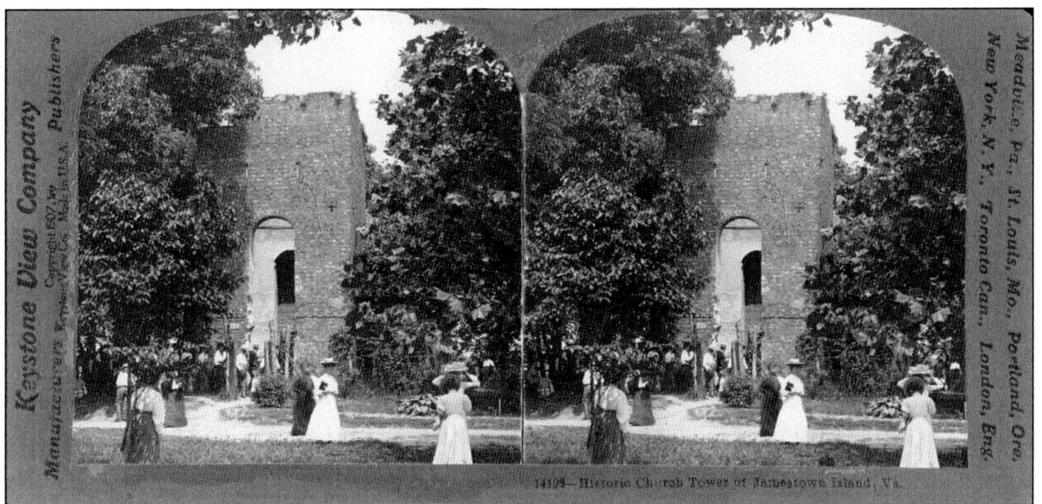

JAMESTOWN CHURCH TOWER, C. 1905. Built around 1680 at the first permanent English settlement, this church tower is all that remains above ground of the original fort. The Association for the Preservation of Virginia Antiquities, the first statewide preservation organization in the United States, was given the tower and 22.5 acres in 1893. An early corporator of the association, Elizabeth Lyons worked diligently to ensure the tower's acquisition. (LOC.)

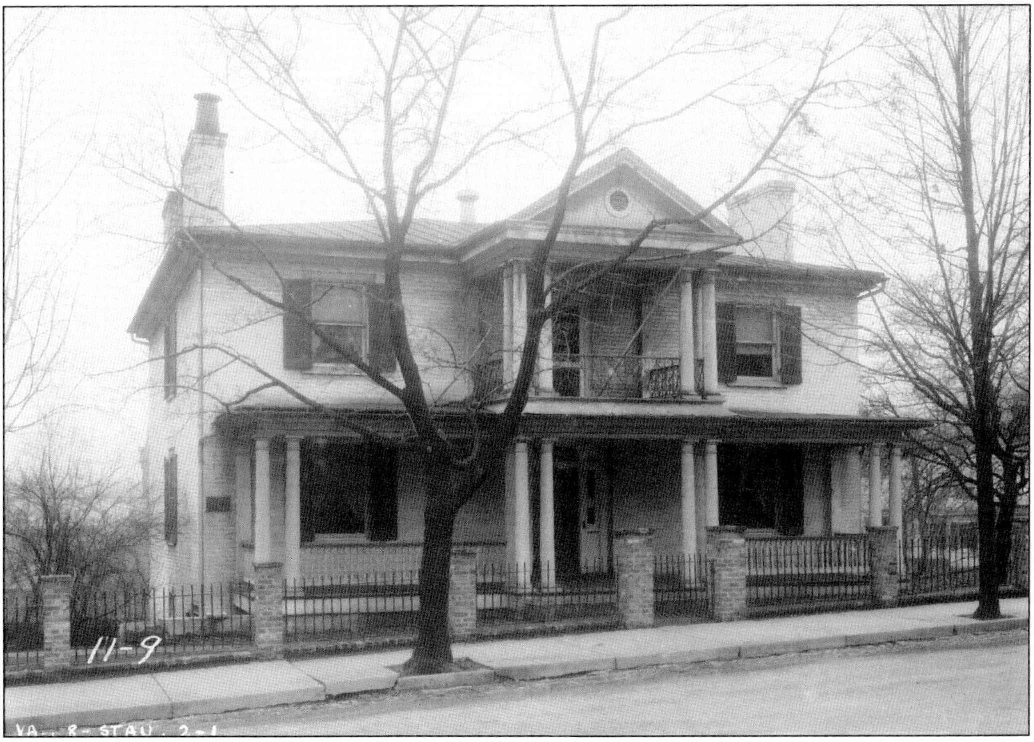

THE MANSE, 1936. Elizabeth and Lucy Henry were both highly educated women. In the 1870s, the sisters attended Augusta Female Seminary in Staunton, Virginia, where they learned foreign languages and advanced writing skills. Possibly designed by the seminary's founder, Rev. Rufus W. Bailey, in 1846, this building housed the pastors of Staunton's First Presbyterian Church. Pres. Woodrow Wilson was born in this house in 1856. (LOC.)

LUCY GRAY AND LOUISE HENRY HARRISON, C. 1898. Lucy Henry Harrison (left) and her husband, Matthew Bland Harrison, gave birth to their only daughter, Louise, in 1888. Young Louise was well traveled, accompanying her mother to Scotland, England, and Switzerland. As a teenager, however, Louise began suffering from mental illness. This image is one of two known photographs of Louise.

MOUNT HOPE RETREAT, C. 1910. Operated as the largest mental hospital in Baltimore, Maryland, Mount Hope Retreat cared for hundreds of "insane, sick, and inebriates" since this building's completion in 1863. Louise Henry Harrison spent her final years here following her diagnosis of schizophrenia. Louise's mother likely paid between $8 and $15 per week for her care until her death at the age of 31 in 1920. (UMBC.)

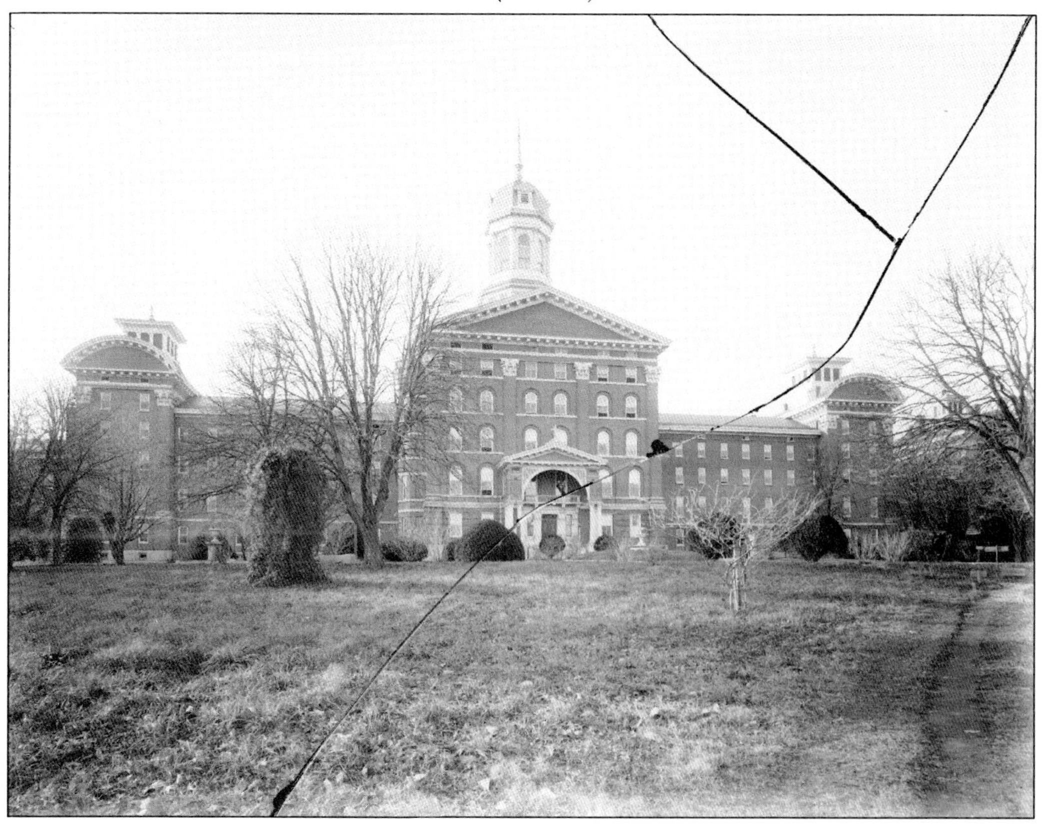

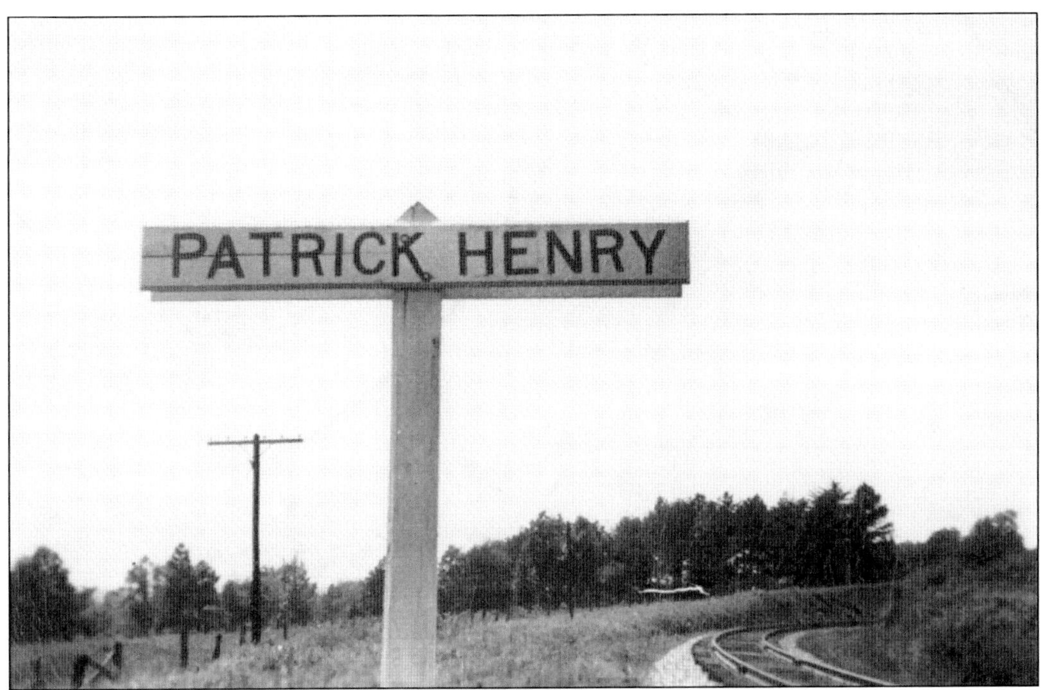

Flag Stop, c. 1948. In 1906, Lucy Harrison sold part of her Red Hill land to the Tidewater Railway Company for over $6,000. A flag stop was established on the conveyed land where trains picked up and discharged passengers. Located a few hundred yards south of the Henry house, the Patrick Henry station was used both by family members and visitors until the mid-20th century. The original iron gates and stone piers seen below still stand.

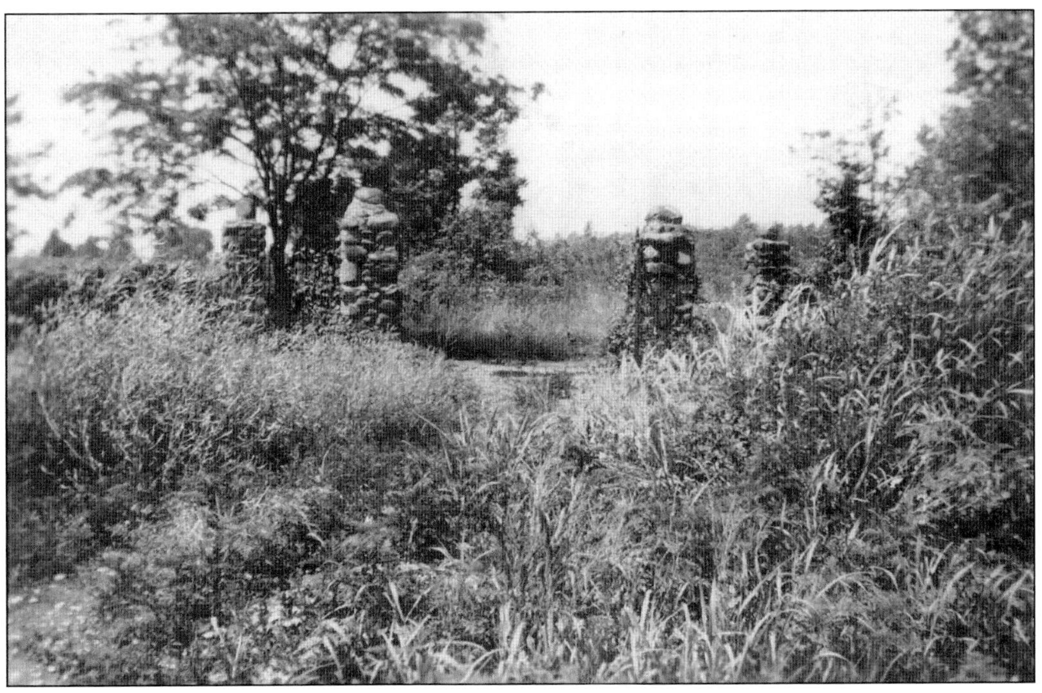

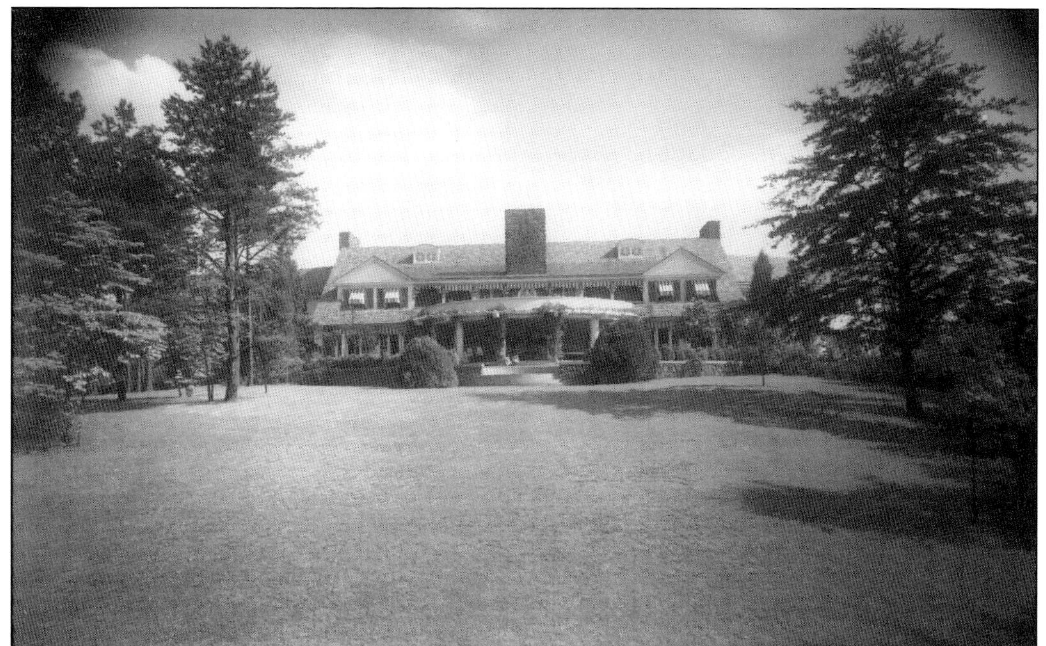

REYNOLDA HOUSE, C. 1920. Charles Barton Keen (1868–1931) was a prolific designer of the American "country house." In 1907, Lucy Harrison hired the Philadelphia architect to design additions to the John Henry house, incorporating the original Patrick Henry house. It took Keen nearly four years to complete Harrison's Colonial Revival mansion. His work at Red Hill led to later successes, including his most famous creation, Reynolda House, built in 1917. (RH.)

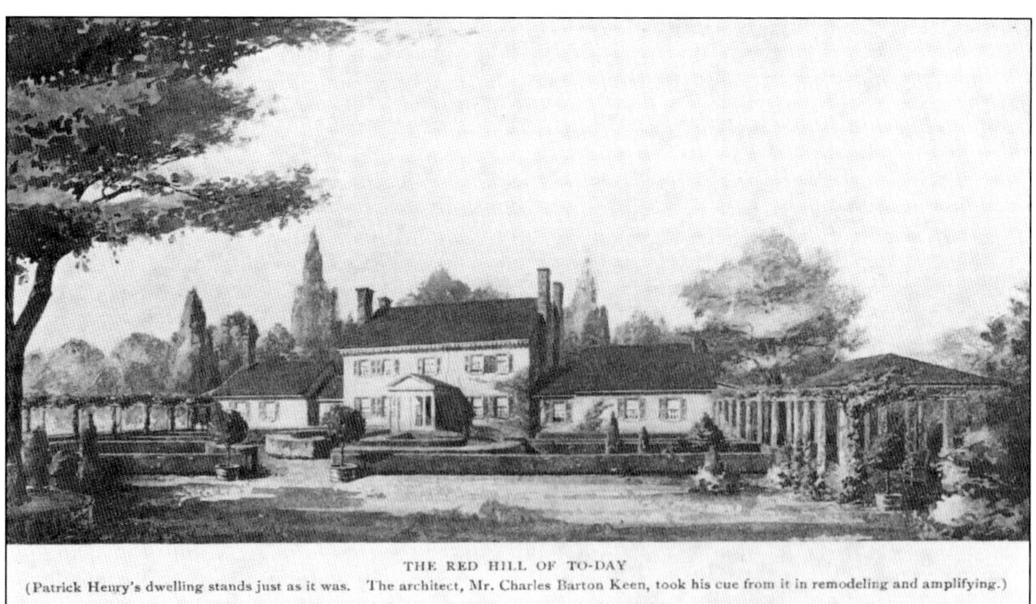

PROPOSED MANSION RENDERING, C. 1907. Architect Charles Barton Keen and his draftsmen painted this rendering of their vision for the new Henry home. However, the final design differed slightly: the grape arbors on either end of the house were never constructed, and the square boxwoods in front were never planted. Such a design was typical of Keen's Colonial Revival tastes.

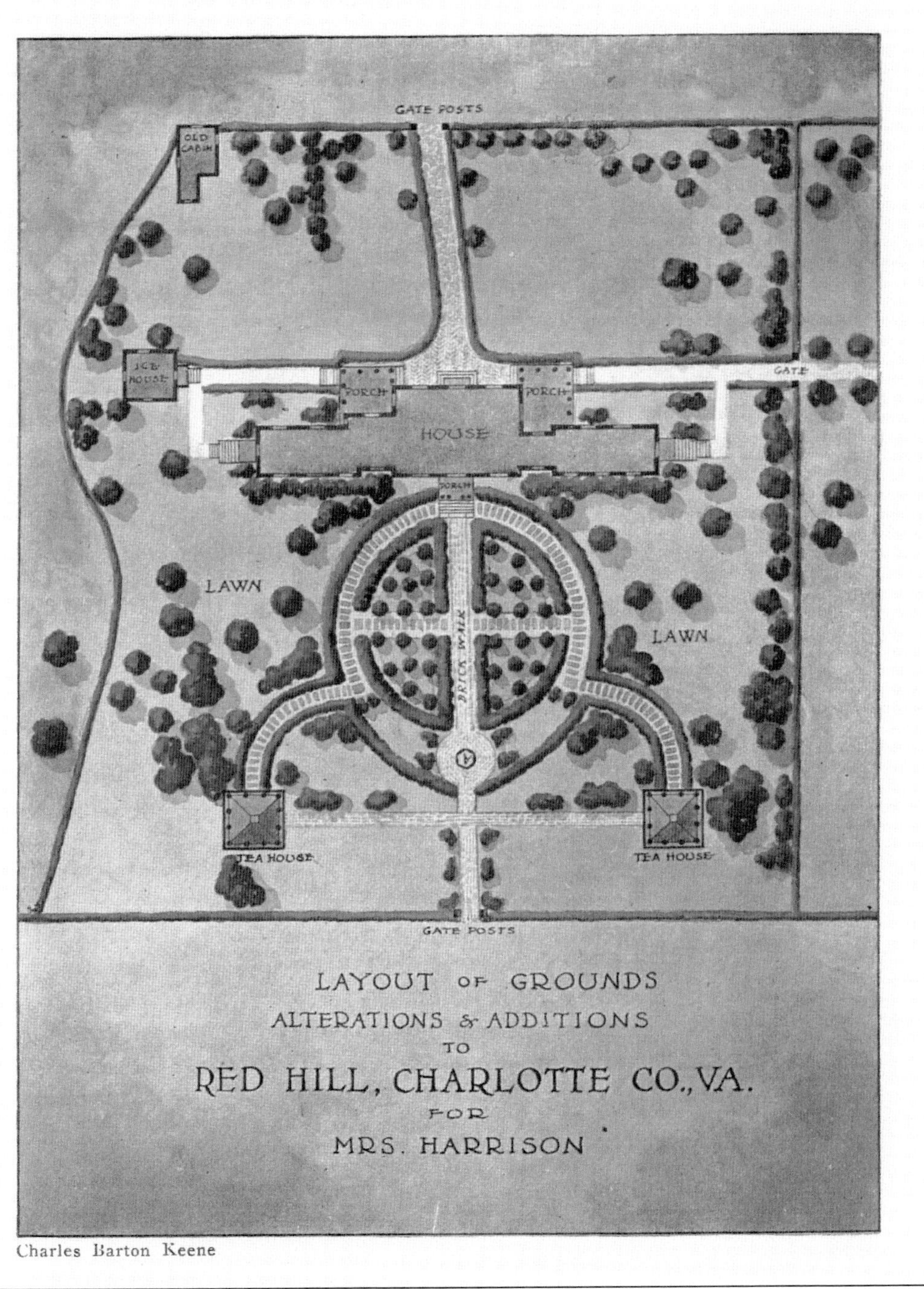

Landscape Renovation Plan, c. 1907. Under the direction of Charles Barton Keen, landscape architect Charles Welan completely transformed the Red Hill gardens. His plan worked in harmony with Keen's architectural creations to expand the 19th-century boxwood garden, lay down new cobblestone walkways, construct matching teahouses, and install plantings of tea, roses, calycanthus, spirea, pear trees, and other flowering shrubs. The plans seen here were never fully realized.

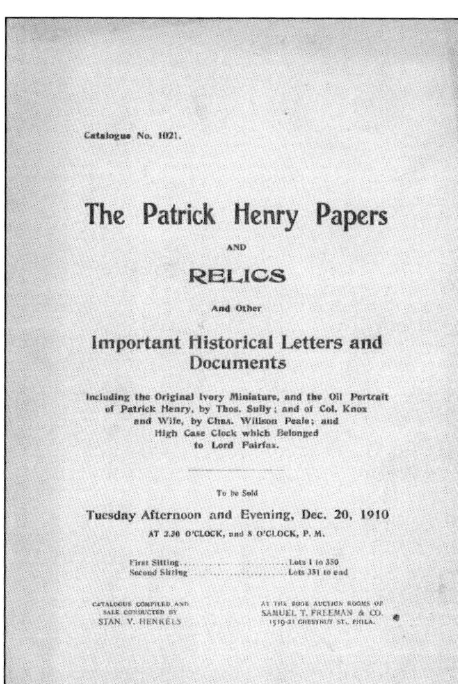

Catalogue No. 1021.

The Patrick Henry Papers

AND

RELICS

And Other

Important Historical Letters and Documents

Including the Original Ivory Miniature, and the Oil Portrait of Patrick Henry, by Thos. Sully; and of Col. Knox and Wife, by Chas. Willson Peale; and High Case Clock which Belonged to Lord Fairfax.

To be Sold

Tuesday Afternoon and Evening, Dec. 20, 1910

AT 2.30 O'CLOCK, and 8 O'CLOCK, P. M.

First Sitting........................Lots 1 to 350
Second Sitting......................Lots 351 to end

CATALOGUE COMPILED AND SALE CONDUCTED BY STAN. V. HENKELS

AT THE BOOK AUCTION ROOMS OF SAMUEL T. FREEMAN & CO. 1519-21 CHESTNUT ST., PHILA.

Auction Catalog, December 1910. To raise money for the expansion of her home into a 21-room mansion, in 1910, Lucy Harrison sold many of her great-grandfather's possessions at auction, including his papers, the chair in which he is said to have died, and his silver spice caster set. Stanislaus V. Henkels conducted the auction at the Philadelphia auction house of Samuel T. Freeman & Co.

Mansion Dining Room, c. 1917. Constructed as part of additions to the main house in 1911, this dining room features Colonial Revival wood paneling and molding, a black marble fireplace, and fashionable furnishings. A secret door to the right of the fireplace leads into the kitchen. Several family heirlooms, including Patrick Henry's silver saltcellars, are also displayed here.

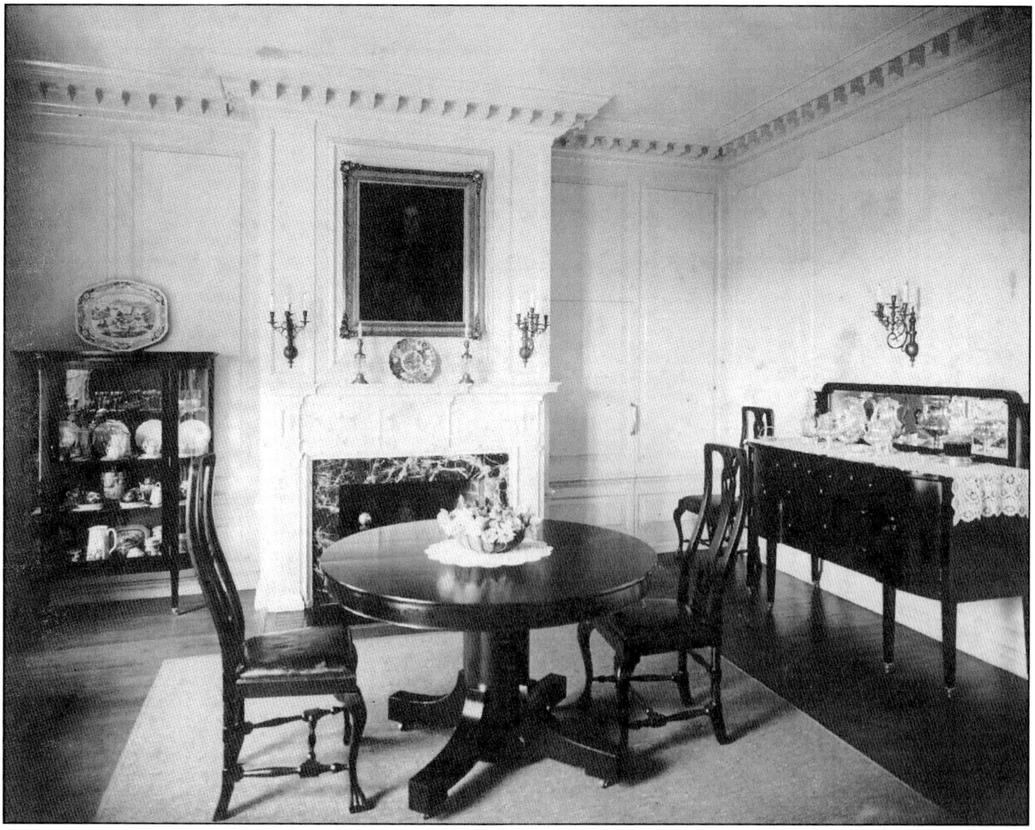

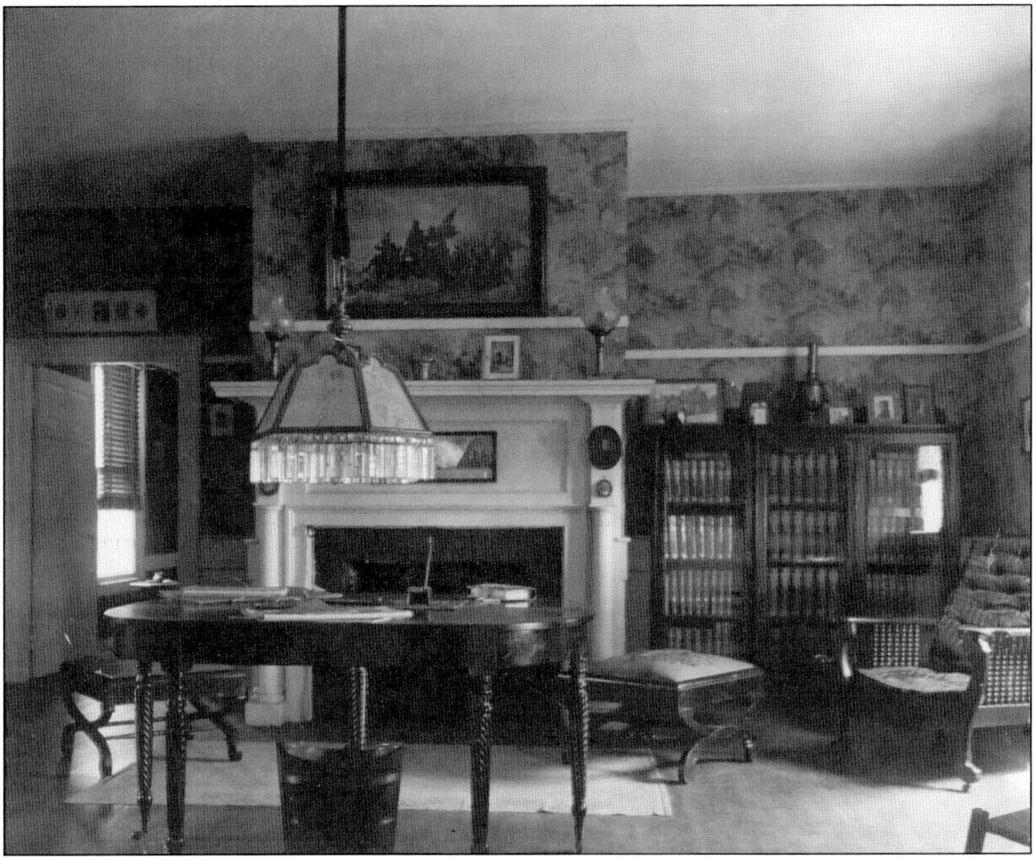

MANSION LIBRARY, C. 1912. While renovating her family home, Lucy Harrison turned the original Patrick Henry house into her library. According to family tradition, the "old chamber," as the space was known, was where Patrick Henry died. On the elegant mantle is a mortar and pestle said to have been owned by Henry and used for grinding herbs and making medicines.

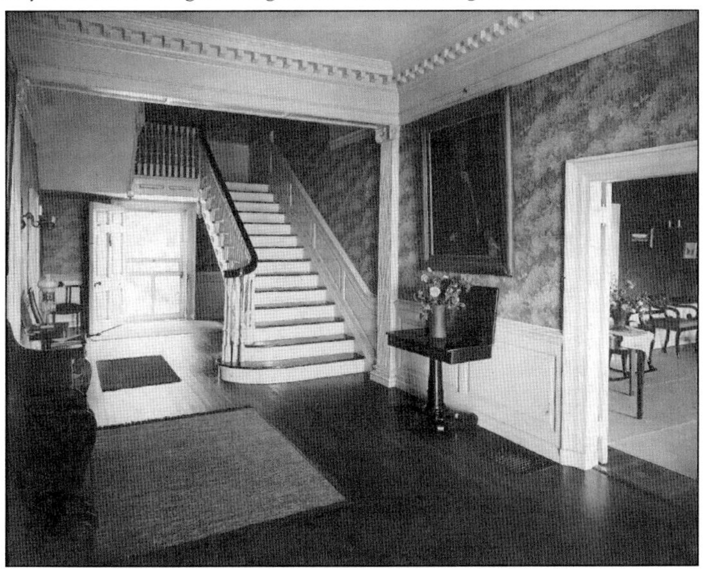

MANSION ENTRANCE HALL, C. 1918. This photograph shows the entrance hall at Red Hill after modifications for Lucy Harrison. A new staircase replaced an older one installed during John Henry's ownership, which was moved to Patrick Henry's law office. The portrait on the wall to the right is of Lt. Gov. Alexander Spotswood, an ancestor of Lucy.

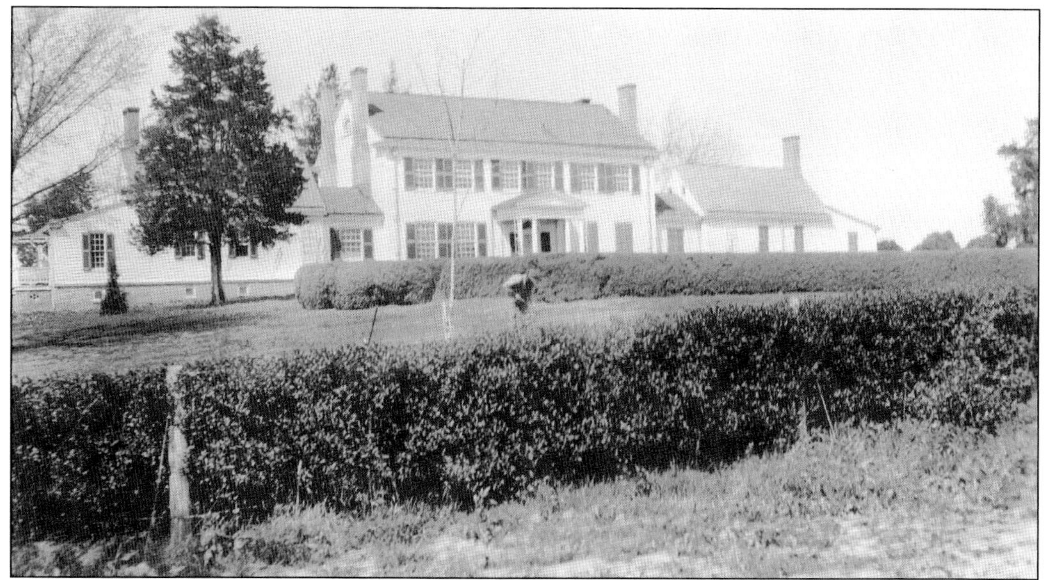

SOUTH FACADE AND GARDENS, C. 1912. The front (south) facade of the Red Hill mansion resembles a white palace rising from the hill. At over 6,400 square feet, the finished home boasted 21 rooms, gas lighting, and an interior kitchen. Walter Cook, a Black caretaker, managed the expansive grounds and gardens for over 25 years from the 1910s until his death in 1940. Cook may be pictured here.

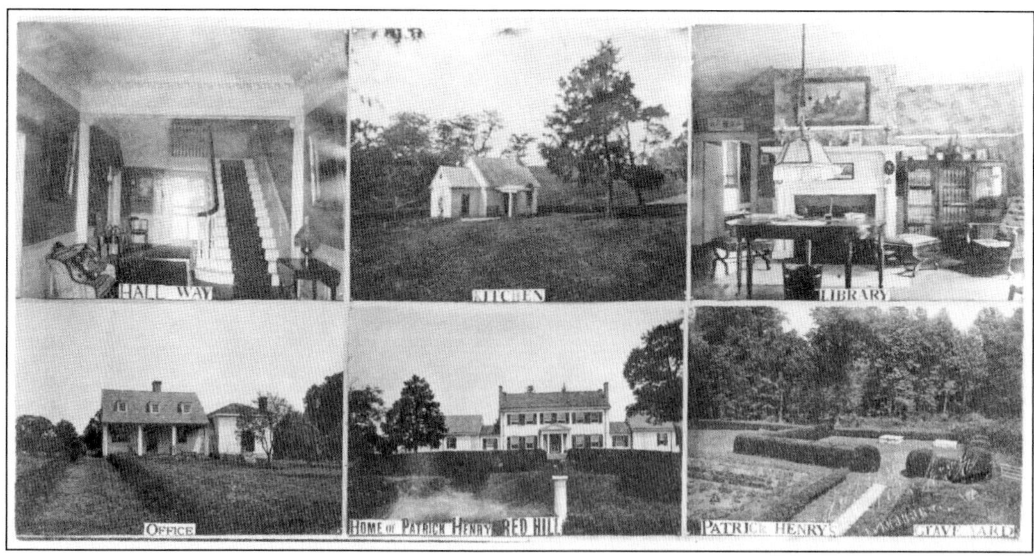

POSTCARD OF RED HILL, C. 1919. This postcard contains a collection of photographs taken between 1912 and 1919. The hallway and library of the Henry family home are shown here, as well as a south view of the Henry mansion taken shortly after its expansion, Patrick Henry's law office, the old kitchen, and the Henry family cemetery.

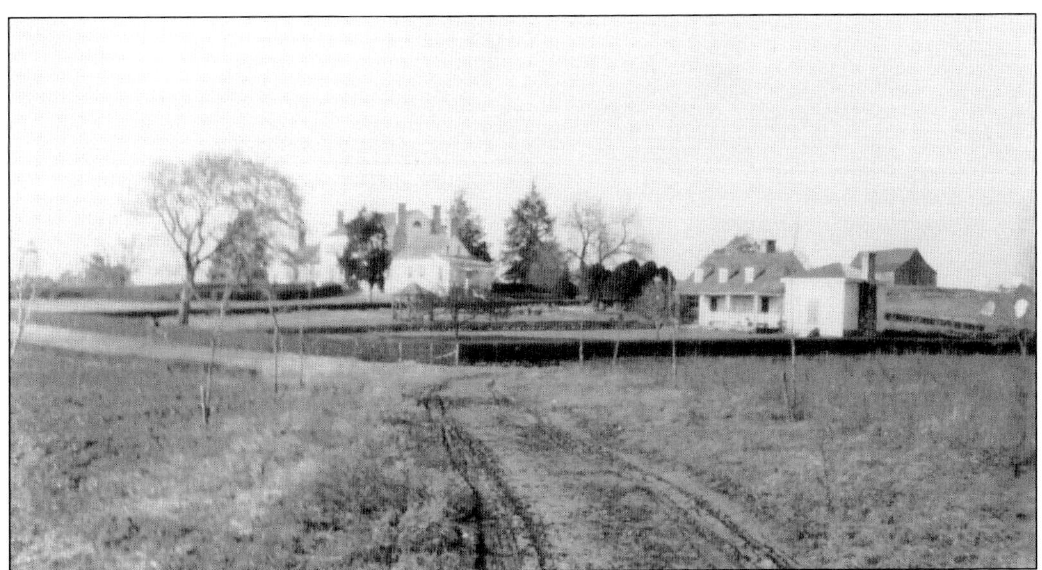

Law Office, Mansion, and Grounds, c. 1912. This photograph of the central grounds was taken from the southeast of a farm road. To the right is Patrick Henry's original law office, with later additions, and a large barn stands in the distance. Privet hedges enclose the lawn. A water tower in the distance at the left supplied water for farming and livestock.

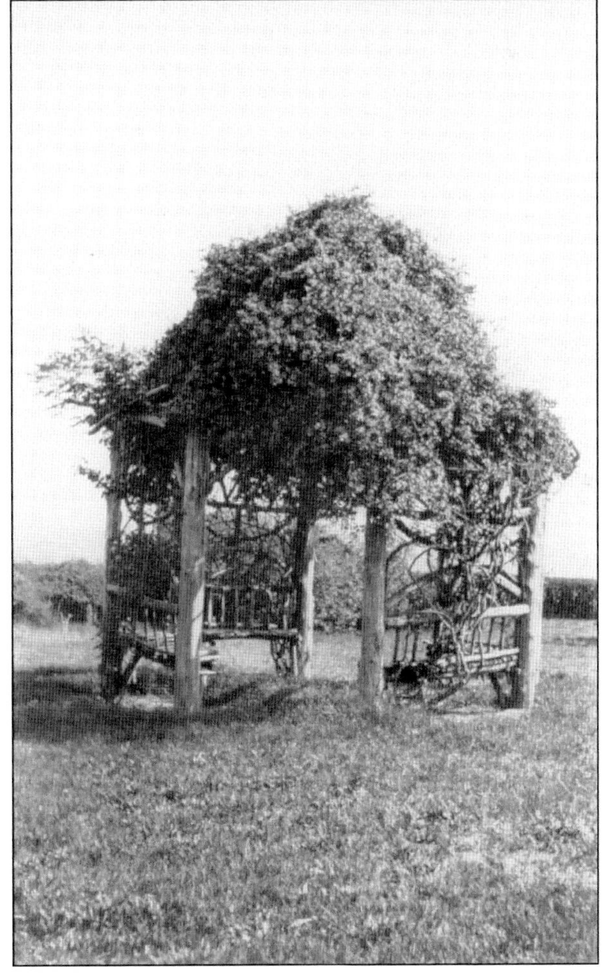

Arbor with Jasmine, c. 1912. After this photograph was taken, Lucy Harrison described, "A yellow jasmine, which is doubtless a hundred years old, covers a summer house with a canopy of gold and its fragrance fills the grounds." Located on the east lawn of the mansion, the arbor commanded a pleasant view of the estate and the river valley. Lucy often enjoyed tea and reading under its shade.

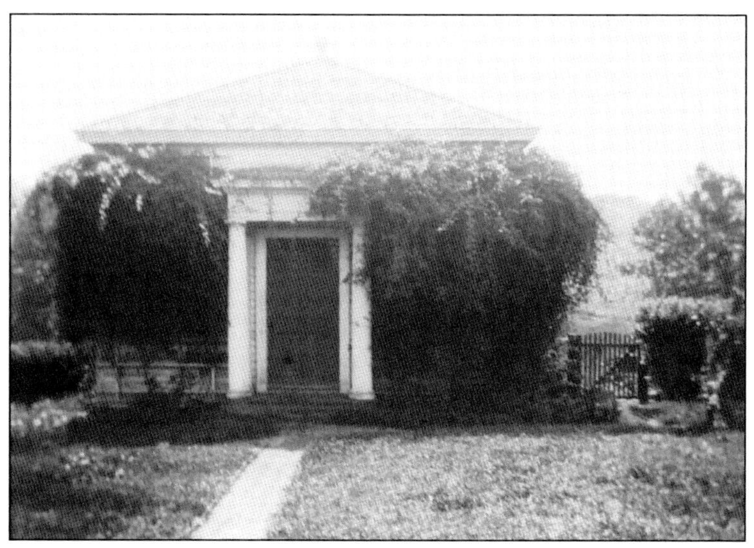

ICEHOUSE, 1918. Built on a slope near the kitchen, this icehouse kept food, dairy products, and beverages cool during the warm months. The above-ground part of the icehouse was designed to enhance and reflect the Colonial Revival architecture of Lucy Harrison's recently enlarged mansion. Ice for the pit was bought or acquired from nearby water sources that froze during the winter.

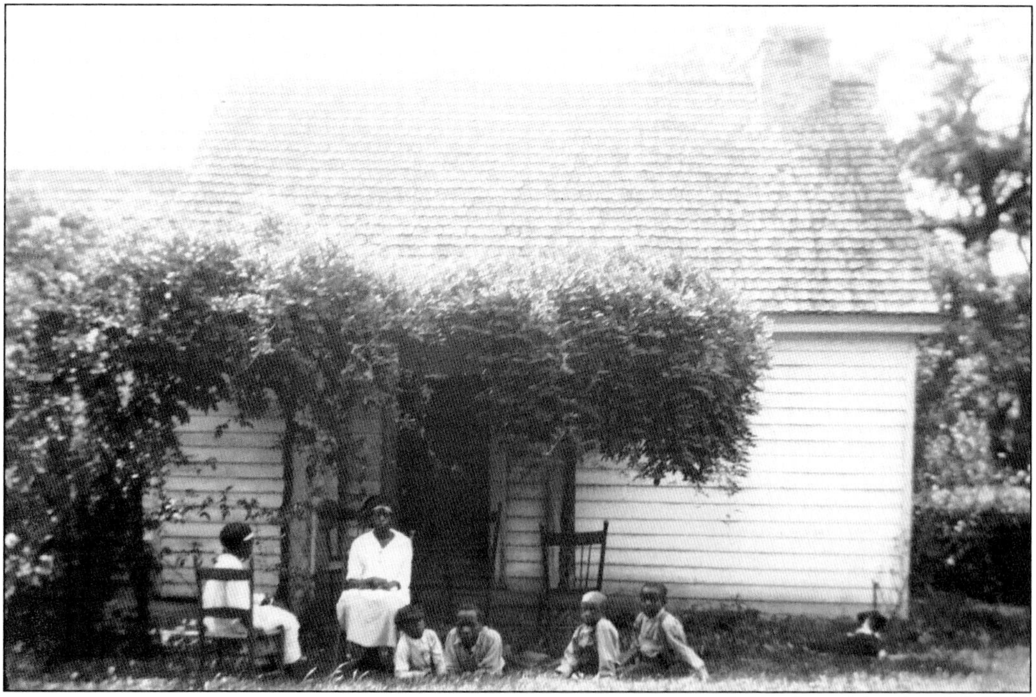

COOK'S HOUSE, 1918. Situated to the rear of the mansion, this building originally served as a kitchen but was later converted into a residence for two Black cooks and their families. The cooks prepared the day's food in the kitchen, which by 1911 had been incorporated into the mansion. This building burned down on Christmas Day in 1928.

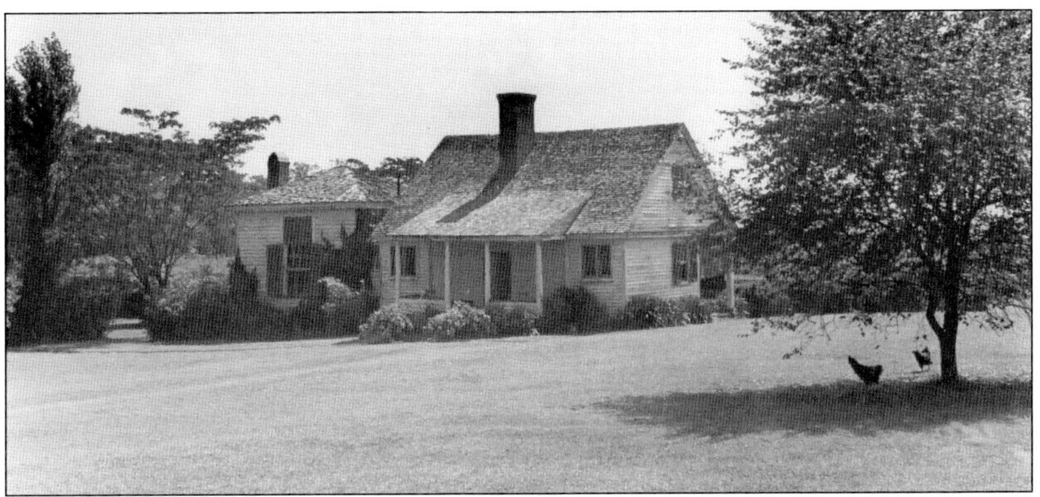

Law Office, c. 1953. During the enlargement of her home at Red Hill, Lucy Harrison took up residence in Patrick Henry's old law office. When the manor home was destroyed by fire in 1919, Lucy moved back into the office, which she had previously enlarged by adding a second floor and porch. She also had her father's one-room law office connected to the building's east (left) side.

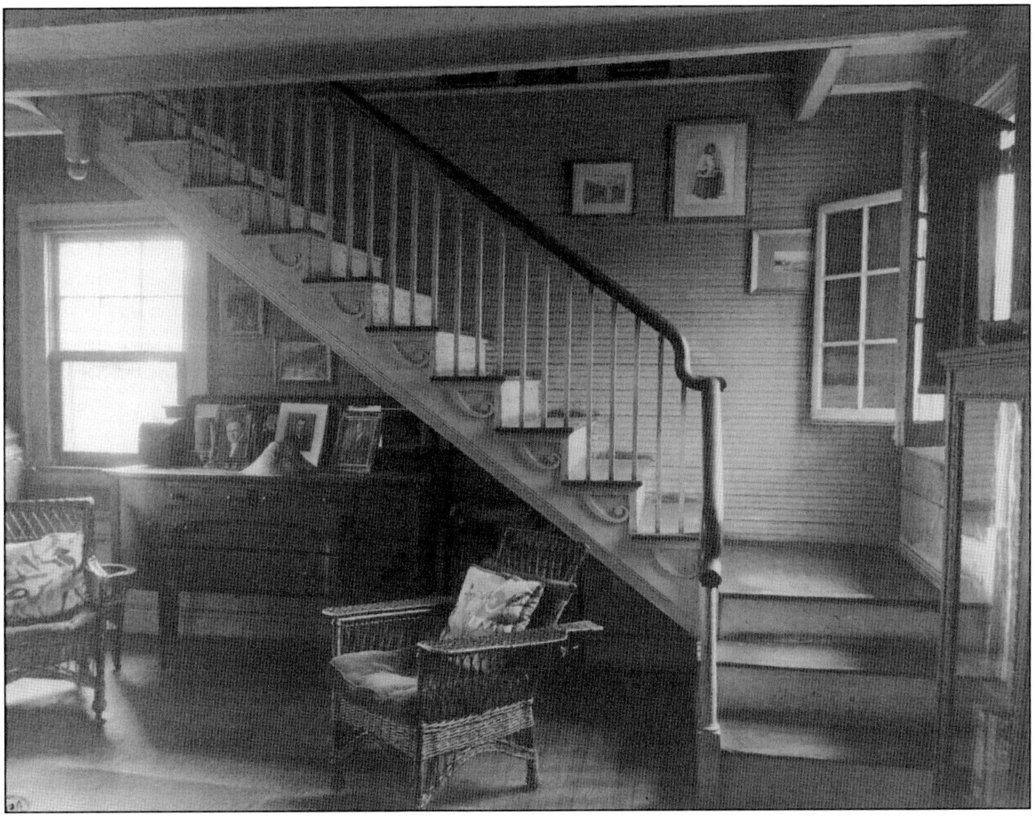

Law Office Parlor, c. 1930. This interior photograph of Patrick Henry's law office, taken during Lucy Harrison's occupancy in the 1930s, shows the staircase leading to the second floor, which had been added to the original structure. In 1961, the law office underwent extensive restoration to return it to its 18th-century appearance, removing much of what is seen here.

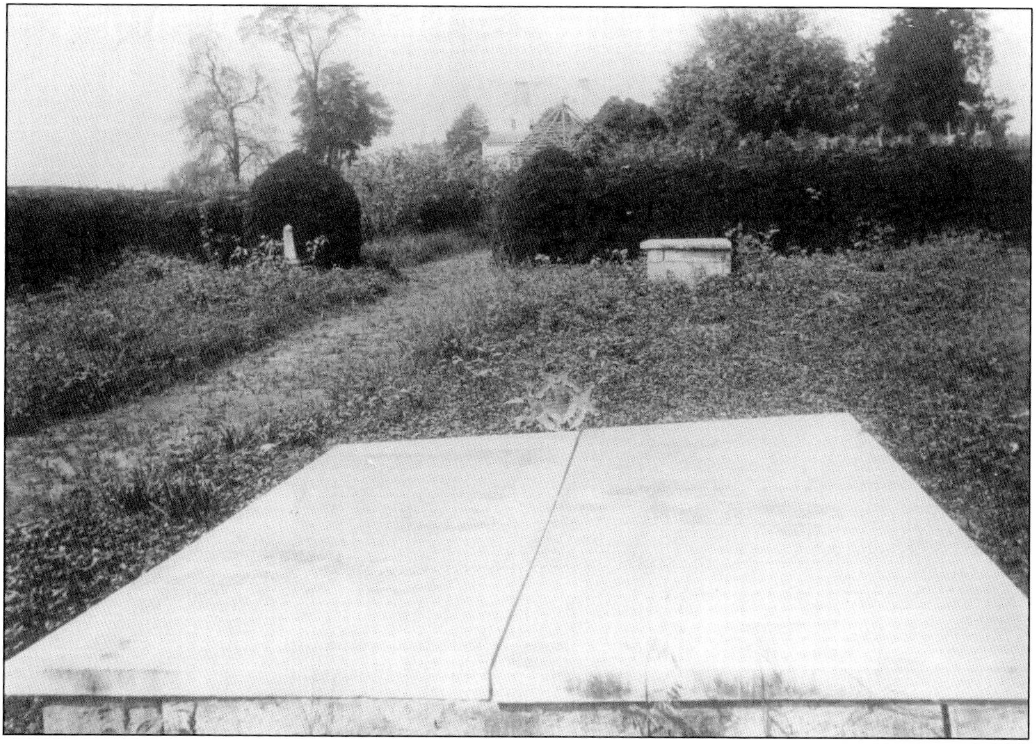

HENRY FAMILY CEMETERY, C. 1907. Among the periwinkle and boxwoods sit the graves of Patrick Henry and his family. Under Lucy Harrison's residency, the cemetery became a site of pilgrimage where visitors from around the country paid their respects to the patriot orator. Lucy, however, refused to let any Henry descendant into Red Hill until they could prove their lineage.

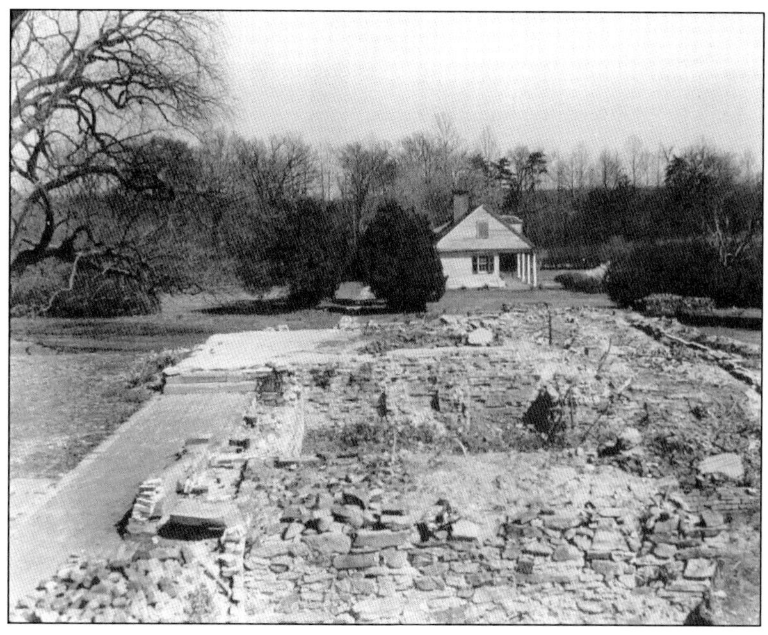

RUINS OF THE MANSION, 1950. After a fire destroyed the Red Hill mansion, it was never rebuilt for unknown reasons. More than three decades later, the ruins still sat charred and crumbled, a reminder of what once was. Lucy Harrison lived in the small building in the background—formerly Patrick Henry's law office—until her death. It was not until 1956 that the ruins were filled in.

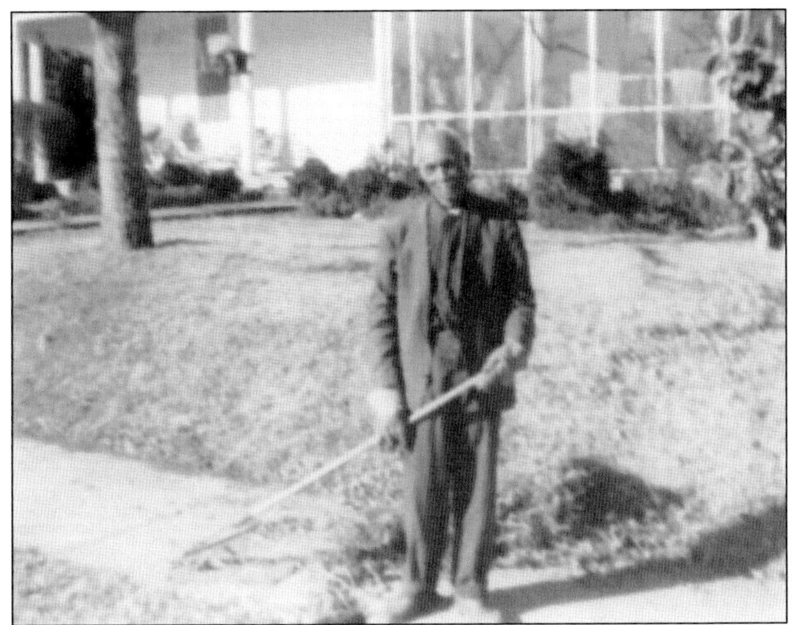

George Ed Britton, 1975. A descendant of one of Patrick Henry's enslaved persons, George Britton was a teenage field hand when he noticed the Henry mansion was on fire on a February morning in 1919. Due to his quick actions, the Henrys got out safely, and many of their possessions were saved from destruction.

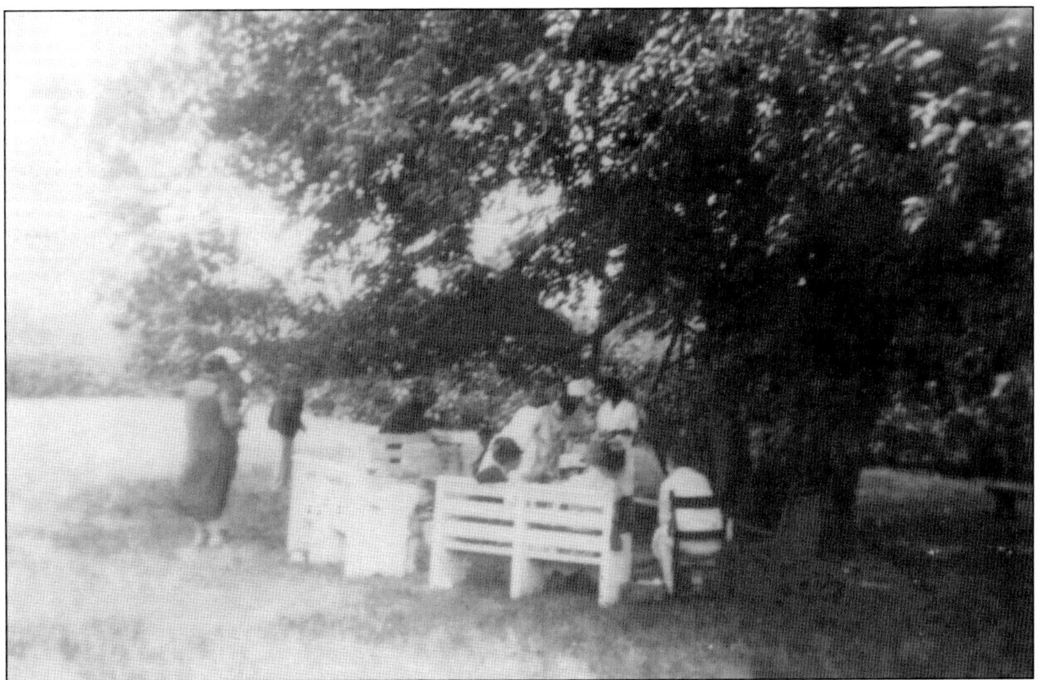

Colonial Dames Picnic, 1926. On a warm summer day, members of the National Society of the Colonial Dames of America picnicked at Red Hill. The Dames visited Patrick Henry's grave and enjoyed lunch under the historic Osage orange tree, where they conversed with Lucy Henry Harrison (far right).

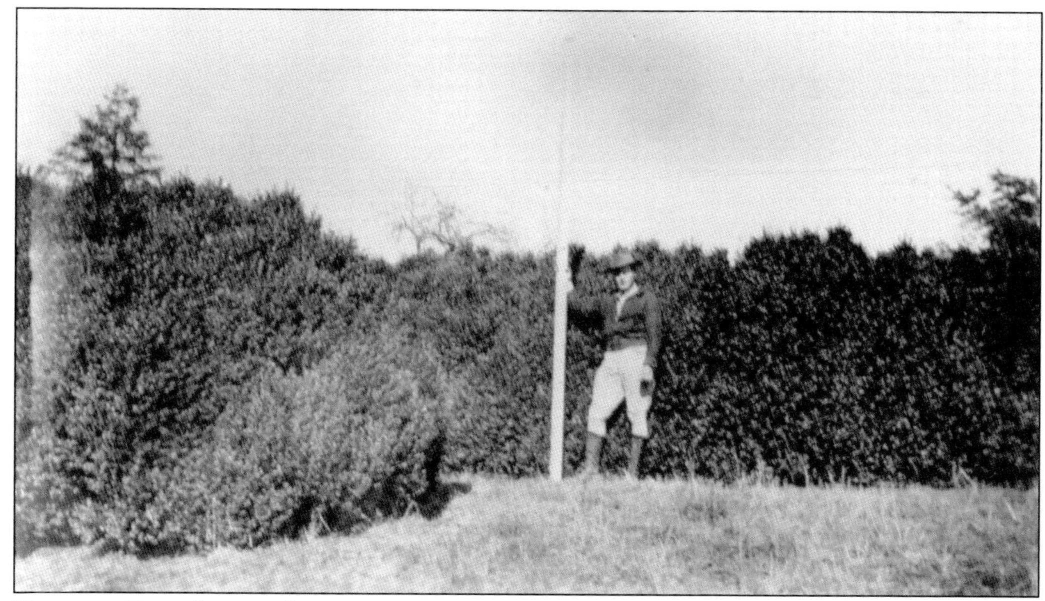

National Park Service Surveyman, 1936. Lucy Henry Harrison realized the importance of preserving Red Hill. She offered to sell the estate to the US government in 1935; the National Park Service surveyed the site before purchasing. Carrying a measuring pole for scale, Park Service engineers photographed everything from buildings to plantings, including the Osage orange tree and the ruins of the burned mansion.

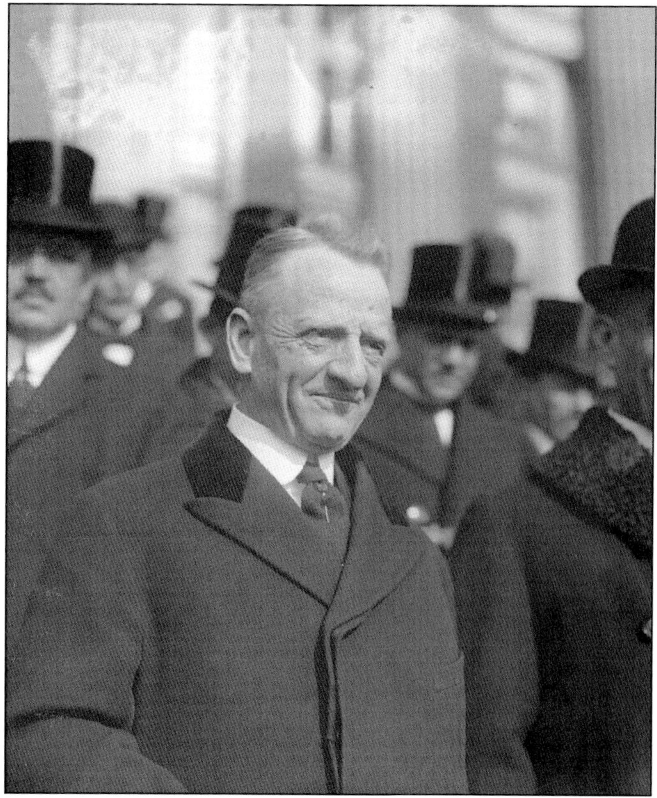

Sen. Carter Glass, c. 1919. During the 1930s, Sen. Carter Glass of Lynchburg sponsored acts in Congress to establish the Patrick Henry National Monument at Red Hill. Due to the "high-handed and arbitrary efforts" of the Department of the Interior to acquire the property at much below its true value, Senator Glass later worked with Sen. Harry Byrd to repeal the previous acts establishing a national monument. (LOC.)

Five

Restoring Red Hill 1945–1975

Established on October 27, 1944, the Patrick Henry Memorial Foundation epitomizes the grassroots efforts to preserve a site of national historical significance.

Following the death of Lucy Henry Harrison, Red Hill fell to the Charlotte County Circuit Court, which appointed commissioners to search for a buyer. Harrison named Elizabeth Kerper—her former nurse—executrix but left no power of sale in her will. This concerned patriotic citizens who did not wish to see Patrick Henry's final resting place fall into the wrong hands.

A Halifax County lawyer, James Stone Easley, believed Patrick Henry to be "the greatest Apostle of Liberty." Easley formed the Patrick Henry Memorial Foundation with Maj. John D. Guthrie as his vice president and nationally recognized figures on the board of trustees, including Sen. Harry F. Byrd, Douglas Southall Freeman, and Gen. George C. Marshall.

The foundation's primary goal was to "establish a perpetual memorial in commemoration of the life and character of Patrick Henry . . . and in particular to purchase, preserve, and maintain the property located in Charlotte and Campbell Counties, Virginia, known as 'Red Hill.'" In July 1945, the foundation achieved this goal when 960.61 acres at Red Hill were purchased for $60,000. Mabel Bellwood, the first caretaker, moved to the estate in 1949 and cleared the overgrown property to welcome the occasional visitor.

It was Bellwood who, in May 1953, welcomed Marylander Eugene B. Casey to Red Hill. The poor state of Henry's burial site shocked the multimillionaire, and he soon offered to "get a house built. In other words, the erection of a living memorial to that great American." Thanks to Casey, the foundation began its principal restoration to bring Red Hill back to the 18th century. By 1955, architect Stanhope S. Johnson had been hired to reconstruct the property, having formerly been employed by Lucy Harrison to build her mansion nearly 50 years earlier.

With its restoration completed in 1965, Red Hill continued to welcome visitors worldwide, but its role as a public museum was only beginning.

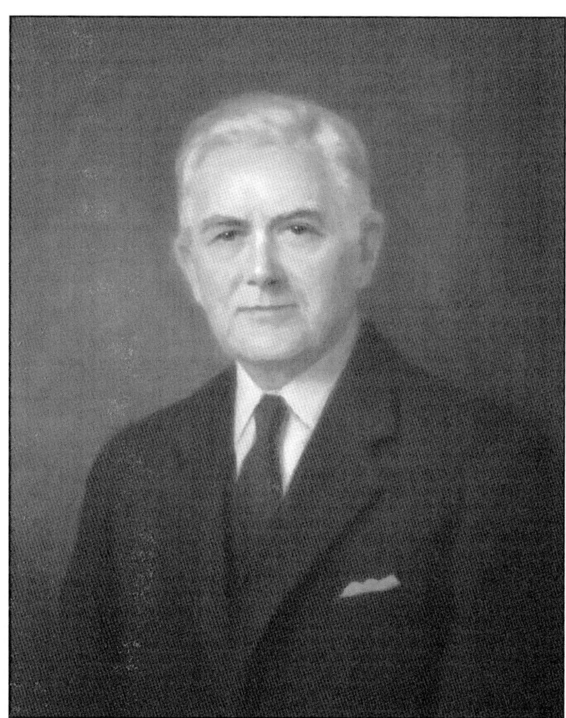

James Stone Easley by David Silvette, 1989. James Easley, a noted attorney from Halifax County, worried for the future of Red Hill after Lucy Henry Harrison's death. Concerned that the Charlotte County Circuit Court would sell the estate into private hands, Easley and other citizens formed the Patrick Henry Memorial Foundation to ensure that Patrick Henry's burial place would be preserved.

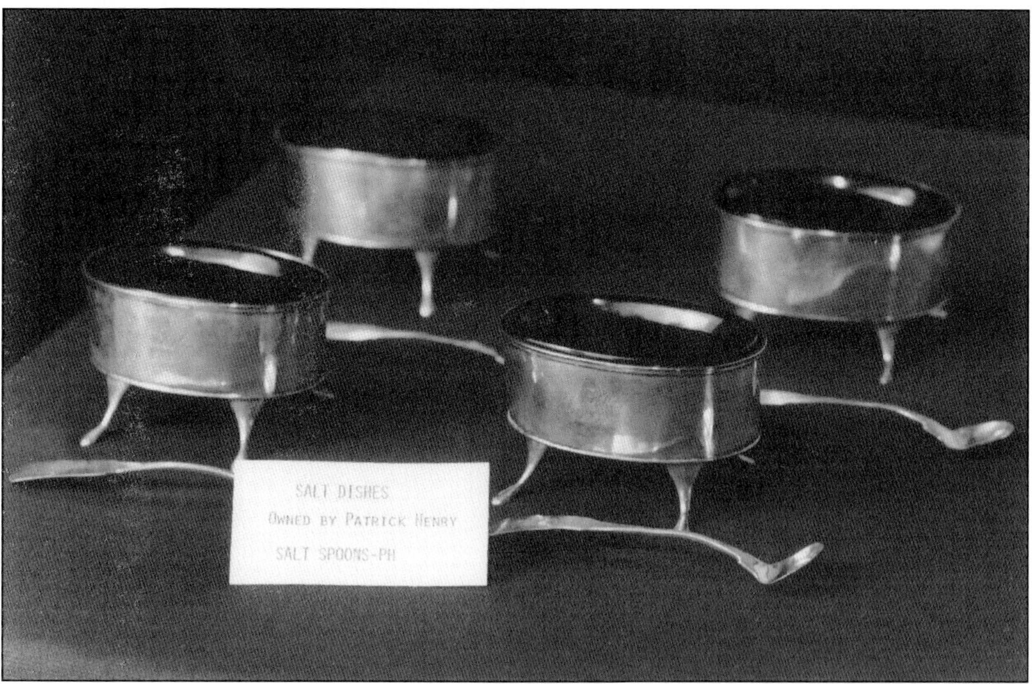

Patrick Henry's Saltcellars, 1977. A sale of Lucy Harrison's estate in June 1945 included many Patrick Henry artifacts the newly formed foundation purchased for its collection, including this set of silver saltcellars. Richmond silversmith Capt. William Richardson crafted this set around 1785. They were later engraved "PH 1777," which may commemorate the year Henry married Dorothea Dandridge. Whether Henry purchased the set or received them as a gift is unknown.

THE IRON WORKER MAGAZINE, 1948. The fall 1948 edition of the *Iron Worker* magazine, published by the Lynchburg Foundry Company, featured an 11-page article on the history of Red Hill and revealed ideas for the proposed restoration of the site. Read by local iron miners and foundry workers, each magazine edition included articles on iron production and history.

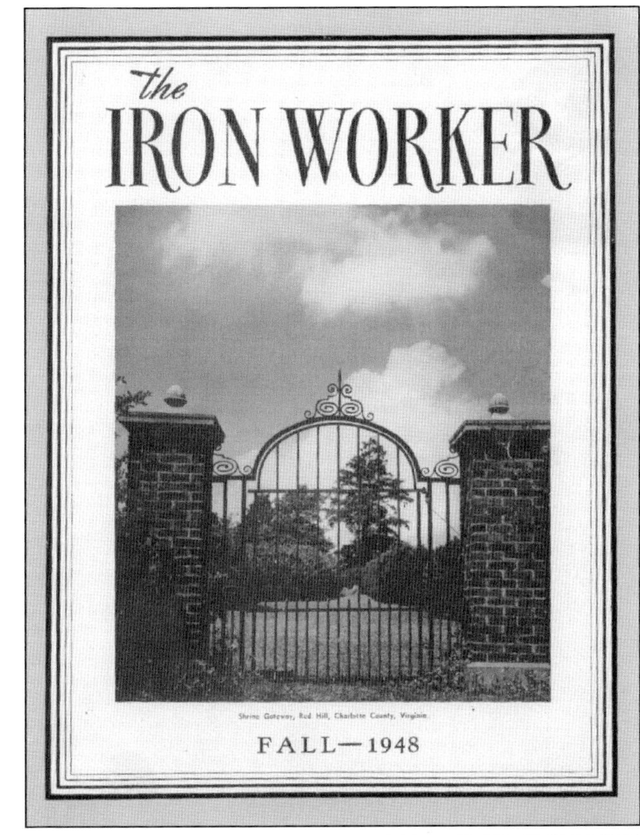

TRUSTEES OF THE PATRICK HENRY MEMORIAL FOUNDATION, SEPTEMBER 1950. These men represent some of the first trustees of the foundation, established six years before this photograph to preserve Red Hill. From left to right, they are Dr. Robert D. Meade, Samuel P. Goodloe, Gov. William M. Tuck, Ralph A. Bard, James S. Easley, Robert S. Chamberlayne, Gerald Cheney, Maj. John D. Guthrie, and Dr. James D. Hagood.

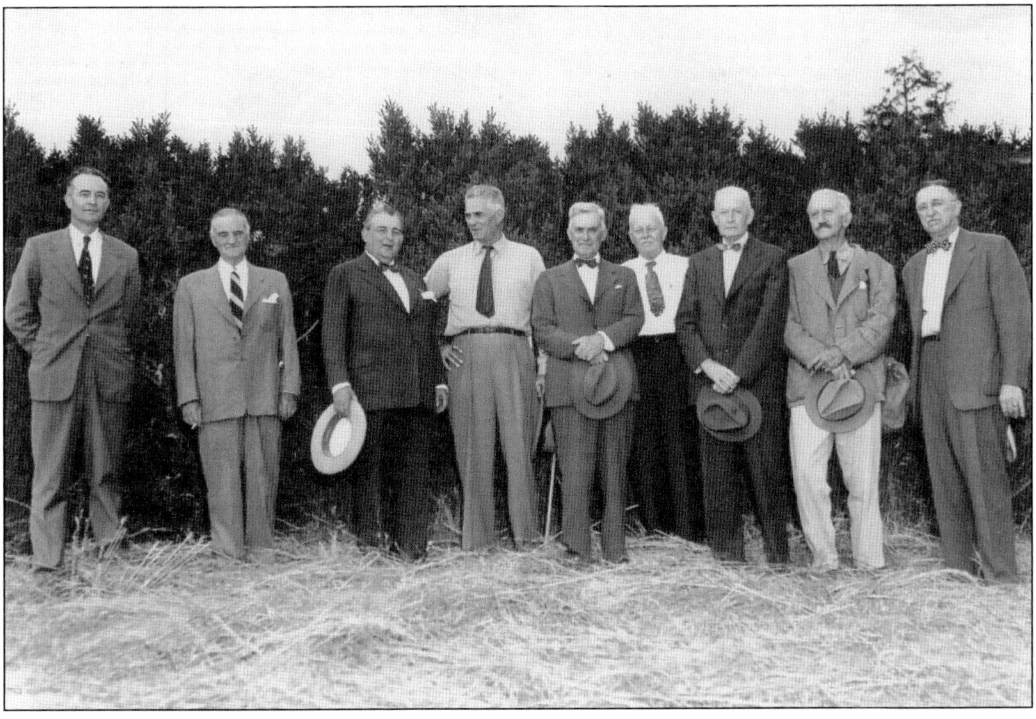

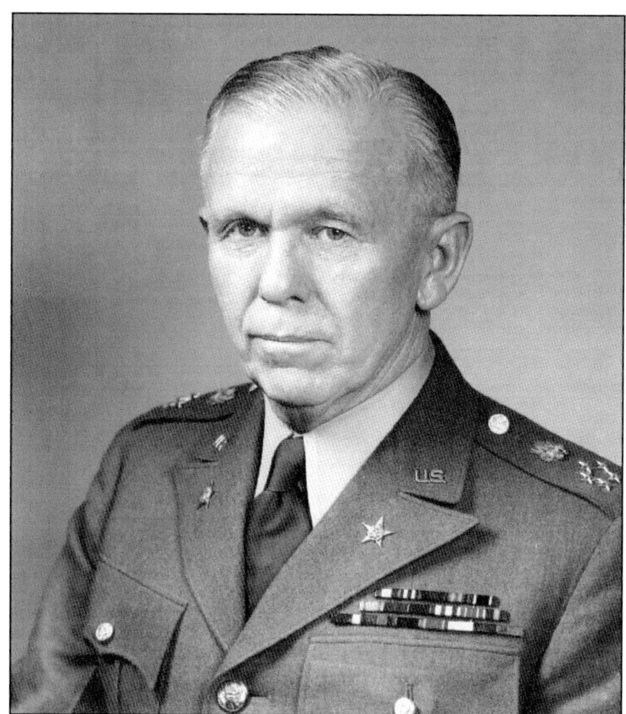

Gen. George C. Marshall, 1945. One of the greatest Americans of the 20th century, General Marshall led Allied forces to victory as US Army chief of staff during World War II. In 1947, Secretary of State Marshall fathered the Marshall Plan to rebuild war-torn Europe. His efforts to preserve international stability earned Marshall the Nobel Peace Prize in 1953. He served as a foundation trustee from 1946 to 1958.

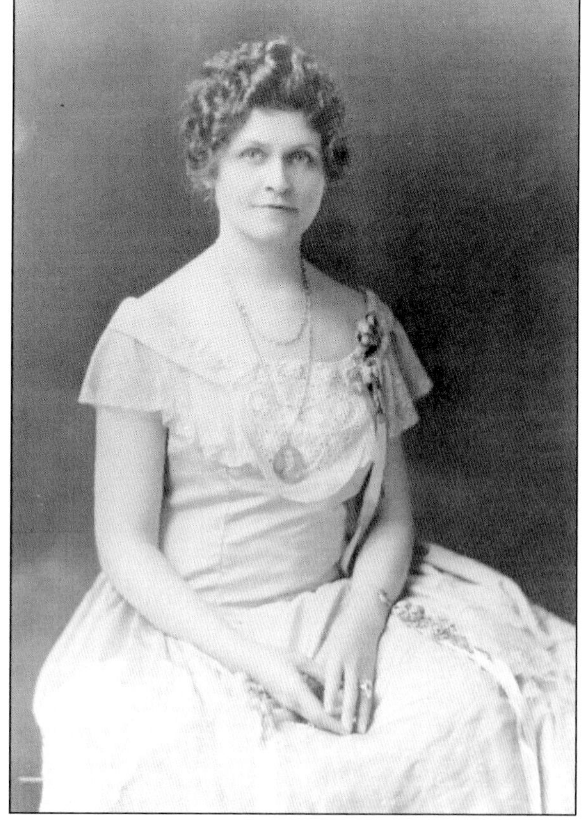

Jessie Ball duPont, 1910. Virginia-born Jessie Ball married into the powerful duPont family, yet she was business-savvy in her own right. After marrying Alfred I. duPont in 1921, she helped lead the family's growing business empire, continuing after her husband's death. Jessie was an early trustee, serving from 1945 to 1967. Her charitable foundation, the Jessie Ball duPont Fund, continues to support Red Hill's efforts to reach historically disadvantaged communities. (SH.)

Capt. Eddie Rickenbacker, 1931. Flying ace Capt. Eddie Rickenbacker was the most decorated airman of World War I, receiving the Medal of Honor and the Distinguished Service Cross. Before the war, Rickenbacker drove race cars and participated in the first two Indianapolis 500s. A successful businessman, Rickenbacker later joined the Patrick Henry Memorial Foundation as a trustee, serving from 1945 to 1960 and 1962 to 1967. (USAF.)

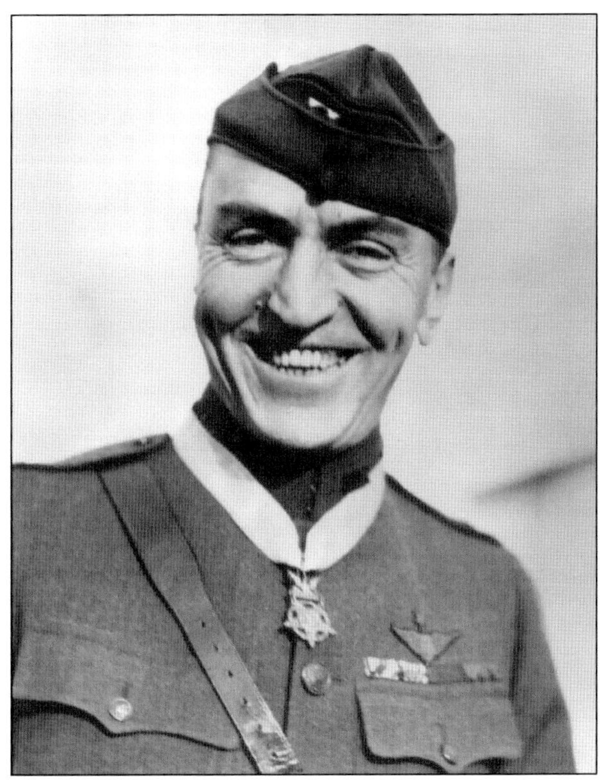

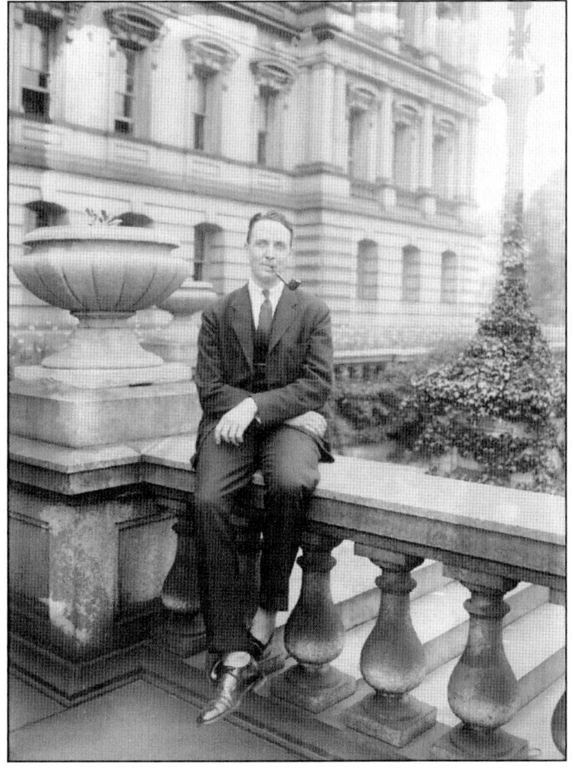

David K.E. Bruce, 1926. David Kirkpatrick Este Bruce was an American diplomat, intelligence officer, and politician. He served as ambassador to France, Germany, and the United Kingdom. Bruce also served as an early foundation trustee and, in 1933, purchased his family estate near Red Hill, known as Staunton Hill. Bruce also purchased Windstone from the estate of Dandridge Yuille Henry in 1950. (LOC.)

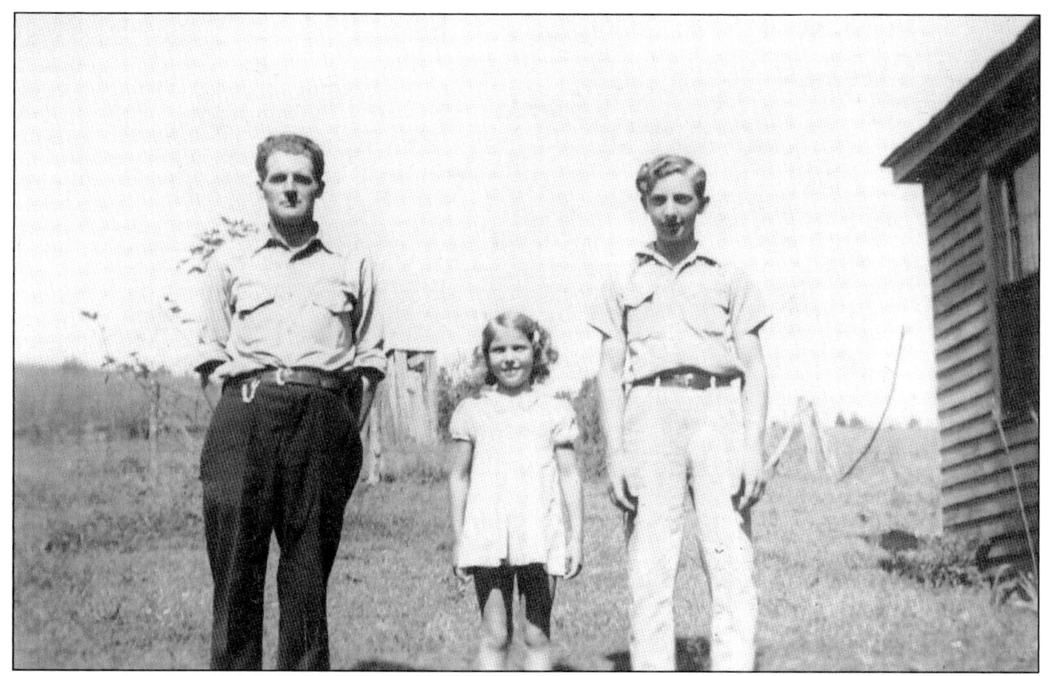

Renters at Red Hill, c. 1948. Before the foundation hired an official caretaker, Patrick Henry's former law office and other buildings were rented out. Samuel Courtney (left) lived in the office with his family in the mid-1940s. Relatives Barbara Collins (center) and Gene Price are visiting Courtney.

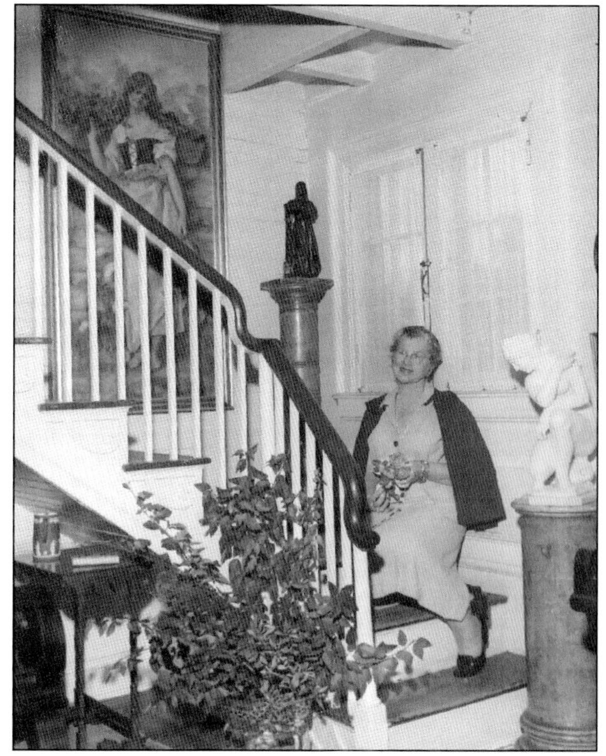

Mabel Oliver Bellwood, c. 1959. In the years after the foundation purchased Red Hill, progress for a complete restoration slowed. In 1949, Mabel Bellwood and her family moved into the former law office, where she would become the first caretaker and curator. Mabel's tenacity broke gender stereotypes by clearing brush, painting buildings, and organizing volunteers. Mabel would retire after nearly three decades of service in 1977.

Ruins of the Mansion, April 1946. When Red Hill was acquired in 1945, much work was to be done. This image shows the ruins of the burned mansion still in their untouched state. It would be over a decade before the Henry house was rebuilt and opened to the public.

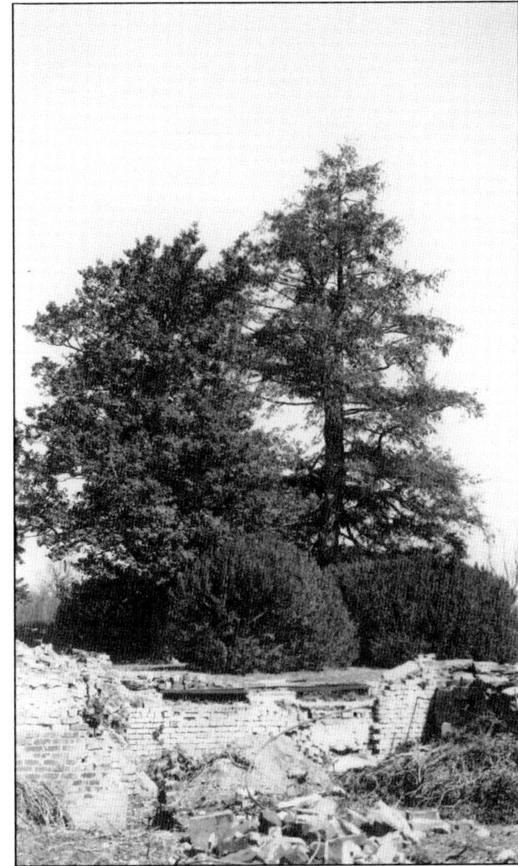

A Dilapidated Law Office, c. 1945. Taken shortly after Lucy Harrison's death, this image shows the disrepair at Red Hill before restoration work began. The once-manicured jasmine arbor has become mangled and rotted, the lawn is overtaken by tall grass, and a rotting building is only years away from irreparable loss.

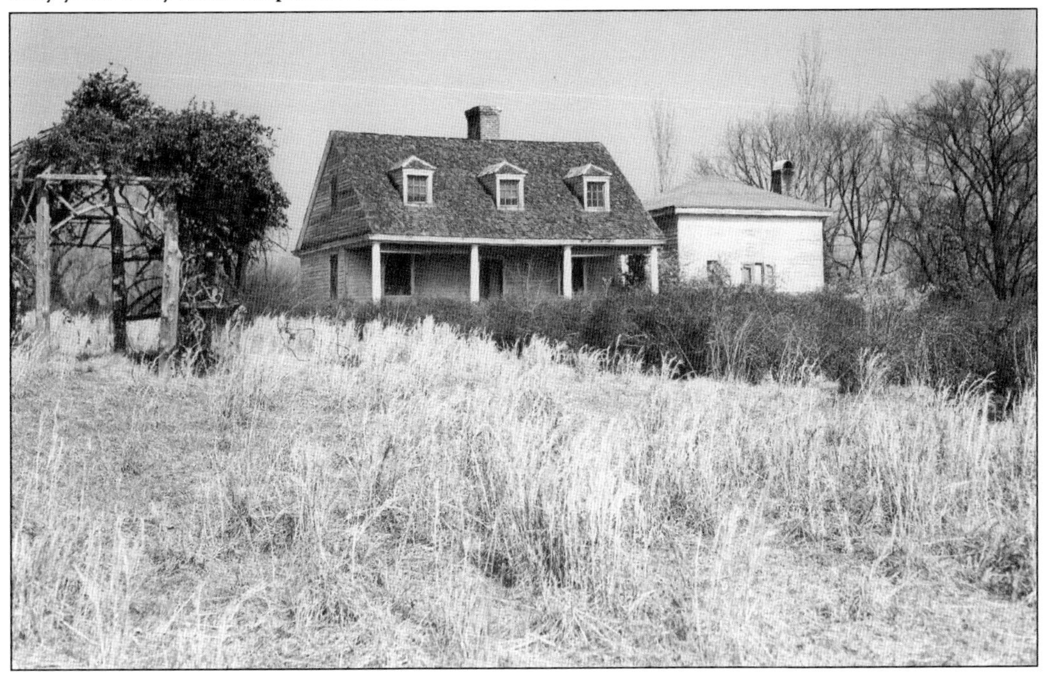

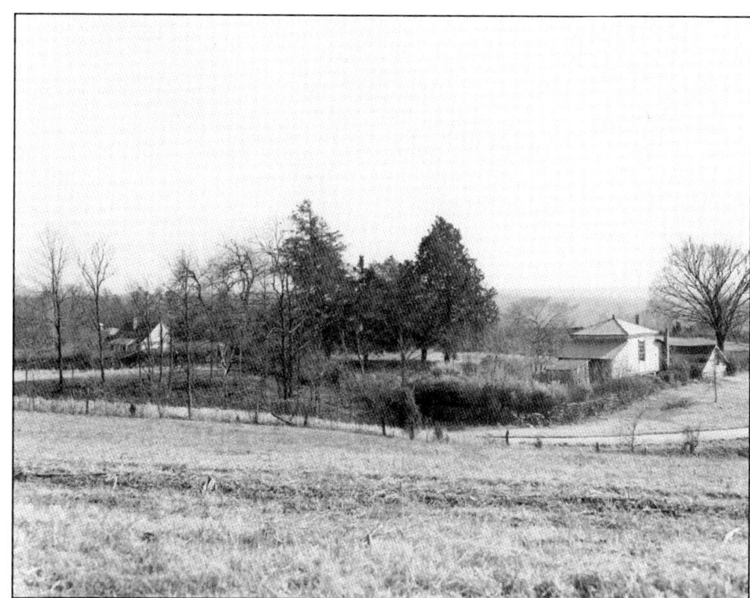

RED HILL GROUNDS LOOKING SOUTHEAST, 1950. This view of the grounds was taken from the hill where the present-day visitor center now stands. To the left can be seen Patrick Henry's expanded law office; to the right are the servants' house and icehouse. Restoration efforts at Red Hill would not commence for another four years.

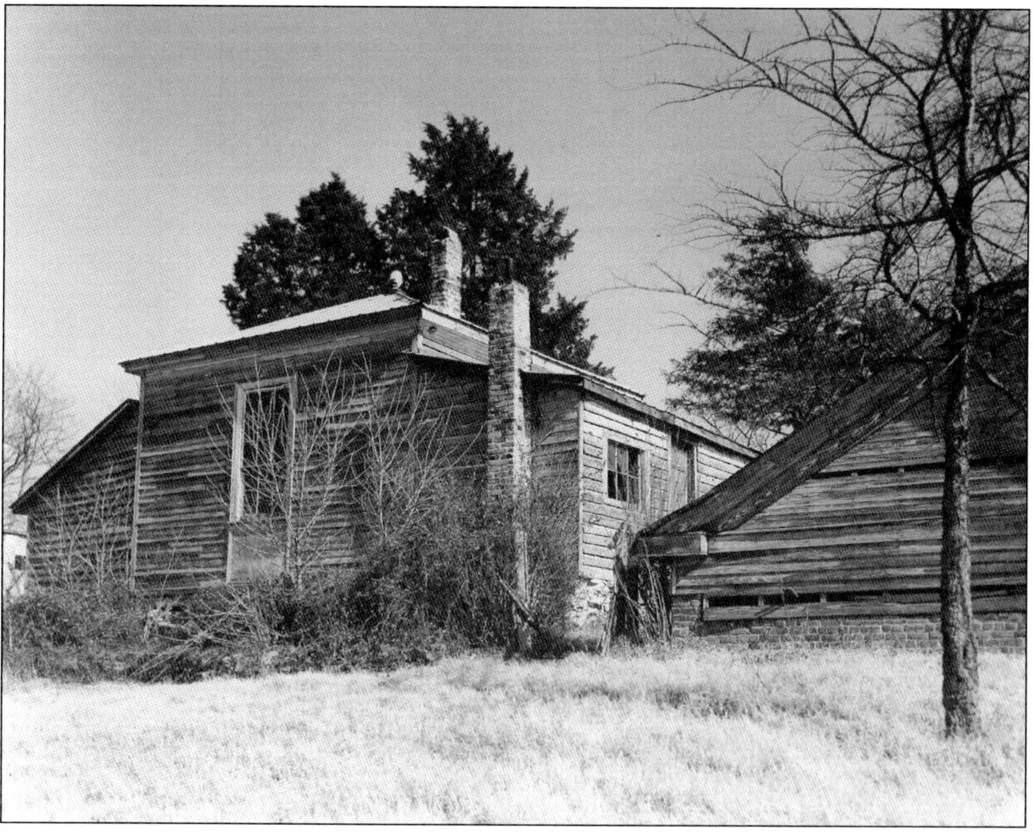

ICEHOUSE AND SERVANTS' HOUSE, 1950. By 1936, the servants' house stood on the property, rented by domestic laborers and field workers under Lucy Harrison's employ. Next to the servants' house stands an icehouse, built into a slope to store the ice underground. Both structures were torn down in the early 1960s during the restoration period.

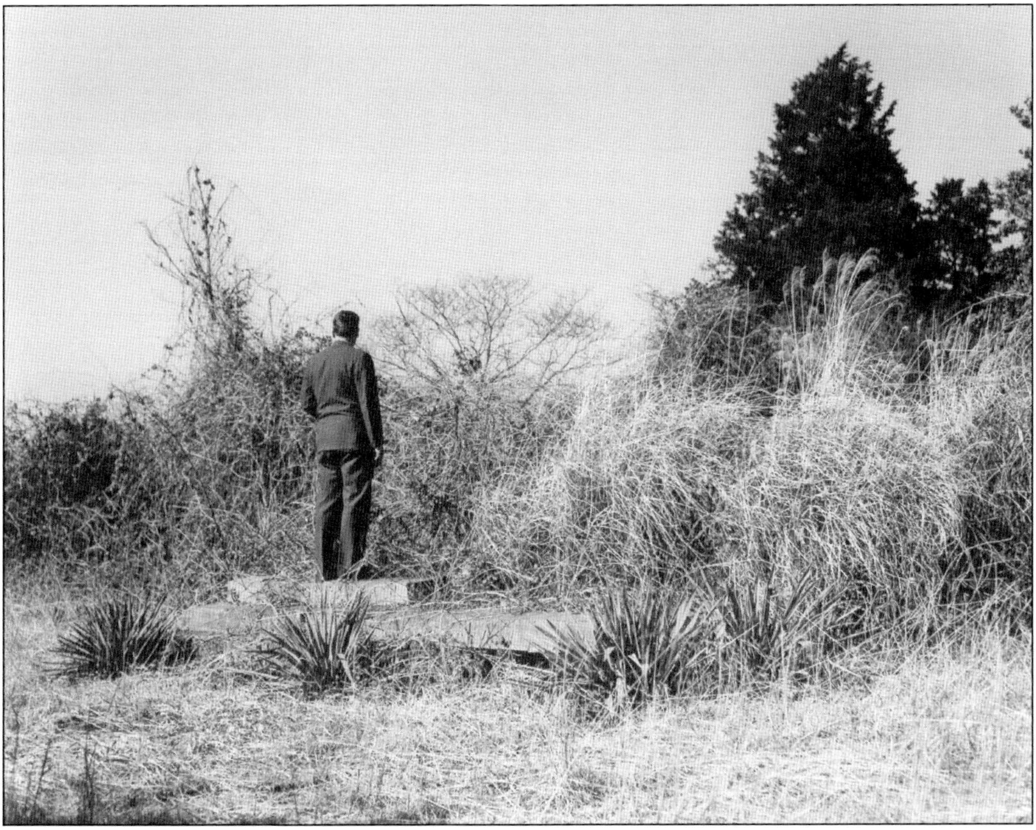

Overgrown Mansion Ruins, c. 1950. An unidentified man sorrowfully views the ruins of what was once the Henry mansion. Overgrown maiden grass and common yucca dot the neglected landscape. This may have been used as a publicity photograph by the foundation to garner support and donations for the restoration of the Henry house.

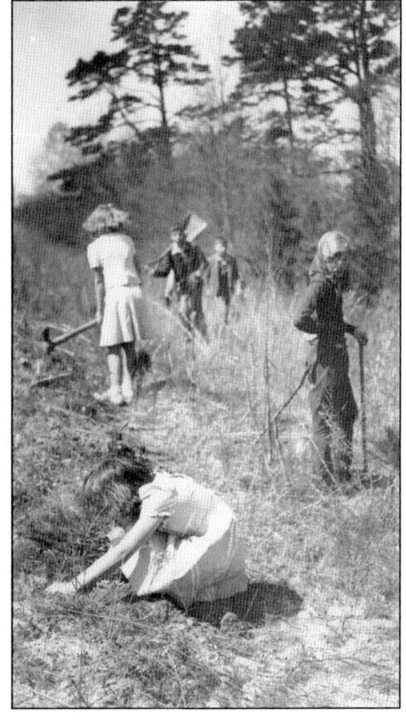

Club Volunteers, April 1946. Volunteering has always been important to the preservation work at Red Hill. Before a dedicated groundskeeper lived on site, Aspen School 4-H Club students held back Mother Nature. Three girls and two boys with farm tools are shown here working to clear part of the property during one of their clean-up days.

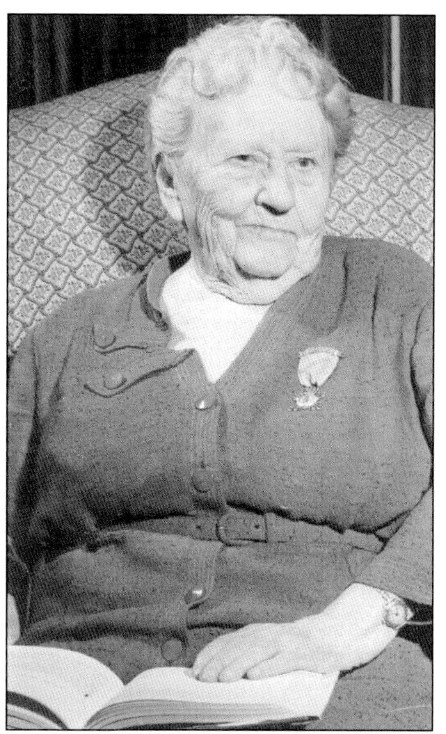

ELVIRA "MISS ELLA" HENRY MILLER, 1955. One of Patrick Henry's last living great-grandchildren, Miss Ella was born at Red Hill as grandchild to John and Elvira McClelland Henry in 1850. Her recollections helped the foundation locate and reconstruct several buildings and record her family's personal stories. Miss Ella also cofounded the Blue Ridge Chapter of the Daughters of the American Revolution in 1895, the sixth chapter to be chartered in Virginia.

FOUNDATION TRUSTEES WITH ELVIRA MILLER, OCTOBER 1950. After years of fund-raising, the Patrick Henry Memorial Foundation celebrated paying off its mortgage at the 100th birthday party of Elvira Henry Miller. A portrait of Elvira's grandmother, Elvira McClelland Henry, and her daughter Emma Cabell hangs to the right. The portrait is now in the Red Hill collection.

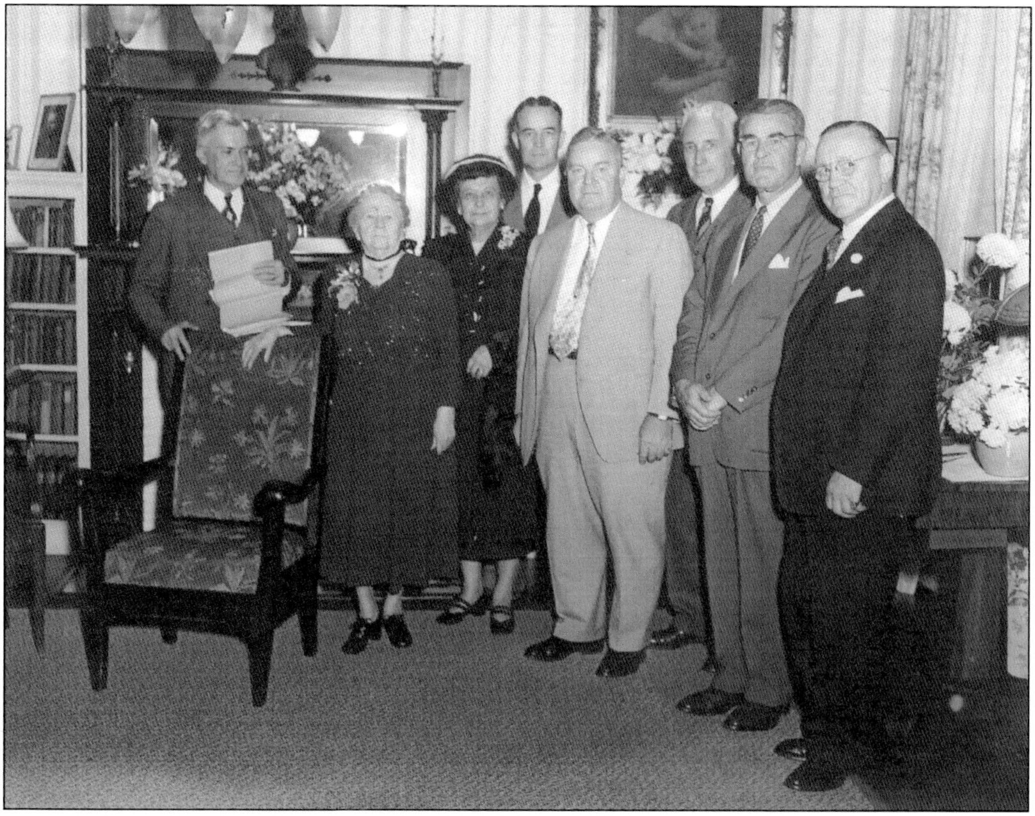

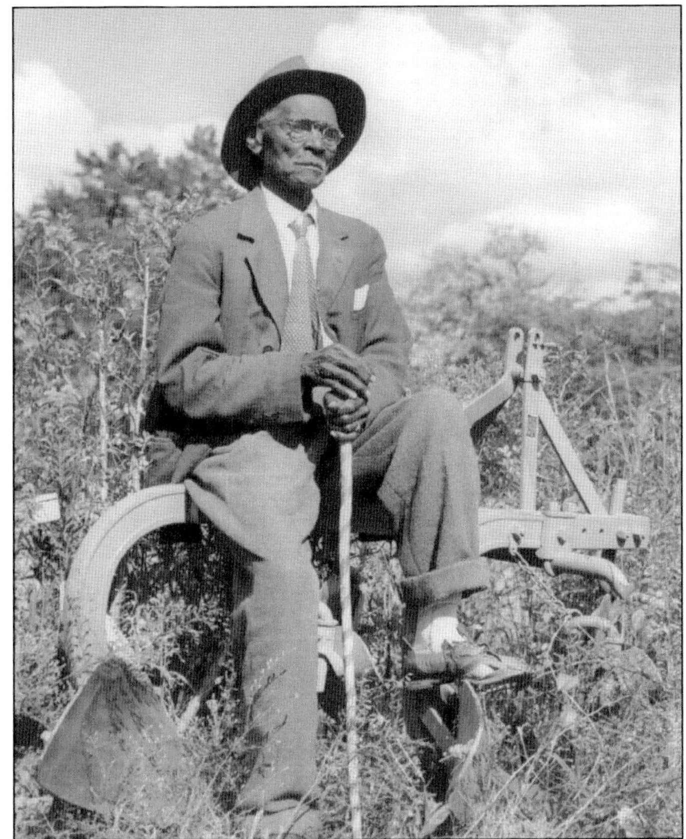

Albert Pannell, October 1950. Born enslaved by John Henry, Albert Pannell lived long enough to see emancipation and the transformation of Red Hill into a museum. He is pictured here at the age of 102, then living in Campbell County as a former sharecropper. Many of Albert's relatives are buried at Quarter Place Cemetery, where their legacy lives on.

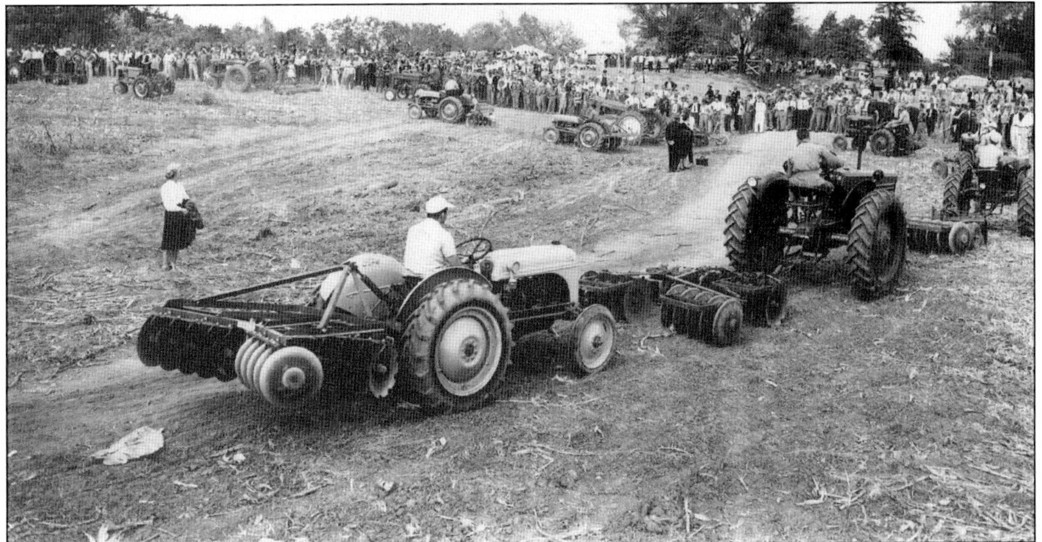

Miracle Day, October 1950. To demonstrate farming practices, the Patrick Henry Boys Plantation, a nearby home for neglected children, hosted Miracle Day to restore nearly 250 acres at Red Hill. Local farmers brought tractors, bulldozers, trucks, and fertilizer as crowds watched the demonstrations. Virginia's governor and other naturalists, including Dr. Thomas S. Buie, attended.

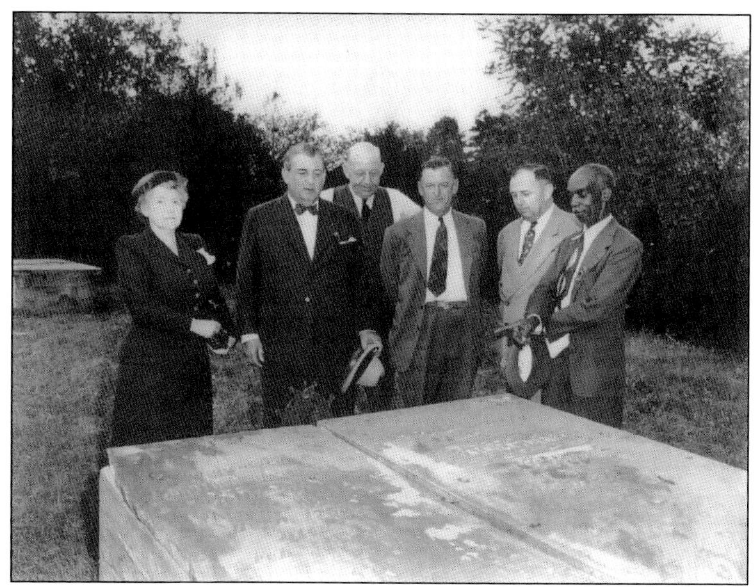

Group at Henry Family Cemetery, October 1950. During Miracle Day, visitors stand at the graves of Patrick and Dorothea Dandridge Henry. From left to right are Henry descendant Susan Hill Dabney, Gov. William M. Tuck, Rev. Ralph Bellwood, unidentified, Dr. Thomas S. Buie, and George Ed Britton. Britton, a descendant of persons enslaved at Red Hill, points toward the graves and addresses the group.

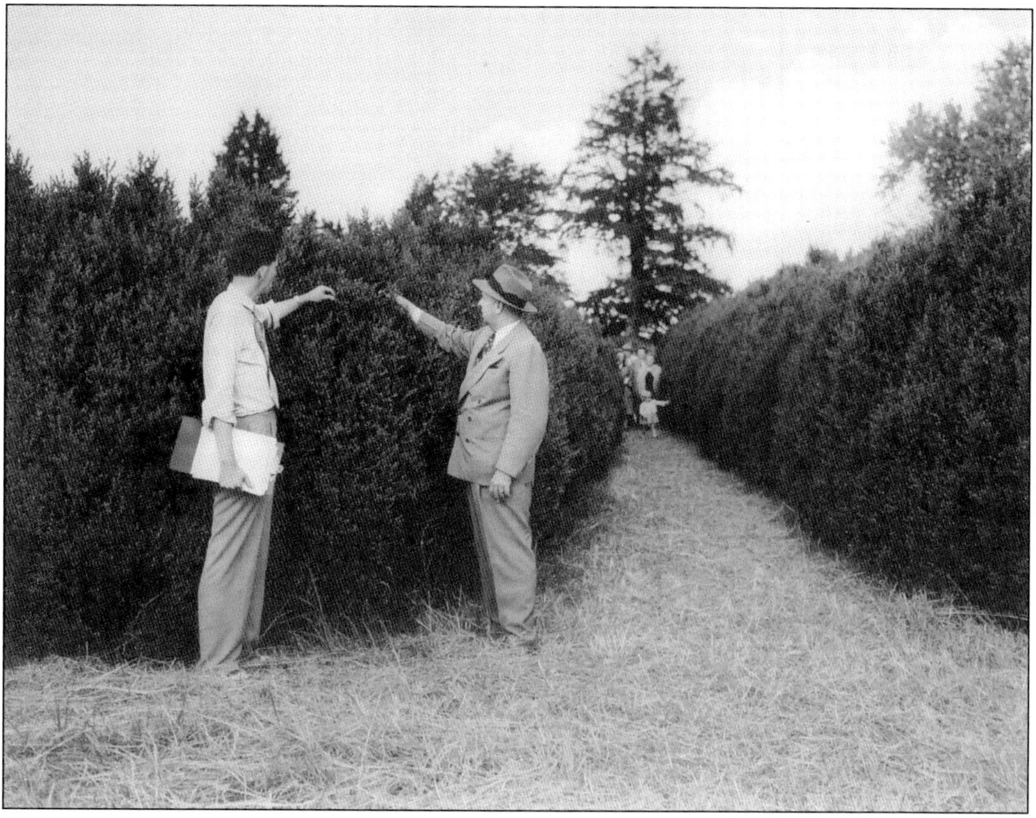

Dr. Thomas Buie with Lyn Shelton, October 1950. On Miracle Day, Soil Conservation Service regional director Dr. Thomas Stephen Buie pauses near the boxwood gardens, approaching where the Henry house once stood. With him is the editor of the *Halifax Gazette*, O. Lyn Shelton, listening to Dr. Buie discuss the unique boxwoods.

S.A. Ozlin Speaks at Miracle Day, October 1950. S.A. Ozlin, chairman of the board of supervisors of the Southside Soil and Water Conservation District, addresses the attendees of Miracle Day in October 1950. Also present is Virginia governor William M. Tuck (seated, left) and foundation president James S. Easley (seated, fourth from right).

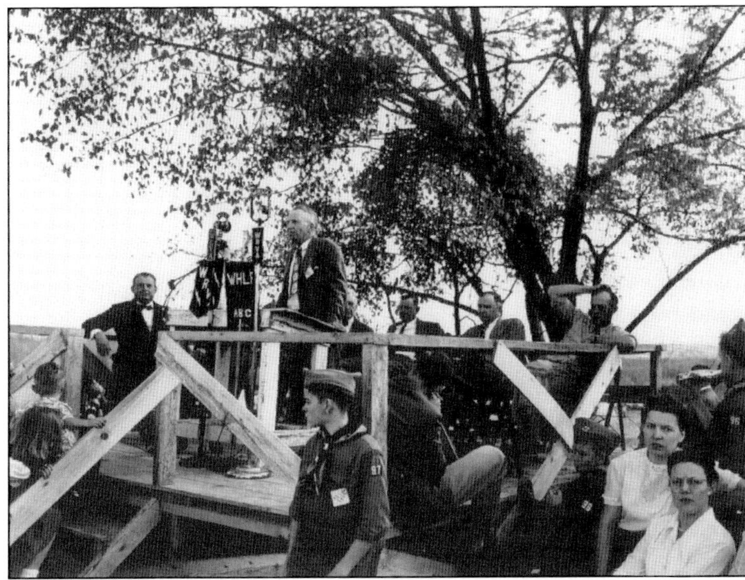

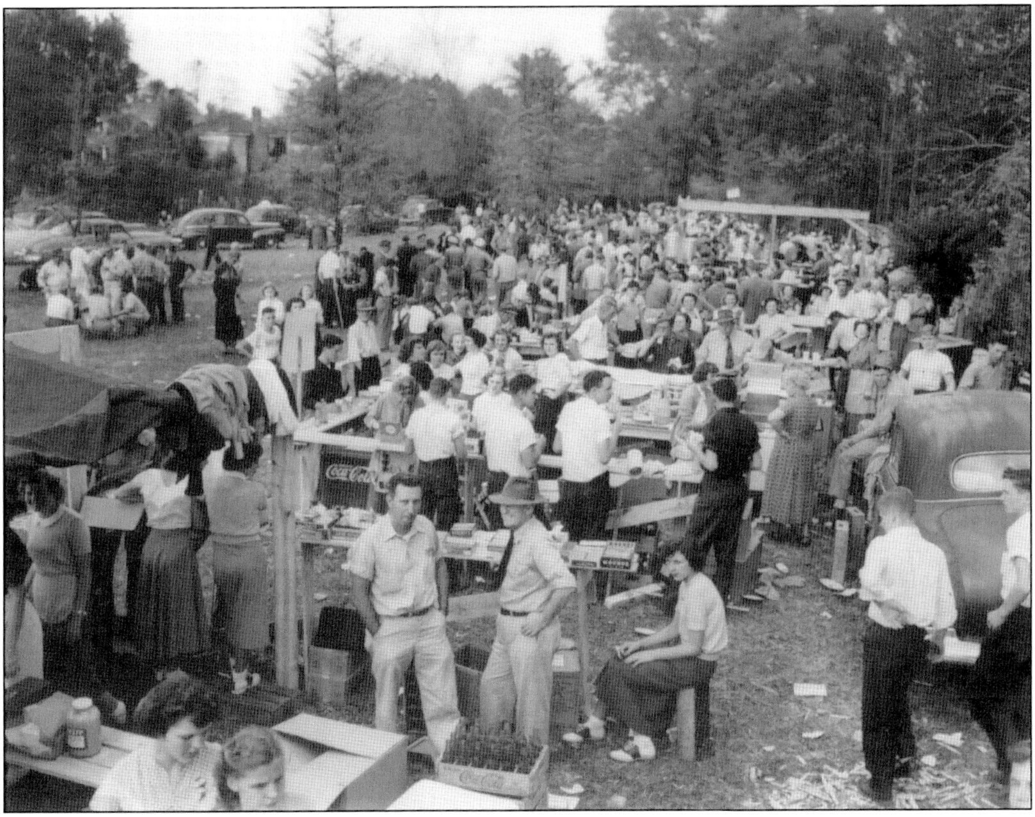

Vending Stands at Miracle Day, October 1950. Visitors at Miracle Day enjoyed the offerings from various vendors who set up for the event. This picture shows that certain treats like Hershey bars and Coca-Cola have stood the test of time. Today, the site where this photograph was taken is near a quiet walking path between the historic grounds and a picnic area southeast of the Henry house.

EUGENE B. CASEY
607 Blandford Ave.
Rockville, Maryland

October 22, 1953

Honorable James S. Easley
South Boston, Virginia

Dear Mr. Easley:

On a recent visit to my daughter, Betsey, who is attending college at Randolph Macon, Lynchburg, we became interested in exploring some of the nearby historic sites and determined upon Appomatox Court House one day and Red Hill, Patrick Henry's former home in Charlotte County, the next.

We visited with the hospitable and kindly reverend who now makes his home on the Henry grounds. Frankly, I was greatly dis-illusioned by the treatment posterity has rendered to a man who was truly the father of American liberty.

However, I was somewhat buoyed through the knowledge that a Foundation had been established for the re-building of the Henry home and complete restoration of the property and grounds.

Being a Marylander, an outlander so to speak, and having been in public life for some period of time and always accepting Senator Byrd as a leader in all categories in the Old Dominion State, I have communicated with him through his son, Harry, with whom I had the honor to serve in the Navy in World War II.

From this correspondence and telephone calls it has been suggested to me by Senator Byrd and his son that I communicate with you as the President of the Foundation. This, I am doing and I would like very much to sit down and talk with you on the Foundation's plans. Perhaps in so doing I will evidence a completely unselfish thought that may expedite the ultimate goal for your association.

I have the definite notion that we can really get something very tangible started and I mean by that concrete footings, brick and mortar, slate roofing and pine trim - -- get a house built. In other words, the erection of a living memorial to that great American who was Virginia's first Governor and who declined every honor that another great Virginian, George Washington, sought to bestow upon him.

Very truly yours,

Eugene Casey

EC/jhj

EUGENE B. CASEY TO JAMES EASLEY, OCTOBER 1953. This letter reflects sentiments that would change the course of Red Hill's history and perhaps the legacy of Patrick Henry himself. Eugene Casey, a World War II veteran and American history buff, visited his daughter Betsey at Randolph-Macon Women's College in Lynchburg, and during that visit, they made a trip to Red Hill, which was still in its neglected state. This letter to foundation president James Easley expresses Casey's feelings about how "dis-illusioned" he was "by the treatment posterity has rendered to a man who was truly the father of American liberty." Understanding that the foundation had acquired the property, Casey became optimistic and provided the initial funding to rebuild the Henry home and other historic buildings in the 1950s and 1960s.

Eugene B. Casey by Peter Egeli, 1976. Following his visit to Red Hill in 1953, real estate mogul Eugene Casey of Maryland promised his financial support to the restoration efforts. Casey's early and generous donations led to the reconstruction of Henry's house, kitchen, and other buildings from 1956 to 1965.

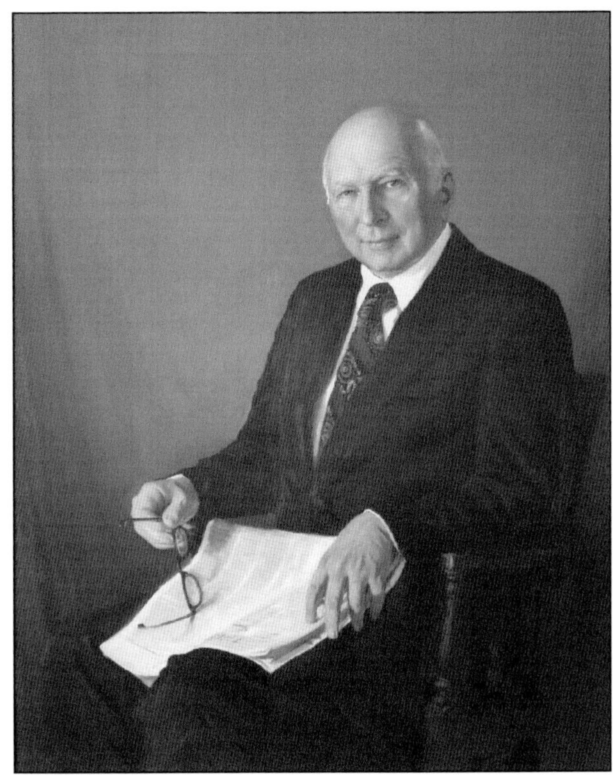

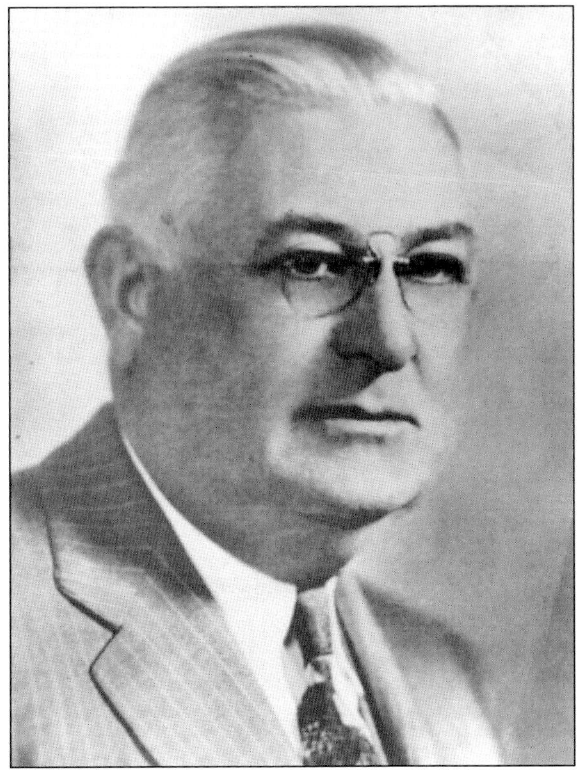

Stanhope S. Johnson, c. 1954. In 1954, the Patrick Henry Memorial Foundation hired Lynchburg architect Stanhope Johnson to direct the restoration of Red Hill. Johnson had previously served as a draftsman under Charles Barton Keen, who had been hired by Lucy Harrison in 1907 to renovate her home. Johnson made detailed measurements and sketches of the house and law office, which he used during the restoration.

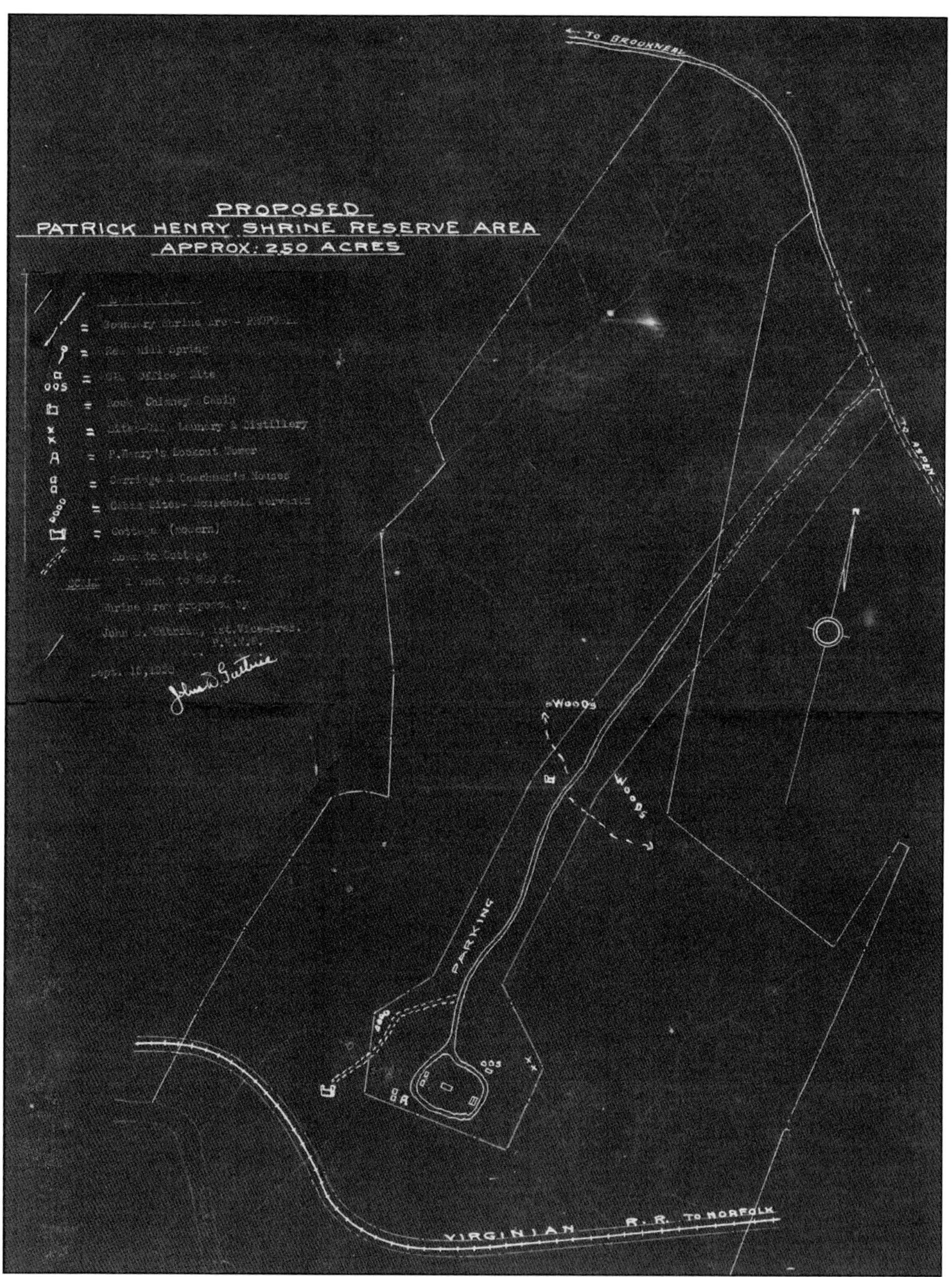

PROPOSED PATRICK HENRY SHRINE RESERVE AREA, SEPTEMBER 1950. This map of the proposed "Red Hill Shrine" was hand-drawn by Maj. John D. Guthrie, who had a civilian and military background in forestry management and construction. At the time, Guthrie served as the first vice president of the foundation. The map shows the layout of buildings and former building locations as they were in 1950. Along with other early drawings and notes, it continues to be valuable for researching the property's history. Major Guthrie served as an early trustee of the foundation for 15 years, from 1945 to 1960. His home, Villeview, was once the home of Henry's grandson William Wirt Henry in Charlotte Court House. For his service in the US Army during and after World War I, Major Guthrie received honors from the United States, France, and Russia.

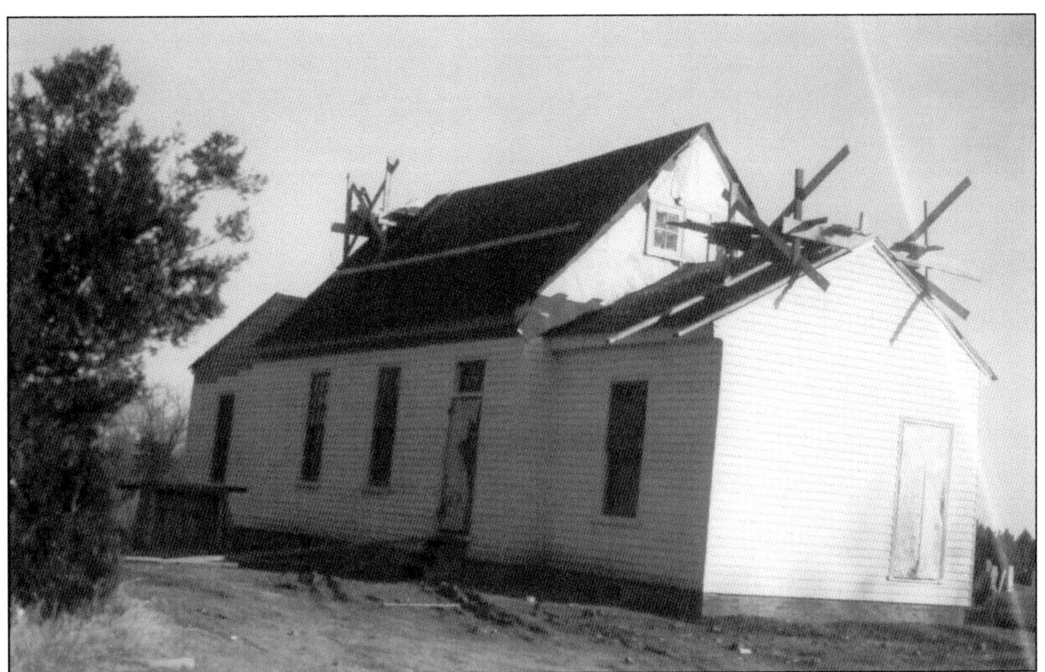

Patrick Henry House under Construction, c. 1956. In 1956, Patrick Henry's house was reconstructed on its original foundations using architect Stanhope Johnson's measurements and early-20th-century photographs. The side additions, built during John Henry's ownership, were mistakenly rebuilt by the architects, who believed them to be part of Patrick Henry's home.

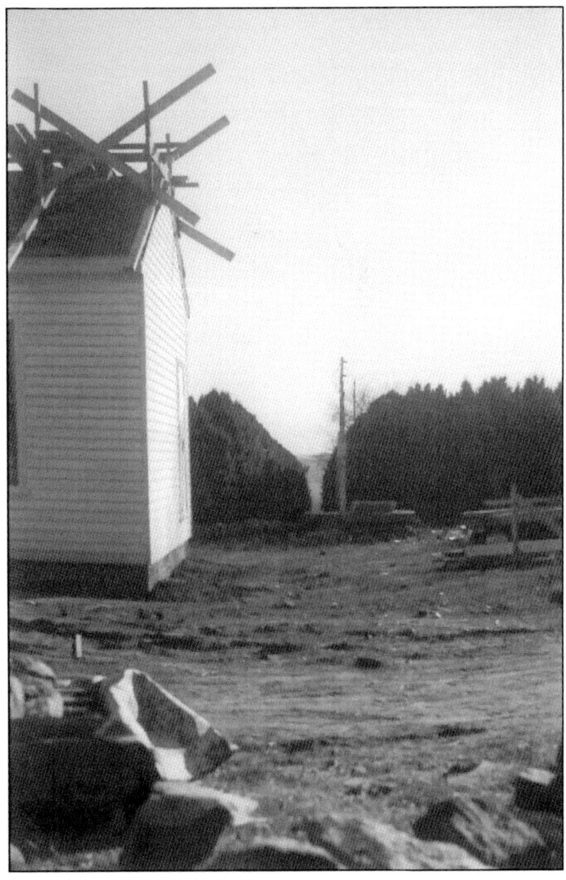

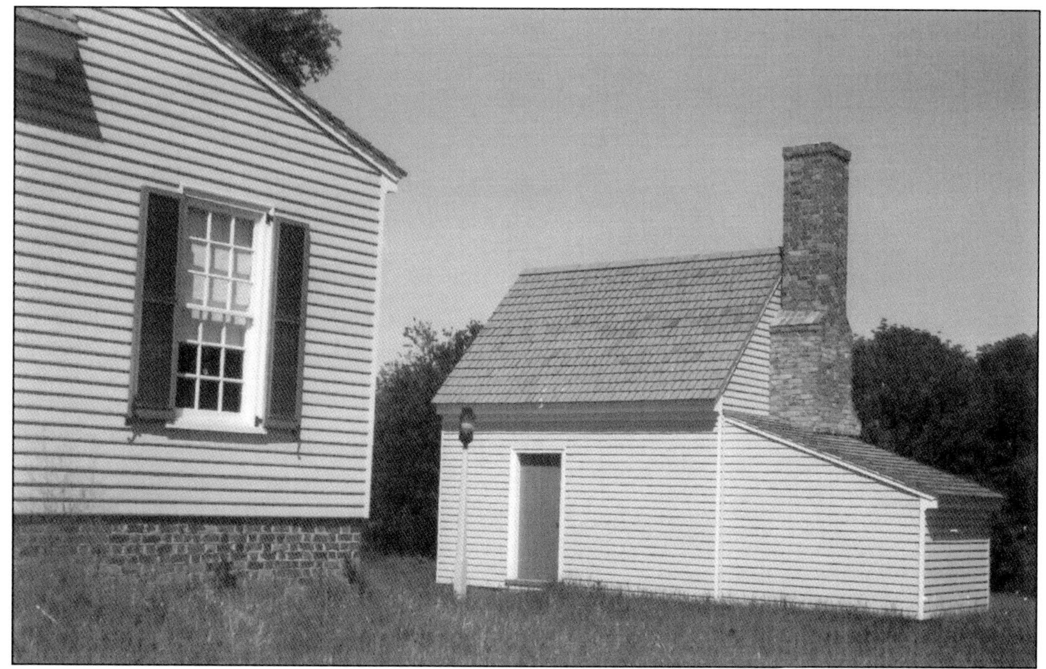

Reconstructed Kitchen, 1957. Kitchens were often separated from the main house to prevent heat, smells, and soot from entering and to segregate the enslaved. The reconstructed kitchen at Red Hill is a one-room frame structure containing a large fireplace, a brick floor, and a lean-to scullery. Recent research indicates that the old kitchen stood slightly northwest of the Henry home.

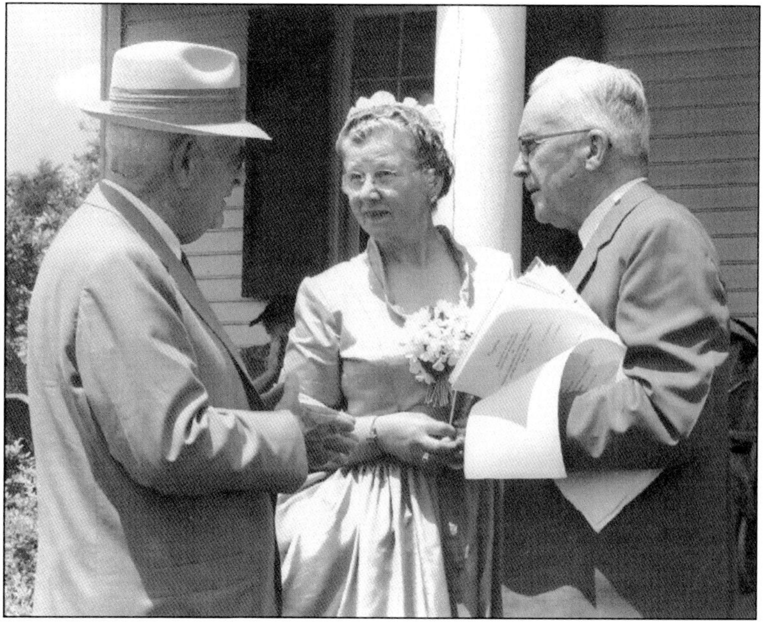

Stanhope Johnson, Mabel Bellwood, and James Easley, May 1959. Standing before Patrick Henry's former law office, Stanhope Johnson (left), head restoration architect; Mabel Bellwood, the first caretaker; and James Easley, foundation president, converse on the occasion of Patrick Henry's 223rd birthday. These individuals contributed to the success of Red Hill as a museum in its early years.

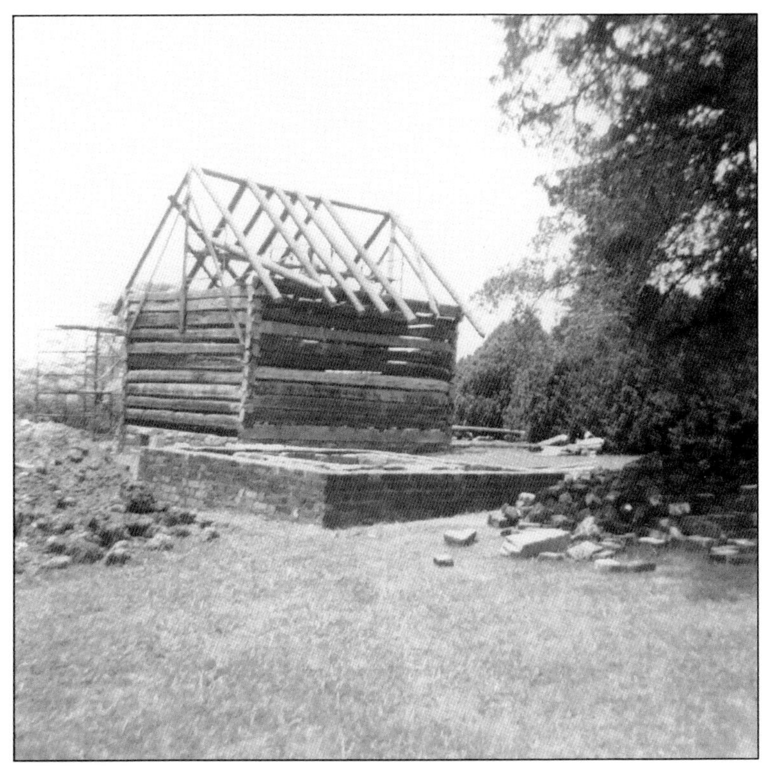

Harrison's Cabin under Construction, June 1961. This one-room log home was given to formerly enslaved coachman Harrison Henry by William Wirt Henry, Patrick Henry's grandson, for his years of service to the family. Harrison's cabin is seen here being rebuilt closer to the Henry home using some logs from the original structure.

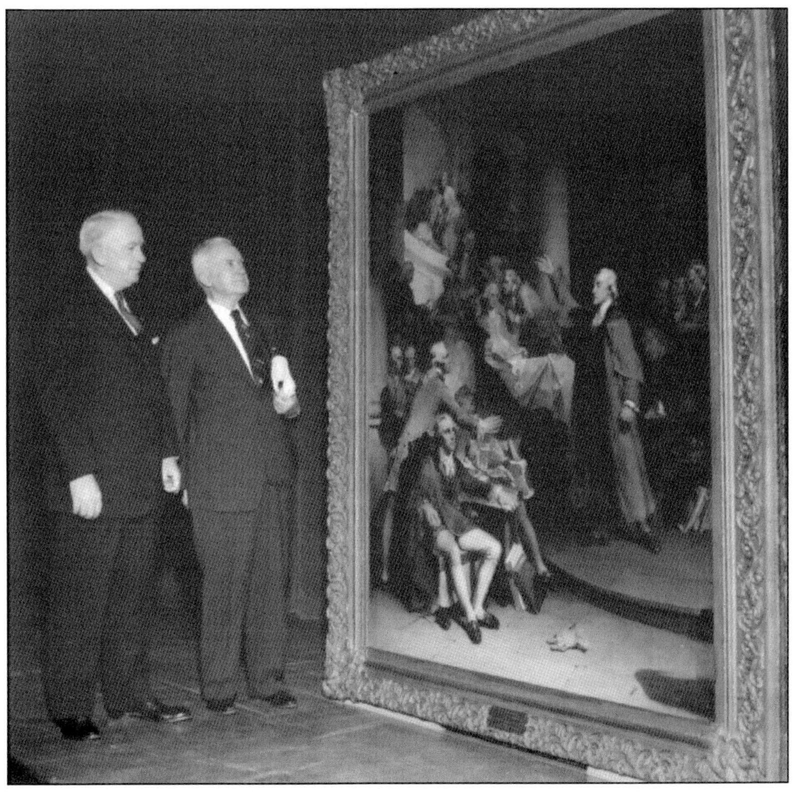

Presentation of *Patrick Henry before the Virginia House of Burgesses*, April 1959. Virginia governor J. Lindsey Almond (left) stands with James S. Easley next to Peter Rothermel's 1851 painting of Patrick Henry defending his resolutions against the Stamp Act of 1765. The painting had been transferred from the descendants of Charles L. Hamilton to the Patrick Henry Memorial Foundation and is now on display at Red Hill.

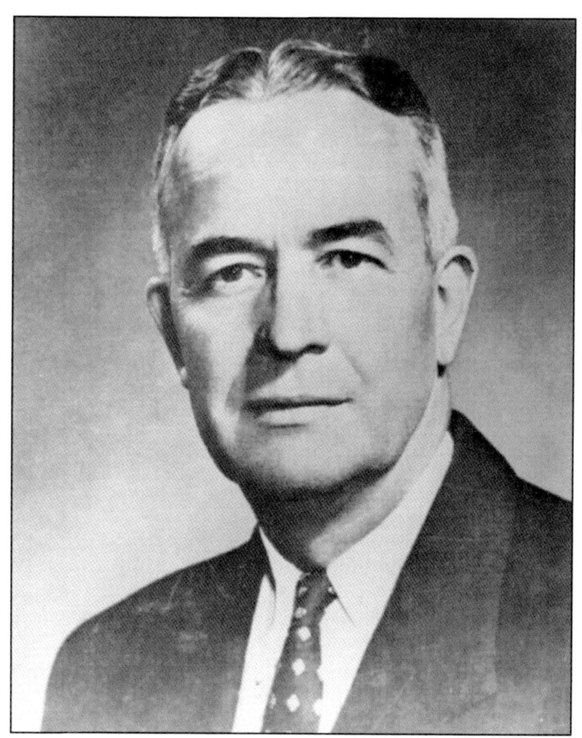

Dr. Robert Douthat Meade, c. 1969. Robert Meade was a professor of history at Randolph-Macon Women's College in Lynchburg, Virginia, from 1936 to 1971 and served as an early trustee of the Patrick Henry Memorial Foundation. Although now out of print, Dr. Meade's two-volume biography of Patrick Henry remains among the most comprehensive.

Launch of USS *Patrick Henry*, September 1959. Named after Founding Father Patrick Henry, USS *Patrick Henry* was a *George Washington*–class nuclear-powered fleet ballistic missile submarine of the US Navy. She was launched from Groton, Connecticut, on September 22, 1959, wrapped in patriotic bunting, now in the Red Hill collection. After 25 years in service, she was decommissioned on May 24, 1984.

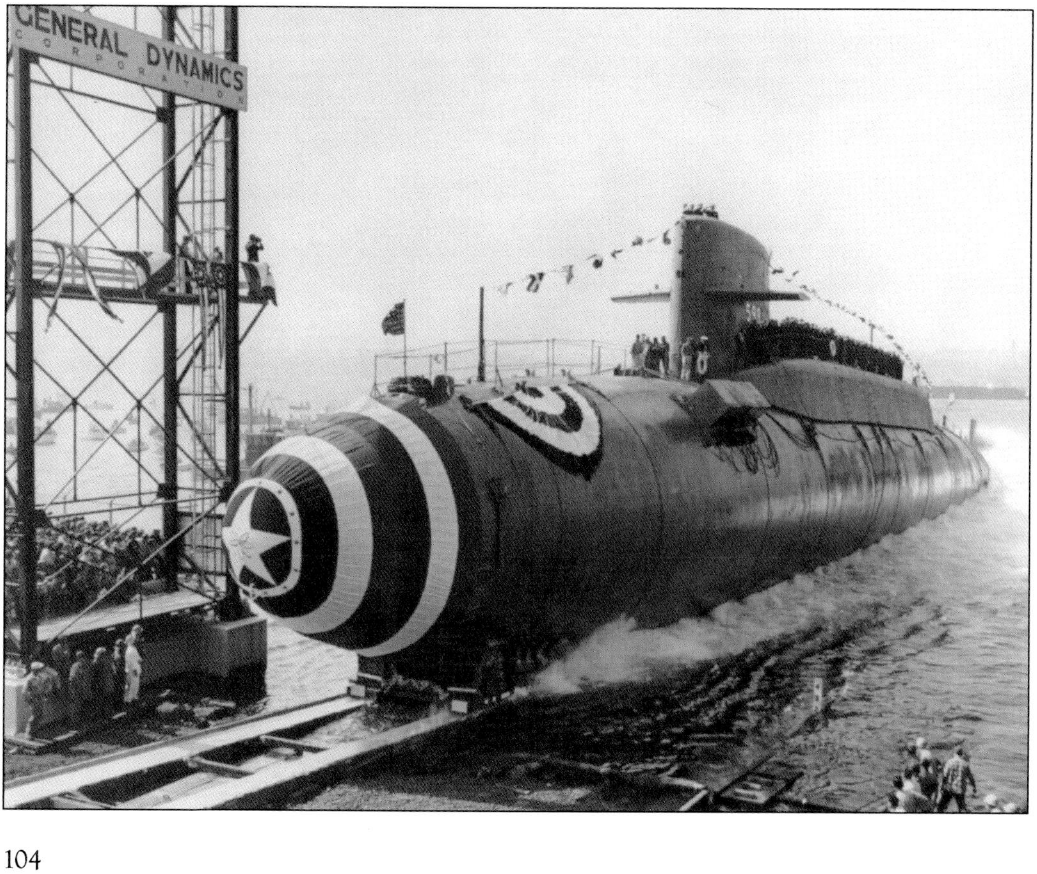

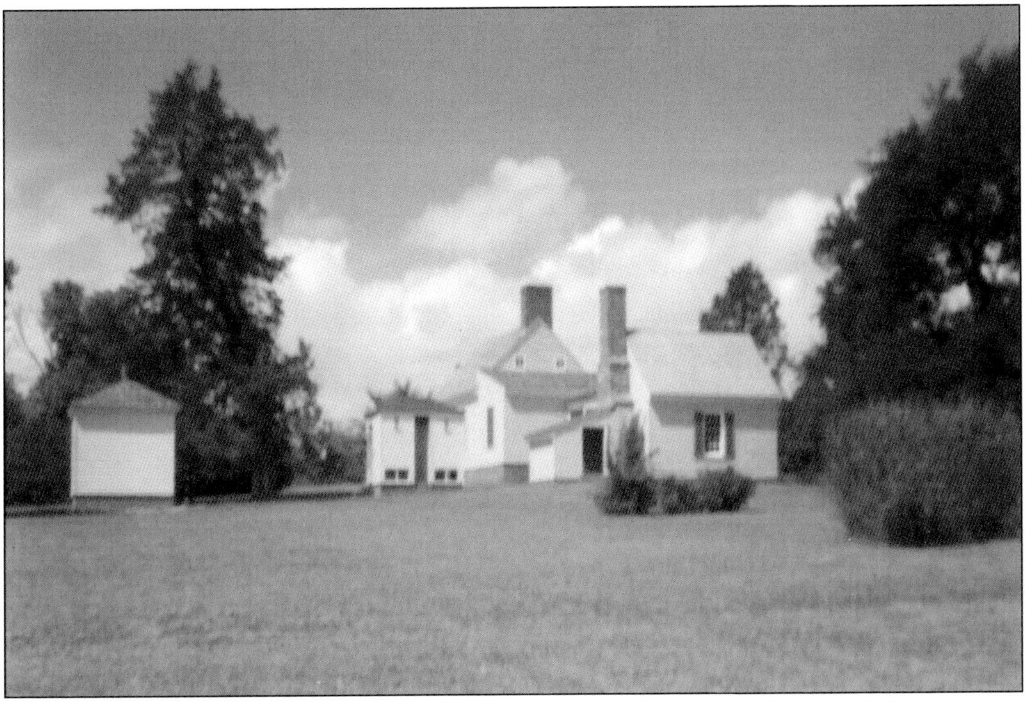

COMPLETED RECONSTRUCTED BUILDINGS, SEPTEMBER 1961. This image of the smokehouse, privy, and kitchen was taken shortly after their reconstruction. The Henry home, rebuilt five years earlier, can be seen behind the kitchen. The National Champion Osage orange tree still stands at the far right.

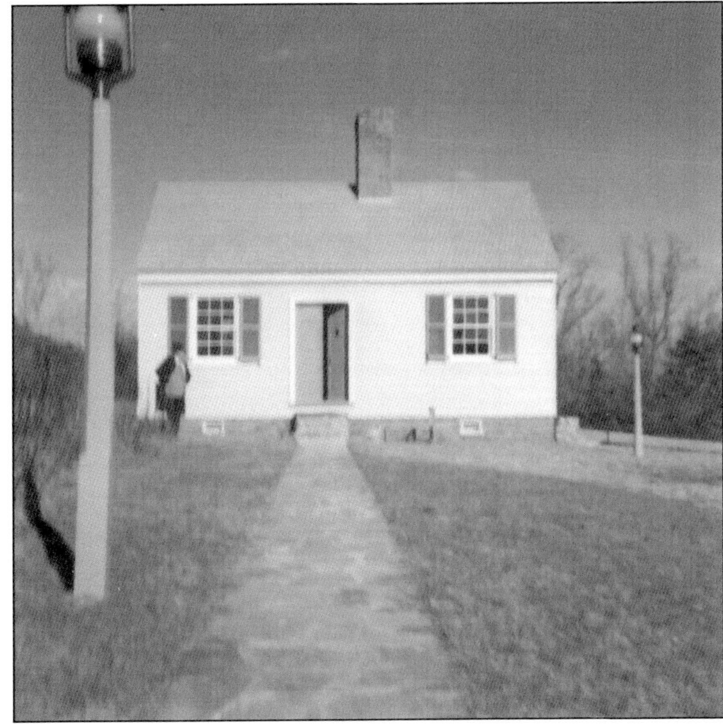

RESTORED LAW OFFICE, DECEMBER 1961. The only surviving 18th-century building at Red Hill, Patrick Henry's law office was restored in 1961 under the supervision of architect Stanhope Johnson and moved closer to its original location on the property. Restoration work focused on removing Lucy Harrison's c. 1911 alterations, such as the second story and portico.

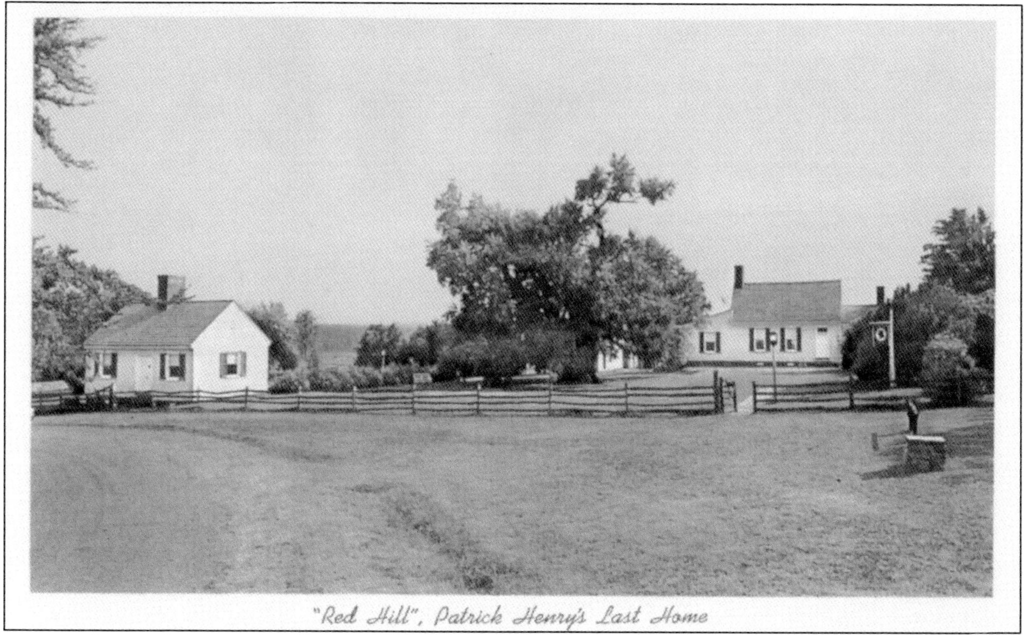

Red Hill Restored, c. 1965. This postcard shows the reconstructed home of Patrick Henry to the right, the Osage orange tree in the middle, and the restored law office on the left. A colonial-style hitching post and stepping-stone are seen near the gate entrance. Although not entirely accurate, the restoration saved Red Hill from destruction and welcomed numerous visitors.

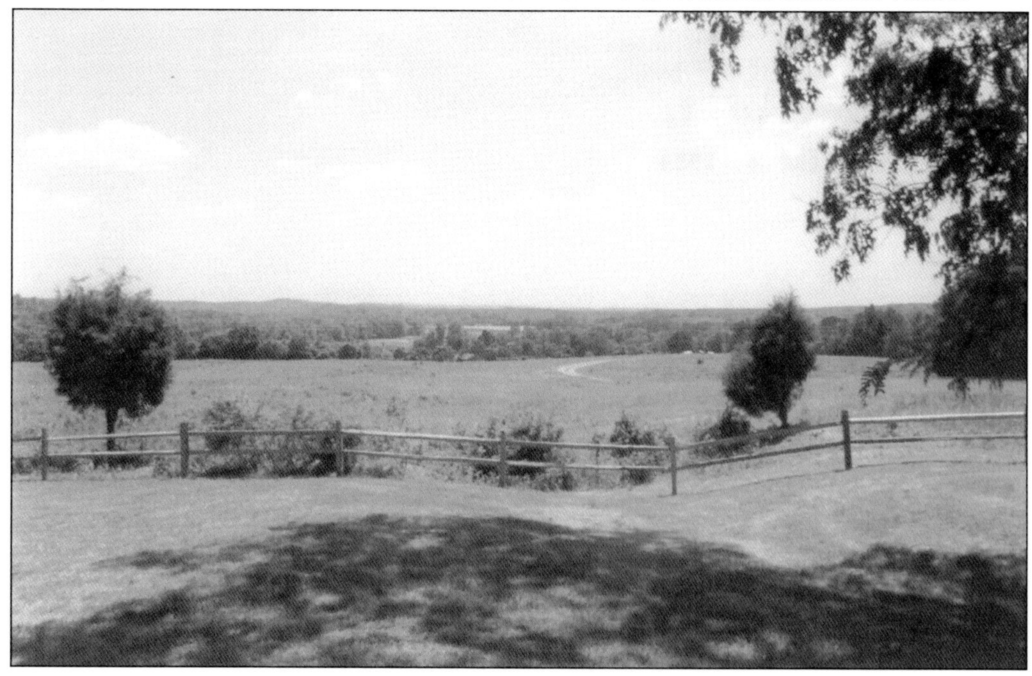

Southern View of the Staunton River Valley, 1999. The view of the slope and lowlands of Red Hill taken from the ridge in front of Patrick Henry's house remained untouched during the restoration. The depression in the ground (center) may be the remnants of an old entrance road. Despite the many changes affecting the property, this view has remained since the 18th century.

Six

A Legacy Preserved 1976–2024

While visitors could experience Red Hill for several years before 1976, that year marked the opening of the visitor center and museum. From then on, the site grew in importance as a historical landmark and a repository for information on Patrick Henry and the property's history. In 1977, the Patrick Henry Memorial Foundation hired its first full-time executive director, Patrick Daily. Daily and two subsequent directors authored biographical works on Patrick Henry that are still respected and referenced today.

The museum began housing artifacts significant to the life of Patrick Henry and the history of Red Hill, which included Indigenous Americans living here long before Henry and his family, as well as the enslaved people. The original 1851 painting of Patrick Henry arguing against the Stamp Act and the paper cutter he held as he proclaimed "Give me liberty or give me death" are staples of the museum, which was expanded in 1996. Today, the collection comprises approximately 3,000 objects rotated for public display. Members of the Patrick Henry Descendants' Branch, established in 1980 to document Henry's lineage, often enhance the museum's holdings.

An act of Congress in 1986 recognized Red Hill as the Patrick Henry National Memorial, making it the only national memorial for a Founding Father in the tri-state area. This recognition has attracted thousands of students and adults to enjoy annual educational events such as Living History Days, naturalization ceremonies, and Independence Day celebrations.

In 2018, Red Hill reacquired Quarter Place, thus opening the door to begin in-depth research on the lives of the enslaved and freed Blacks who lived and worked there during its 150-year history in the Henry family. A portion of that property houses a cemetery where the remains of 147 African Americans are interred. Ongoing research continues to identify those buried at Quarter Place and connect their living descendants.

The Patrick Henry Memorial Foundation continues its work without government funding, perpetuating the legacy of the Voice of the Revolution, the memory of those he enslaved, and the long and complex history of Red Hill.

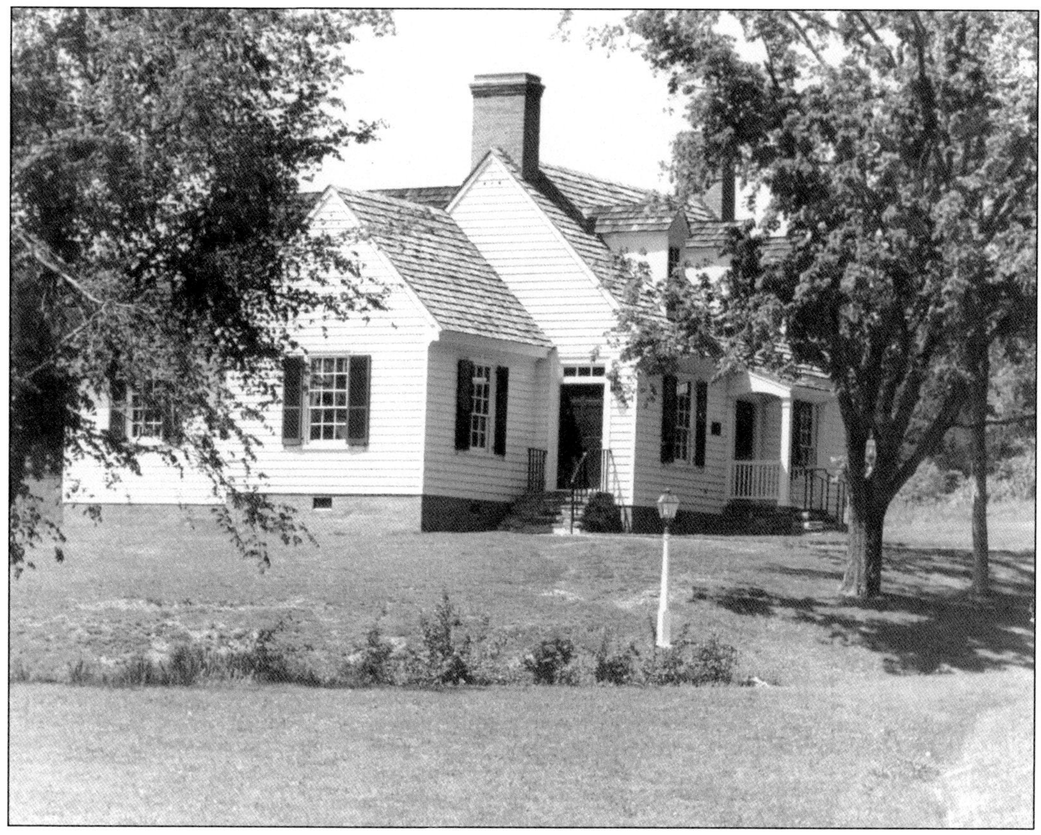

VISITOR CENTER AND MUSEUM, 1979. In 1976, the visitor center and museum at Red Hill was officially opened to the public. The building also served as the administrative offices and a gift shop. The specially designed museum would eventually house the largest known collection of Patrick Henry and Red Hill artifacts.

Nº 2800

Patrick Henry
Shrine

RED HILL, VIRGINIA

Adults $1.00

ADMIT
ONE

Nº 2800

PATRICK HENRY SHRINE

Red Hill, Virginia

Adults — $1.00

ADMISSION TICKET, C. 1977. In the 1970s, a "Red Hill Shrine" ticket cost only $1. In the days before its designation as a national memorial for Patrick Henry, the site was called the Red Hill Shrine. Through the years, admission to Red Hill has been kept reasonable to make the site accessible to as many people as possible.

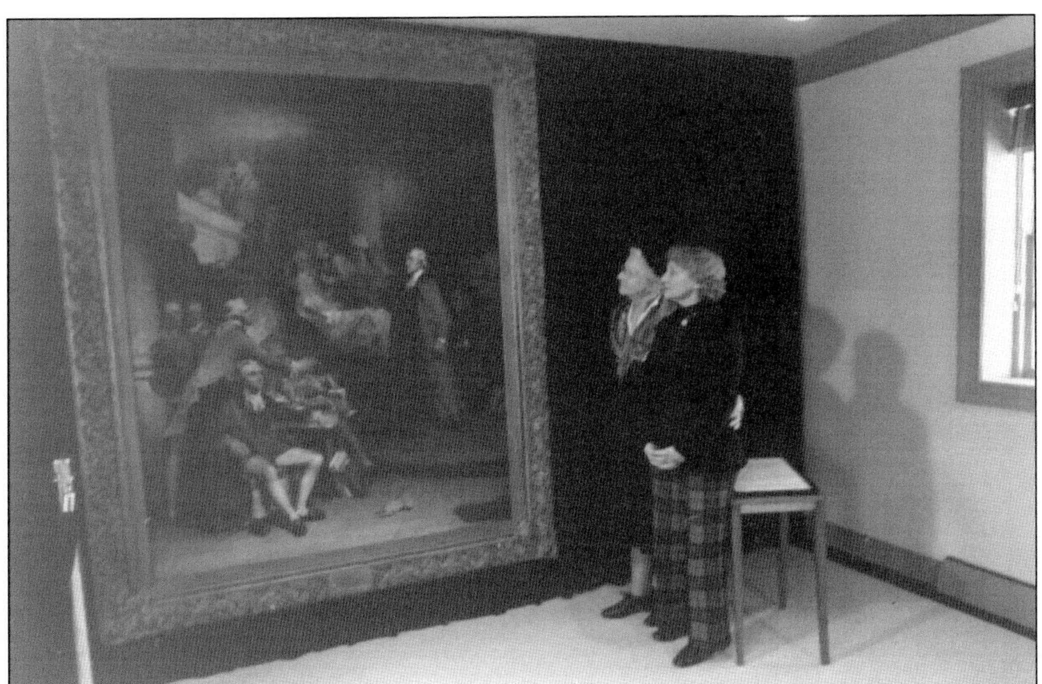

Mabel Bellwood and Marie Reveley with Patrick Henry Painting, 1977. The Red Hill curatorial team of Mabel Bellwood (left) and Marie Reveley admire the original Rothermel painting. Since Red Hill had no physical place to store or display the massive painting, it had been on loan to the Virginia Historical Society since its acquisition in 1959. With the museum's opening in 1976, the Rothermel painting found its permanent home.

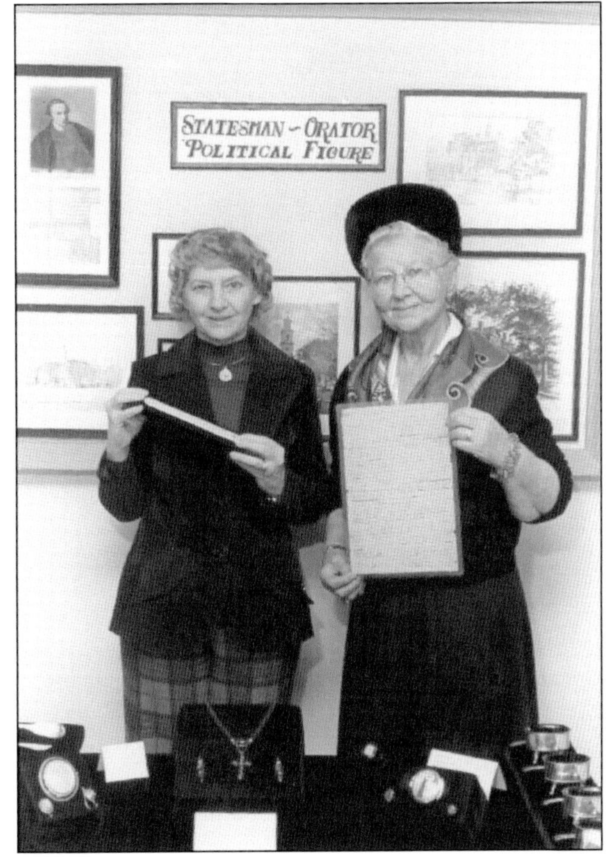

Mabel Bellwood and Marie Reveley Holding Artifacts, 1977. Shortly after the museum's opening, Curator Mabel Bellwood (right) poses with a letter from Patrick Henry to George Washington, while staff member Marie Reveley holds the paper cutter Henry held during his "Liberty or Death" speech. Much is owed to Bellwood for beginning to collect artifacts for the museum.

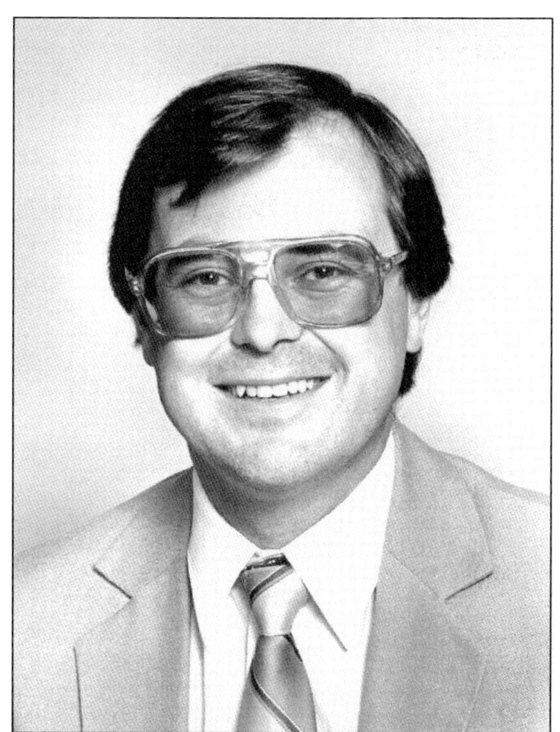

Patrick Daily, 1977. The first professional director of Red Hill (1977–1988), through Patrick Daily's leadership, the museum became a national memorial by an act of Congress in 1986. Daily also served as the secretary-treasurer of the Governor's Commission to commemorate Patrick Henry's 250th anniversary. In 1980, he led the effort to establish the Patrick Henry Descendants' Branch. Daily is the author of *Patrick Henry: The Last Years* (1986).

Elizabeth Taylor Visits Red Hill, May 1977. Sen. John Warner of Virginia, accompanied by his wife and movie star legend, Elizabeth Taylor, laid flowers at the grave of Patrick Henry during a ceremony celebrating the patriot's birthday. Eight years later, John Warner introduced a resolution before the US Senate to make Red Hill the Patrick Henry National Memorial.

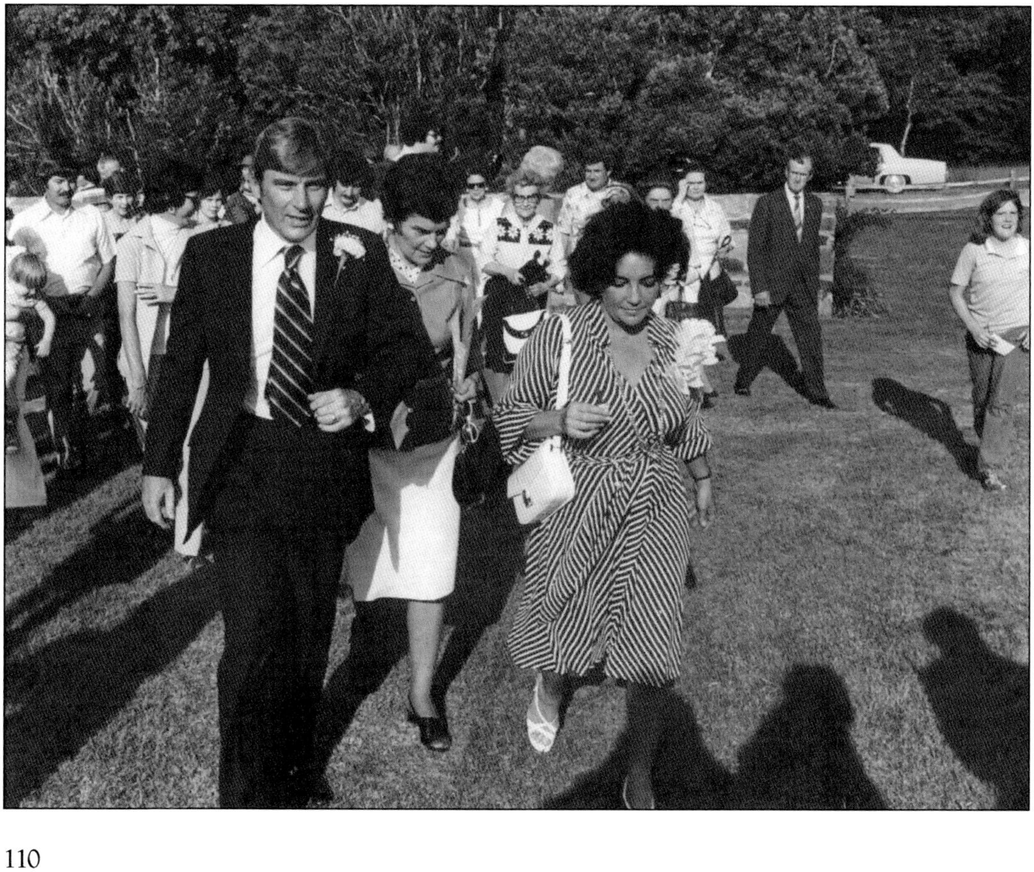

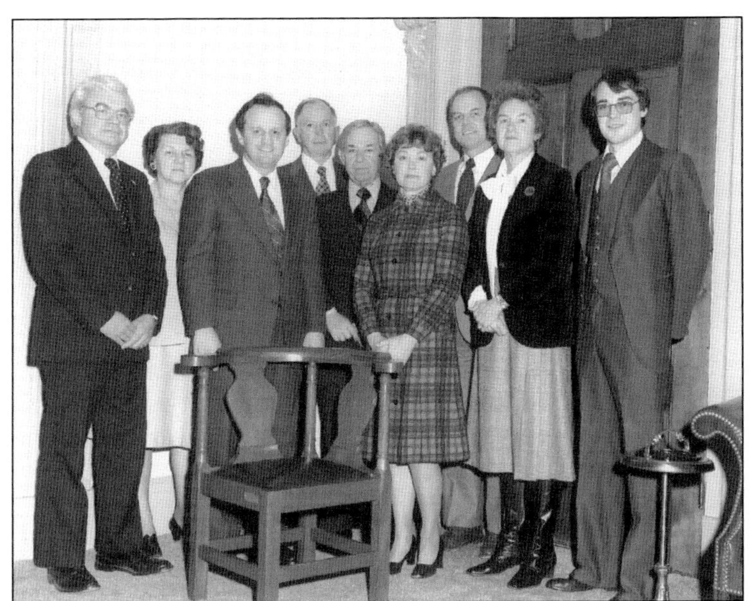

Patrick Henry Corner Chair Reproduction Presentation, February 1979. A reproduction of Patrick Henry's corner chair, made by the Patrick Henry Boys Plantation, is presented to Virginia governor John Dalton at the governor's office in Richmond. Standing next to the governor are members of the state legislature and officials of the Patrick Henry Memorial Foundation.

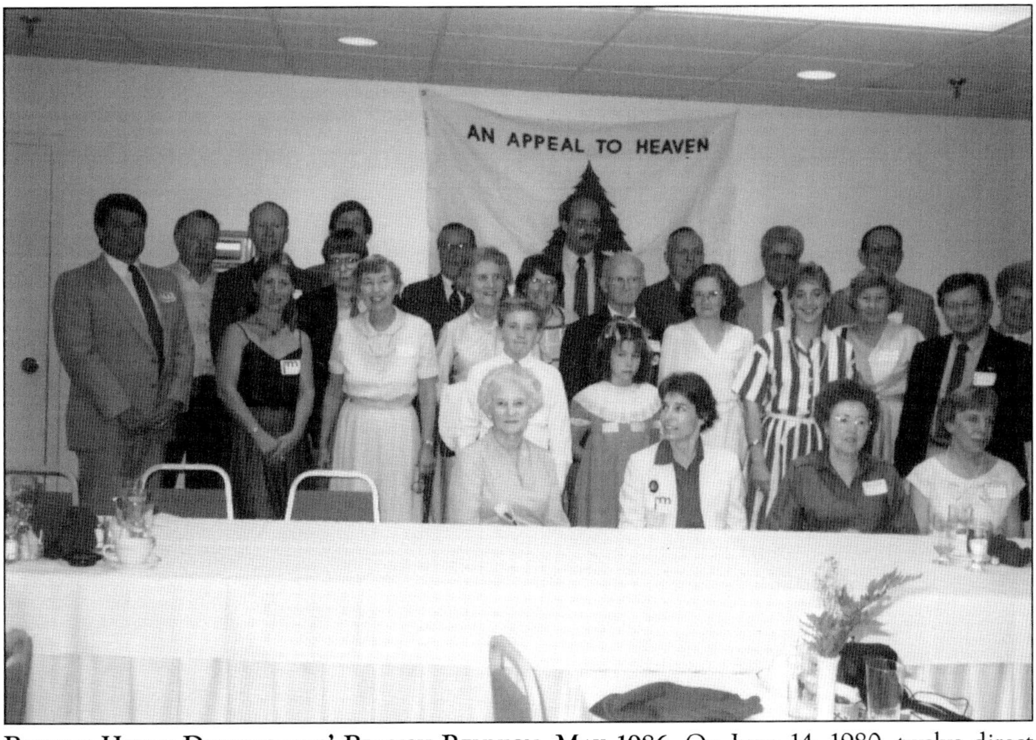

Patrick Henry Descendants' Branch Reunion, May 1986. On June 14, 1980, twelve direct descendants of Patrick Henry gathered under the Osage orange tree at Red Hill by invitation of executive director Patrick Daily and formed a support group for the Patrick Henry Memorial Foundation. Since then, the Descendants' Branch has grown significantly in importance and numbers. The group holds annual family reunions at places associated with their famous ancestor.

S. J. Res. 187

Ninety-ninth Congress of the United States of America

AT THE SECOND SESSION

Begun and held at the City of Washington on Tuesday, the twenty-first day of January, one thousand nine hundred and eighty-six

Joint Resolution

Designating Patrick Henry's last home and burial place, known as Red Hill, in the Commonwealth of Virginia, as a National Memorial to Patrick Henry.

Whereas Patrick Henry was a great orator and leader of the Revolutionary cause in the struggle for independence and in the establishment of a new Government of the United States of America; and

Whereas, fifty years ago on August 15, 1935, the Congress authorized establishment of Red Hill, Patrick Henry's last home and burial place, as a national monument in tribute and recognition of his service to his country, and the authorization was repealed in 1944 due to insufficient appropriations during distressful times; and

Whereas the Patrick Henry Memorial Foundation in 1944 acquired Red Hill, located in Charlotte County, Virginia, and has both reconstructed his home and restored his original cottage law office and grounds as a shrine and museum, in commemoration of the entire life of Patrick Henry; and

Whereas Red Hill is listed on the National Register of Historic Places; and

Whereas the Virginia General Assembly, in its 1985 legislative session, has enacted Senate Joint Resolution 82, calling for national recognition and stewardship of Red Hill by the Federal Government; and

Whereas Scotchtown, Saint John's Church, and Hanover County Courthouse are designated National Historic Landmarks, due to their historical significance, integrity and representation of key moments of Patrick Henry's revolutionary contributions; and

Whereas May 29, 1736, was the birthdate of Patrick Henry, and Scotchtown, Saint John's Church, and Hanover County Courthouse and Red Hill are together planning commemorative activities for the two hundred and fiftieth anniversary of Patrick Henry's birth during 1986; and

Whereas it would be appropriate for Congress, as part of the 1986 commemorative activities, to honor for the benefit of present and future generations the entire life of Patrick Henry by a national memorialization of this American Patriot's burial place at Red Hill, where are also preserved his original cottage law office, his reconstructed home, and museum articles depicting his life and work: Now, therefore, be it

Resolved by the Senate and House of Representatives of the United States of America in Congress assembled, That the last home and burial place of Patrick Henry in Charlotte County, Commonwealth of Virginia, known as Red Hill, is hereby designated as a National Memorial to Patrick Henry, and shall be known as: the Red Hill Patrick Henry National Memorial. The Secretary of the Interior is authorized and directed to take appropriate action to assure that this Memorial is announced in the Federal Register, and that

FIRST PAGE OF THE JOINT RESOLUTION OF CONGRESS, MAY 1986. On August 15, 1935, Pres. Franklin D. Roosevelt signed Public Law 277. Sen. Carter Glass of Lynchburg had presented the bill. It made provisions for the federal government to purchase and maintain Red Hill as a national monument for Patrick Henry. During the next few years, negotiations for the sale of Red Hill were held between officials from the Department of the Interior and Patrick Henry's great-granddaughter Lucy Henry Harrison. However, due to the inability to agree on financial terms, the bill was repealed in 1944.

S. J. Res. 187—2

official records and lists are amended, in due course, to reflect this addition as being included along with other national memorials established by Act of Congress.

SEC. 2. The Secretary of the Interior, with the concurrence of the owner of the property, is authorized and directed to place at the gravesite on or by June 6, 1986, the anniversary of Patrick Henry's death, an appropriate plaque or marker bearing an inscription commensurate with the contributions of Patrick Henry to the American Revolution and with the patriotism his words and deeds continue to inspire in all Americans: *Provided,* That the ownership of Red Hill remains non-Federal, and that the costs of such plaque or marker, and of its inscription and maintenance, as well as the costs of operations and maintenance for the estate shall be borne from non-Federal funds, services, or materials.

Thomas P. O'Neill

Speaker of the House of Representatives.

Strom Thurmond

~~*Vice President of the United States and*~~
President of the Senate Pro Tempore

APPROVED

MAY 12 1986

Ronald Reagan

SECOND PAGE OF THE JOINT RESOLUTION OF CONGRESS, MAY 1986. Four decades after President Roosevelt repealed Public Law 277, an act of Congress recognized Patrick Henry's leadership during the "struggle for independence and in the establishment of a new government of the United States of America" on May 12, 1986. The estate would become known as the Red Hill Patrick Henry National Memorial. Although an affiliate site of the National Park Service, Red Hill does not receive federal funding to support its preservation or educational efforts.

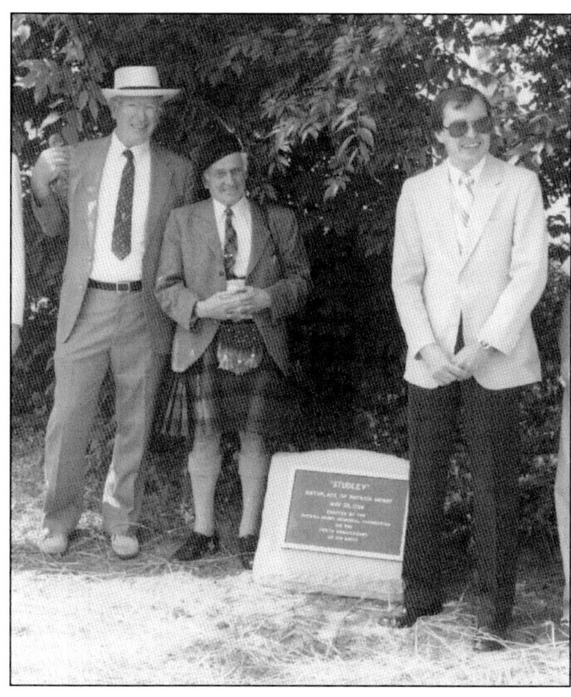

Lord Dunmore Dedicates Plaque, May 1986. Kenneth Murray, 11th Earl of Dunmore, a direct descendant of Virginia's royal governor John Murray, 4th Earl of Dunmore, assists in dedicating a plaque at Studley commemorating the 250th anniversary of Patrick Henry's birth. Murray was invited to Virginia by the Patrick Henry Commission to "revoke" his ancestor's proclamation against the patriot in 1775.

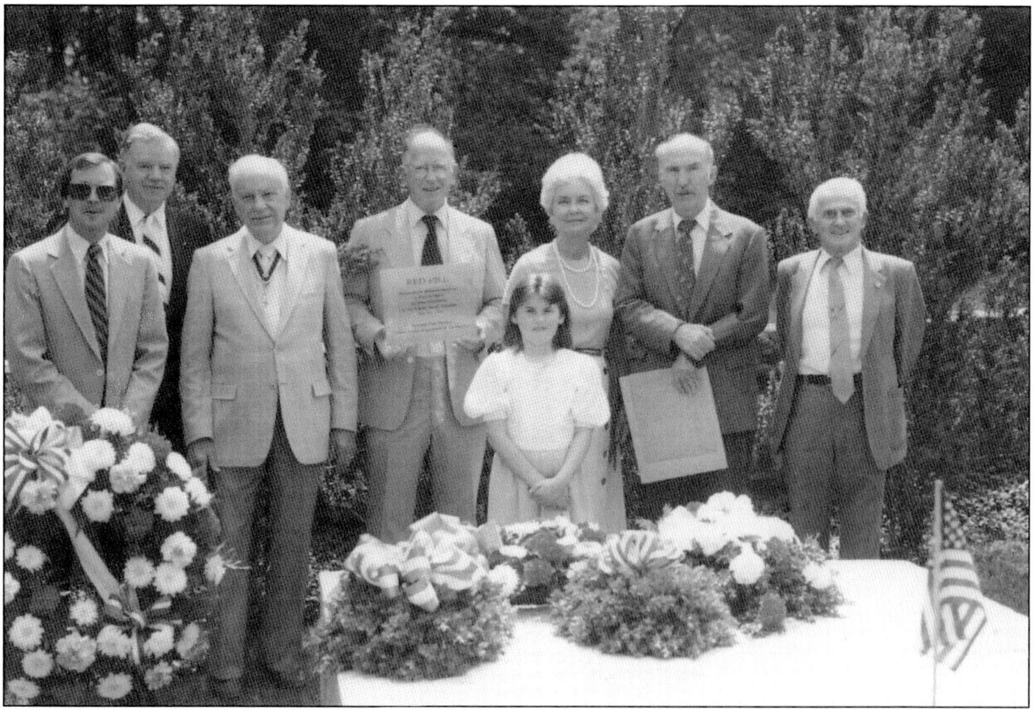

Lord Dunmore Visits Red Hill, May 1986. The Earl of Dunmore visits Red Hill on Patrick Henry's 250th birthday anniversary. In his speech before the celebrators, his Lordship acknowledged that Henry "stood in the forefront of man's battle for human rights, liberty, and religious freedom, and by his unequaled oratory and exemplary leadership inspired his countrymen." Then-executive director Patrick Daily stands at the far left.

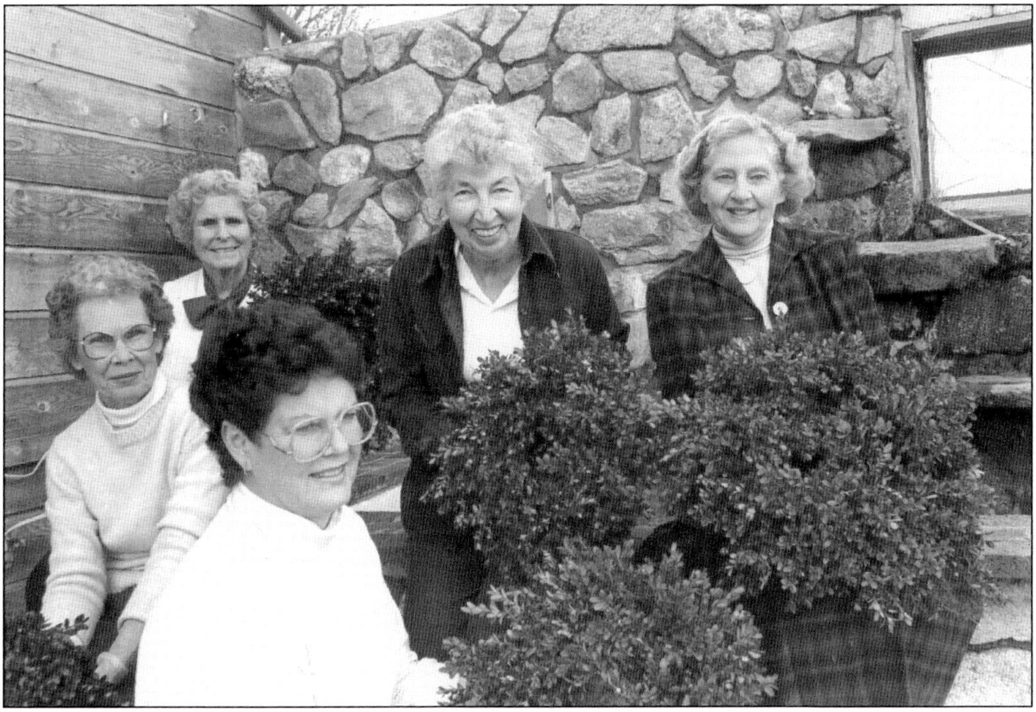

PATRICK HENRY AUXILIARY WREATH-MAKING, 1987. Members of the Patrick Henry Auxiliary—from left to right, Iris Scott, Carolyn Lusardi, and Clara Herndon—make seasonal wreaths from boxwood cuttings. The Patrick Henry Auxiliary is a membership-based volunteer organization that supports the foundation's mission in various ways, including serving as tour guides, museum aides, and interpreters of 18th-century crafts and skills during Living History Days.

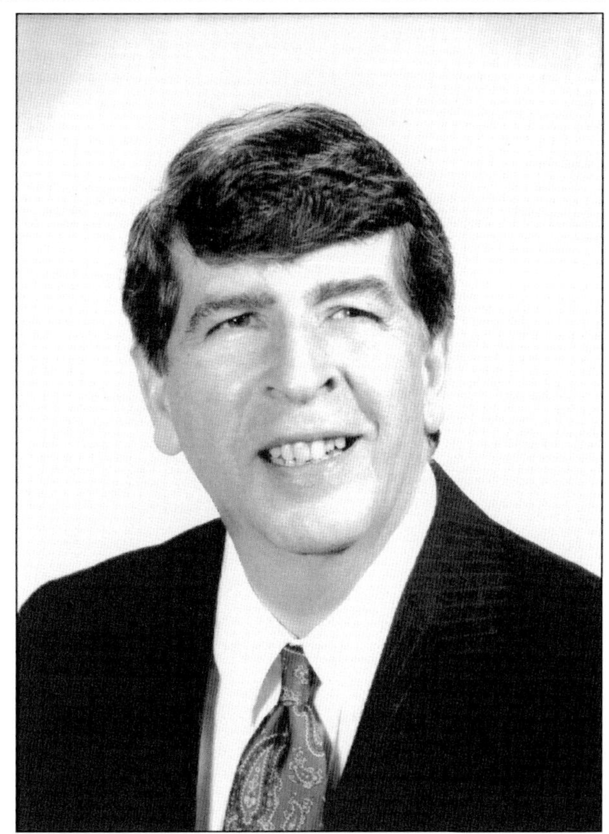

DR. JAMES ELSON, 1995. A graduate of the Juilliard School in New York City and a Fulbright Scholar from West Virginia University, Dr. Elson became executive vice president of the foundation in 1988. His tenure focused on restoring the property, removing inaccurate architectural details, and professionalizing Patrick Henry scholarship. Dr. Elson also edited two books: *Patrick Henry and Thomas Jefferson* (1997) and *Patrick Henry in His Speeches and Writings* (2007).

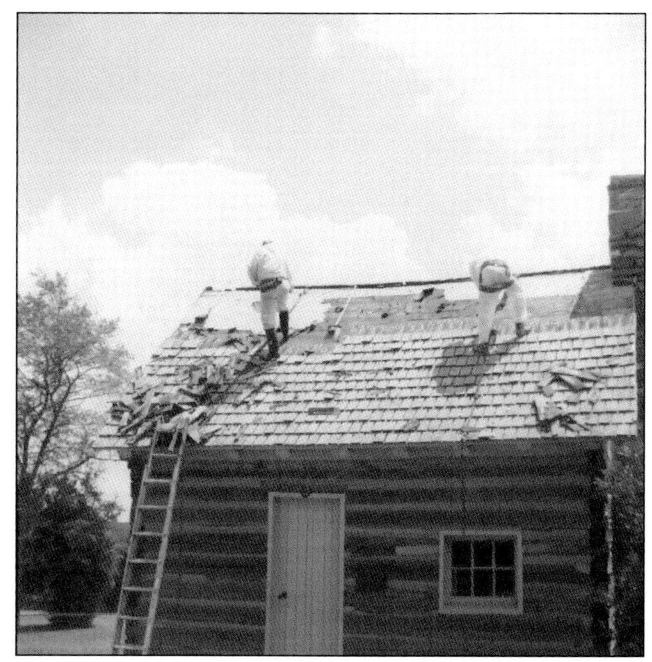

Historic Building Restoration and Asbestos Abatement, 1991. Over the last three decades, continuous research has improved the accurate appearance of the reconstructed historic buildings. Between 1991 and 1992, architects Everette Fauber and Nathaniel Neblett removed inappropriate Colonial Revival details such as wallpaper, light fixtures, and paint colors. Dark varnished flooring was removed in the Henry house and law office to replicate an 18th-century appearance (below). Asbestos roof sheathing, a common fire-resistant material installed in the 1950s and 1960s, was also removed (left).

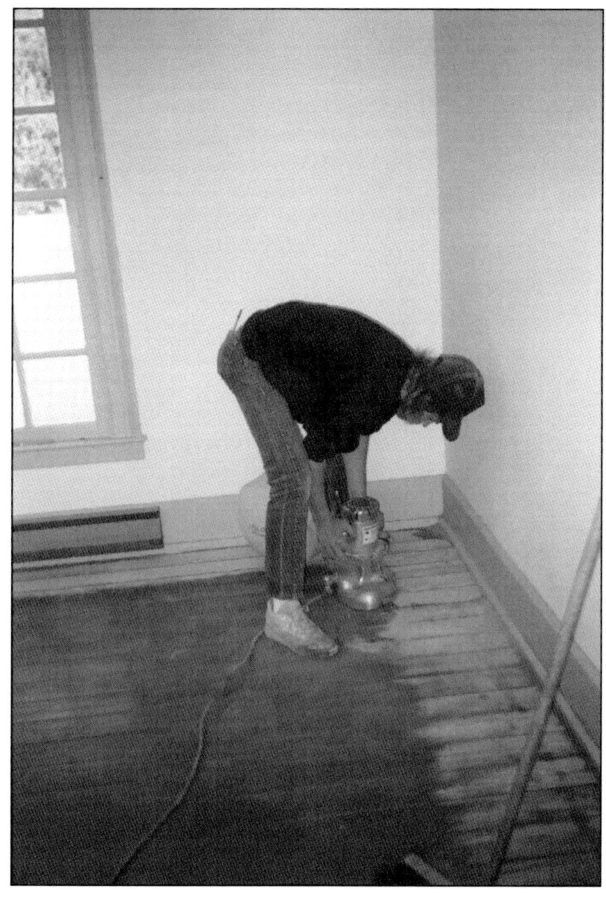

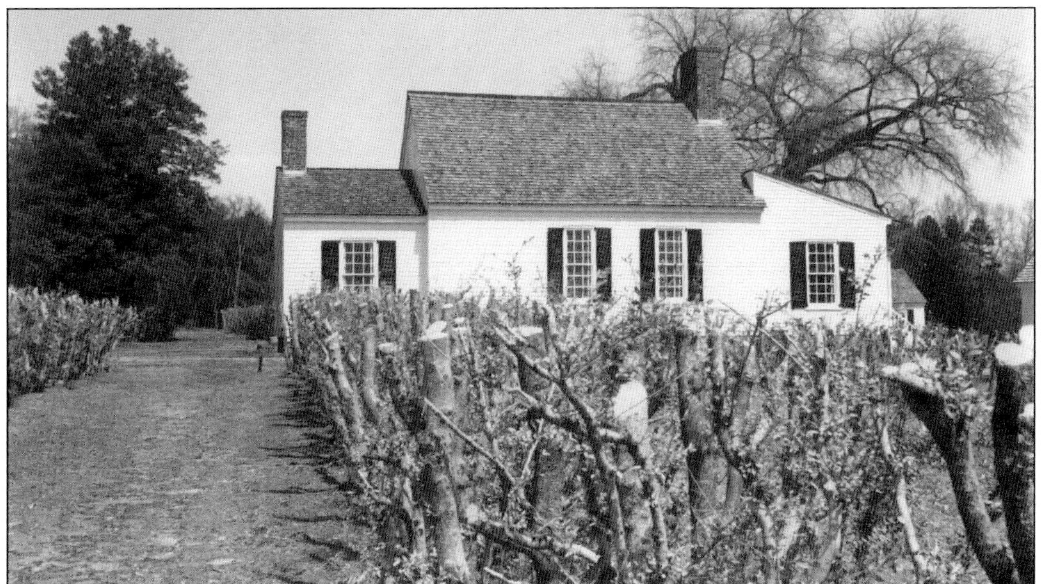

BOXWOOD GARDENS PRUNED, FEBRUARY 1993. During John and Elvira Henry's occupancy and up to 1944, the Henry family kept the boxwood garden at a height of approximately four feet. After that, the bushes were neglected and grew to almost 10 feet over the years, obscuring both the design and the view of the Staunton River valley. In 1992, the foundation cut the boxwood back to the earlier four-foot height.

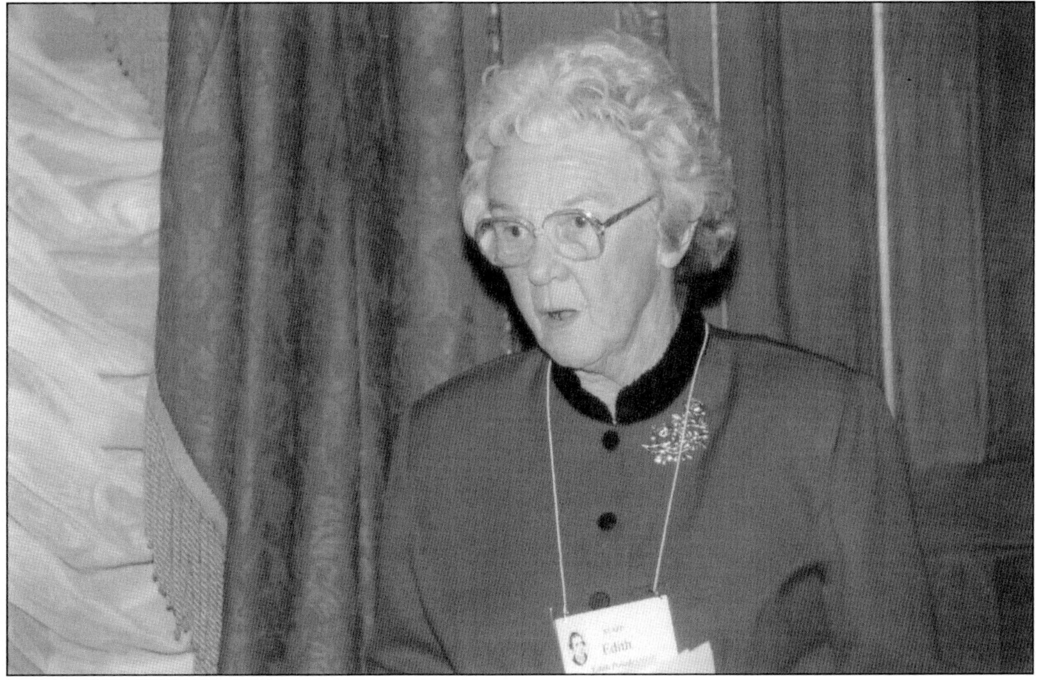

EDITH C. POINDEXTER, C. 1993. Dedicating over three decades of her life to Red Hill, Edith Poindexter, affectionately known as "Miz P," served as the foundation's administrative assistant, curator, and genealogist. An authority on Patrick Henry's family, Poindexter helped establish the Patrick Henry Descendants' Branch and was made an "honorary descendant" by its members.

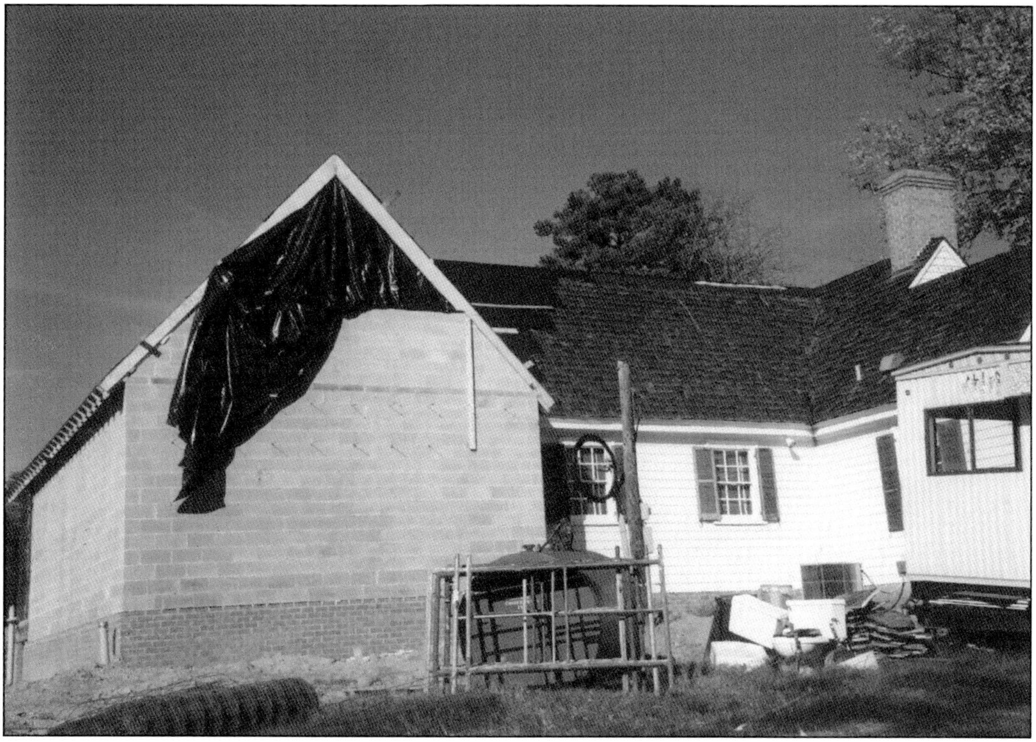

MUSEUM ADDITION CONSTRUCTION AND OPENING, 1996. The expanded and remodeled visitor center opened to the public on May 29, 1996, coinciding with Patrick Henry's 260th birthday. Originally built in 1976, the visitor center had become too small to accommodate staffing, display, and storage needs. The new museum included state-of-the-art temperature and humidity controls, fire-resistant construction materials, and a visitor orientation room. As a result of these improvements, the visitor center doubled in size and became the first accessible building at Red Hill.

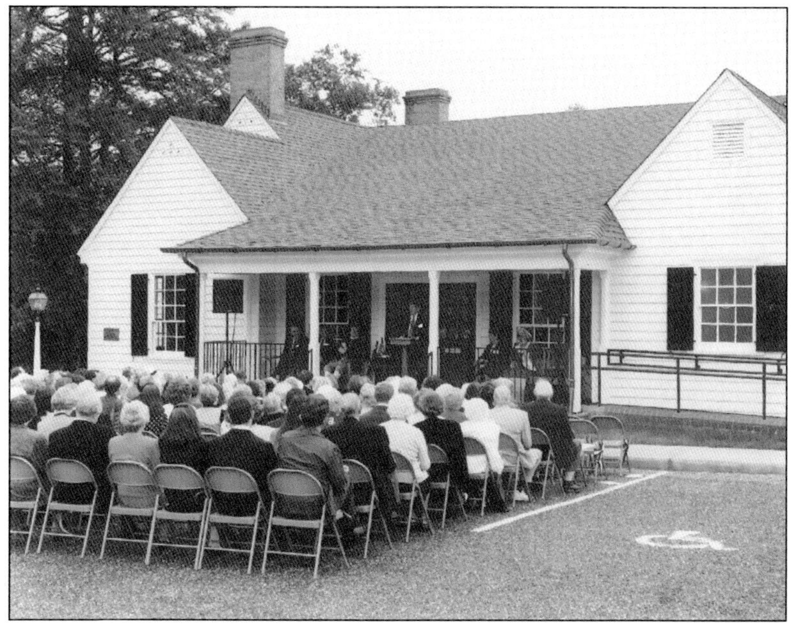

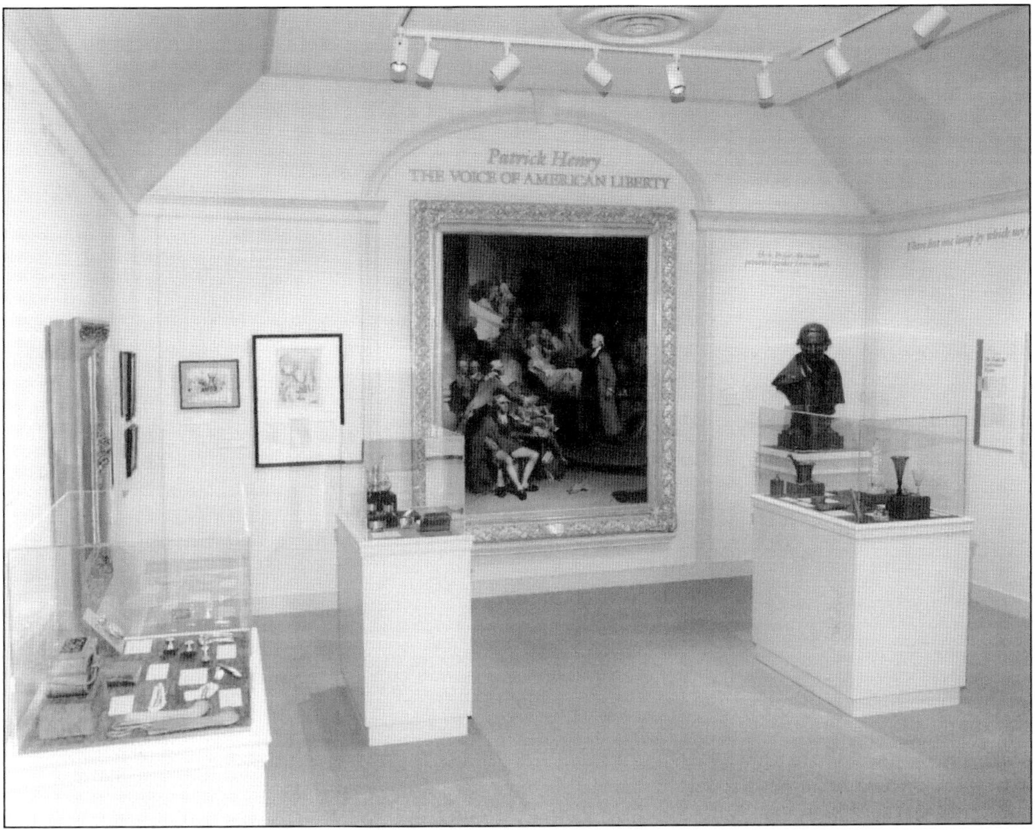

Museum Exhibition Space Opened, May 1996. Inside the new E. Stuart James Grant Museum Room, hundreds of artifacts could be displayed, many for the first time. At the opening ceremony on May 29 (below), foundation trustees, from left to right, Robert Dean, William Carr, and Thomas Ward, inspect Henry family artifacts inside their new exhibit cases. The museum houses the world's largest collection of Patrick Henry artifacts, including letters, documents, portraits, books, and furniture. It is also the permanent home of Peter Rothermel's *Patrick Henry before the Virginia House of Burgesses.*

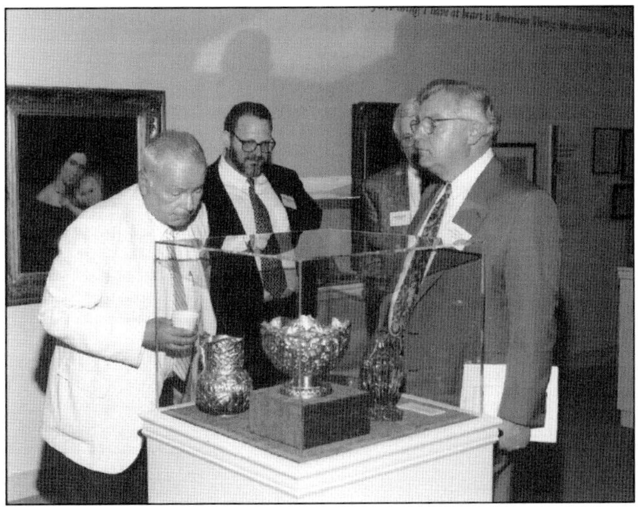

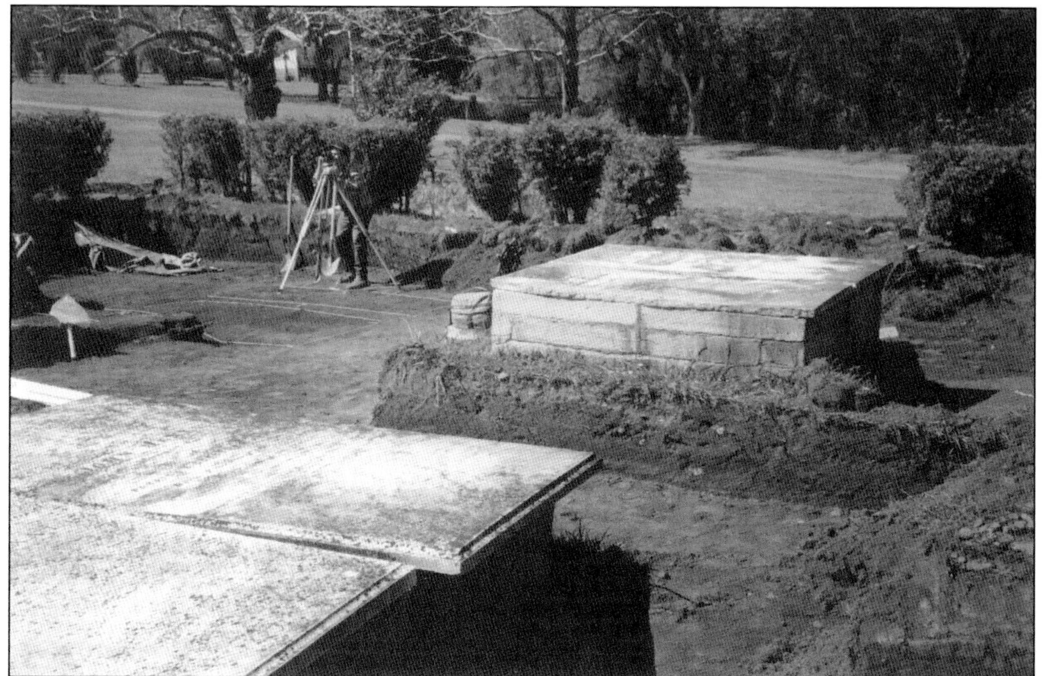

HENRY FAMILY CEMETERY EXCAVATION, MAY 1997. The College of William and Mary excavated the Henry cemetery to locate potential unmarked graves. Although it did not disturb any burials, the excavation revealed three additional ones, two adults and one infant. Unfortunately, no burial records exist for the three outlined burials (below), but research has revealed several likely names: Fayette Henry, son of Patrick Henry; his wife, Anne Elcan; Alexander Spotswood Henry, son of Patrick Henry; Fayette Jr., son of Fayette Henry; and Jane Robertson Henry, daughter of Patrick Henry. The graves of Patrick and Dorothea Henry are in the background (above), while John and Elvira Henry's graves are in the foreground.

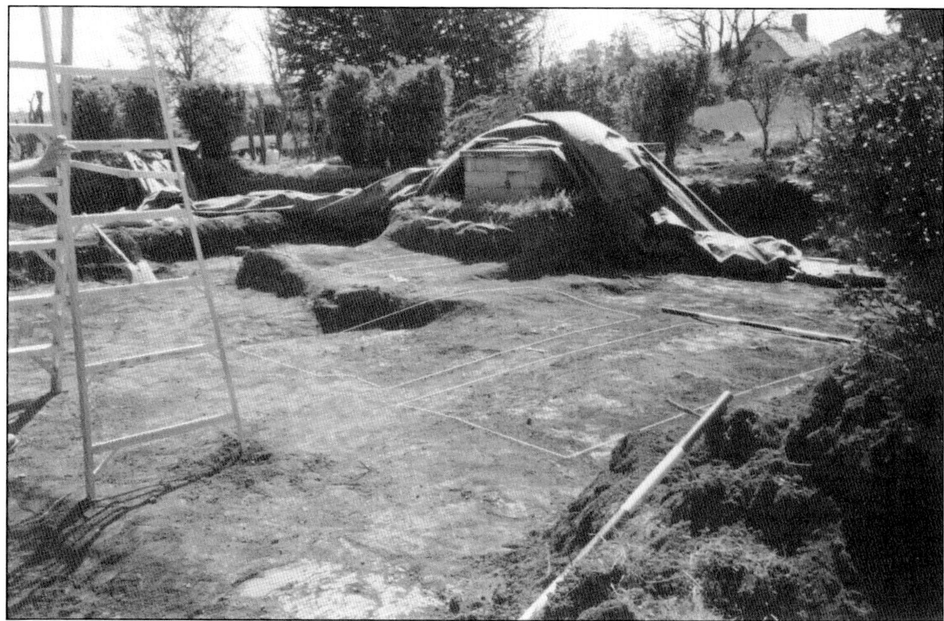

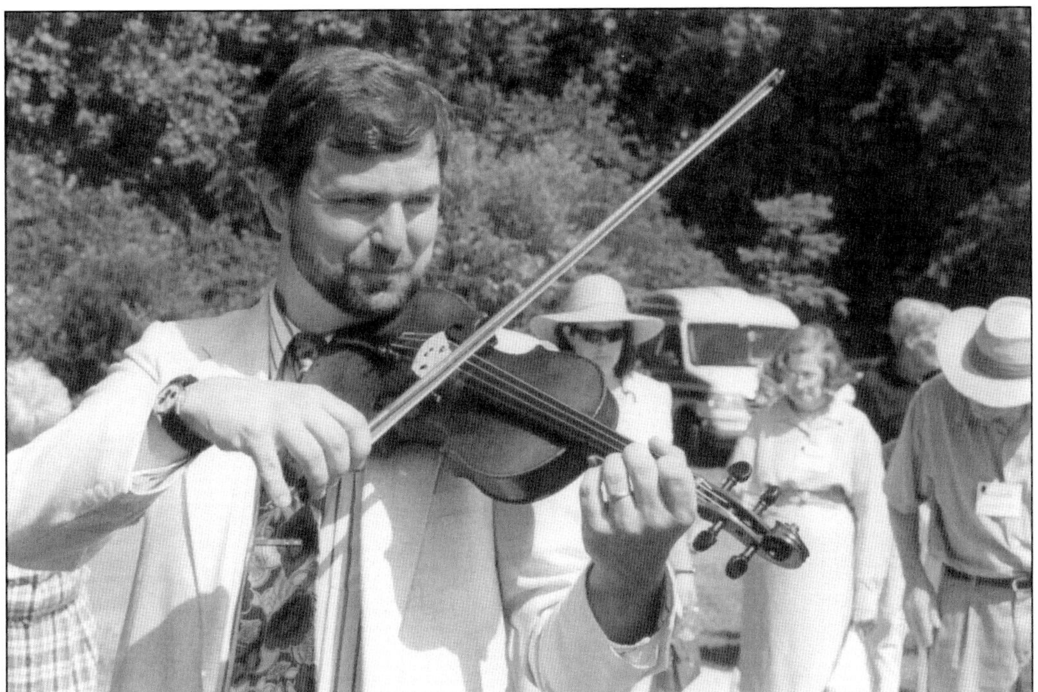

Two Hundredth Anniversary of Patrick Henry's Death, June 1999. June 6, 1999, marked the 200th anniversary of Patrick Henry's death at Red Hill. On that date, a public graveside ceremony was held commemorating the passing of Henry, one of Virginia's most influential Revolution-era leaders. In honor of their ancestor, nearly two dozen descendants traveled from around the country to pay their respects to their "Grandpa Henry." The ceremony included music performed by descendant Patrick Henry Jolly, who played the violin belonging to Henry's son John. After the service, Lt. Gov. John H. Hager proudly posed holding the violin (below).

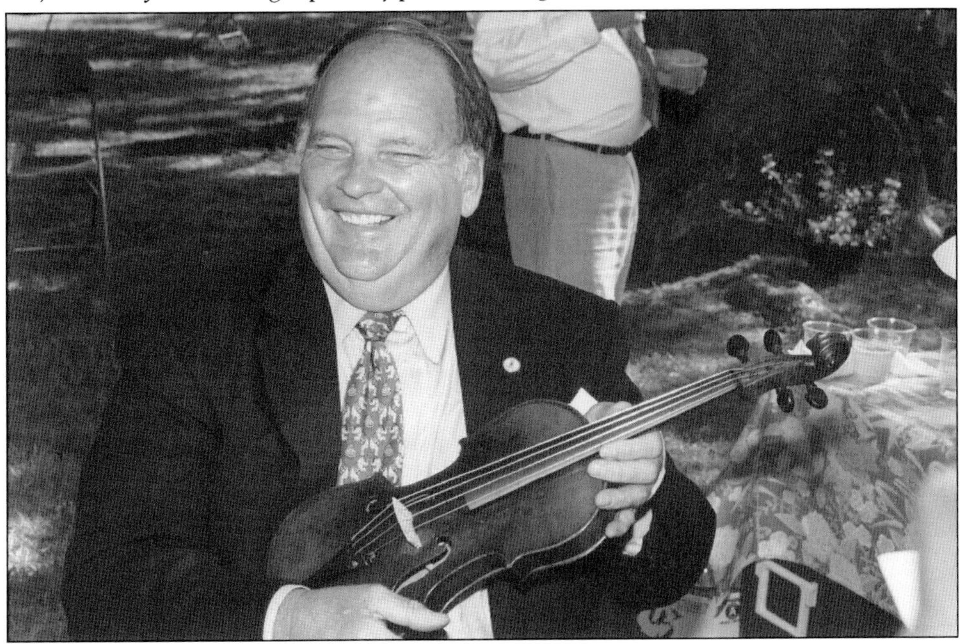

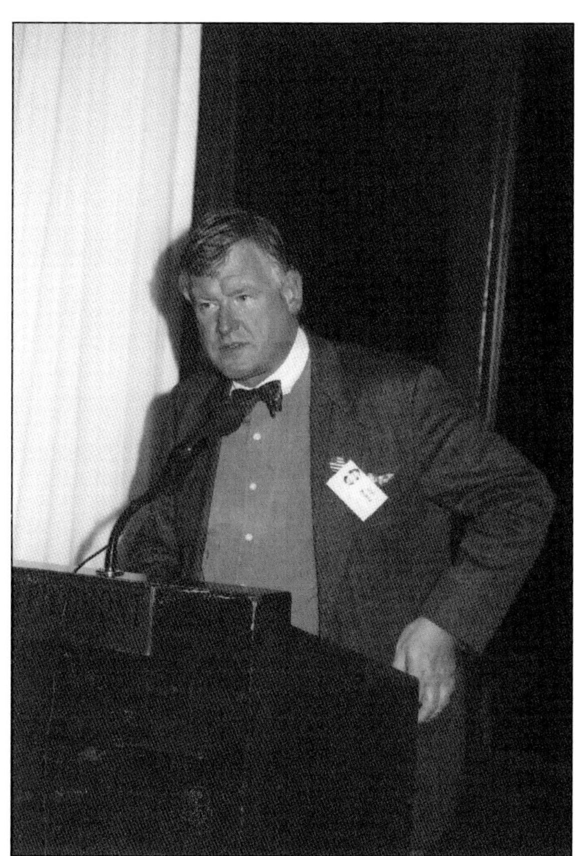

Dr. Jon Kukla, 2001. After receiving his doctorate in history at the University of Toronto, Jon Kukla became the assistant director of the Library of Virginia and then directed the Historic New Orleans Collection in the 1990s. From 2000 to 2007, Kukla served as the executive director of the Patrick Henry Memorial Foundation. He later authored the acclaimed biography *Patrick Henry: Champion of Liberty* (2017).

Historic Greenhouse Discovered, 2001. In 2001, archaeologists uncovered the stone floor of Elvira Henry's greenhouse, constructed a few yards south of Patrick Henry's home around 1840. Elvira's greenhouse contained orange and lemon trees and other tropical plants. The trees were rolled out in large tubs in the summer and placed in suitable spots around the plantation. Enslaved cooks used the fruits from these trees to make pies and preserves.

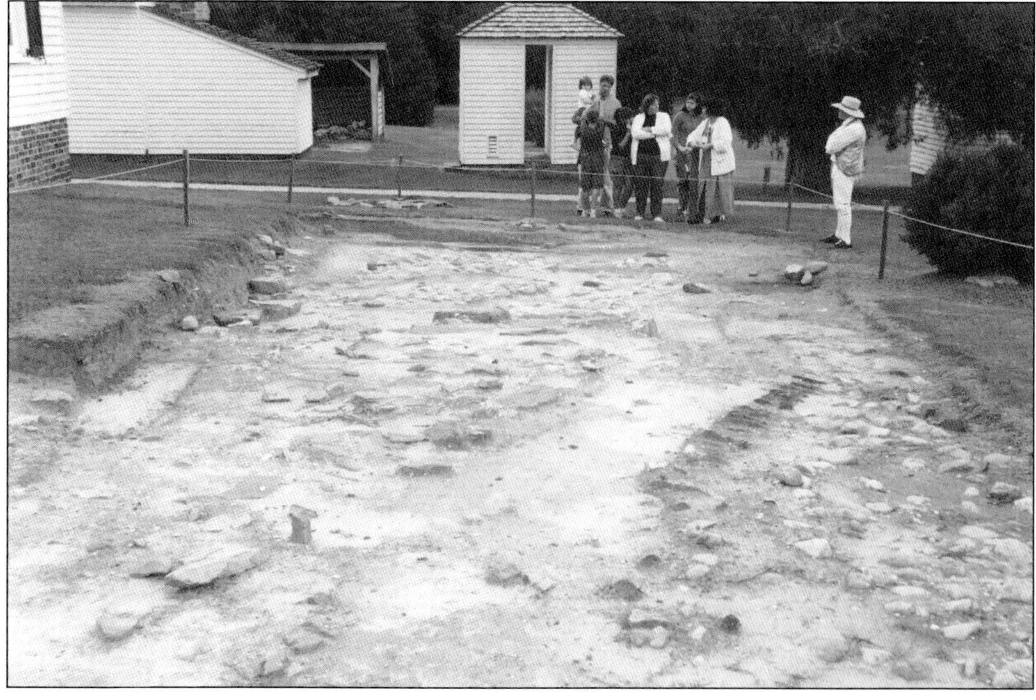

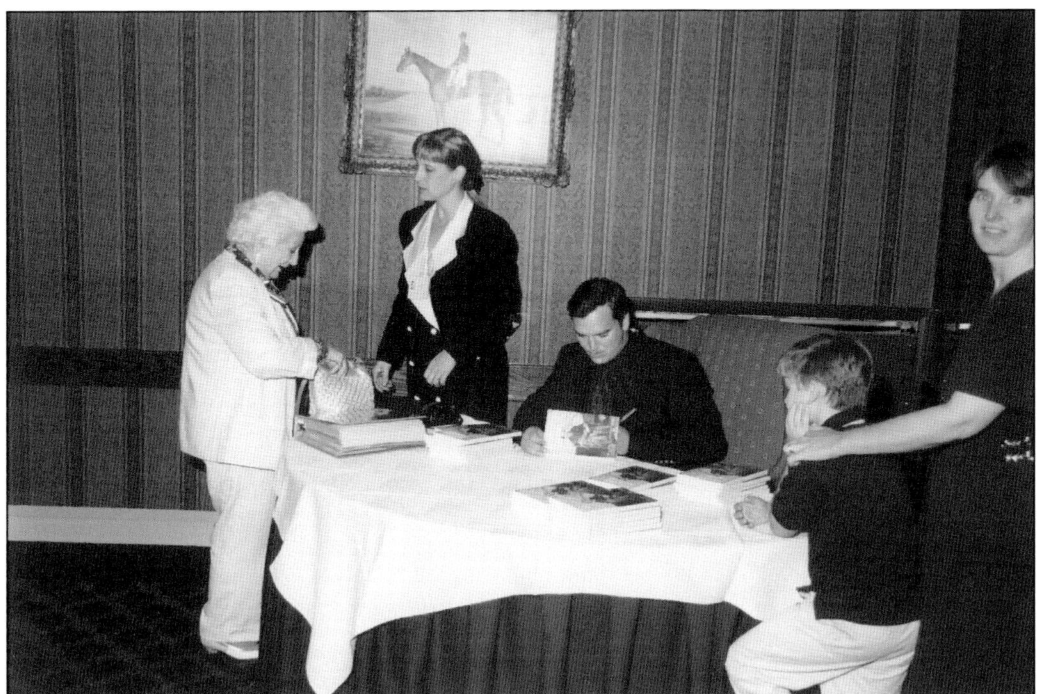

Mark Couvillon Book Signing, September 2001. Historian Mark Couvillon signs copies of his first book, *Patrick Henry's Virginia*, at the 2001 Descendants' Branch meeting at the Piedmont Club in Lynchburg. Part of the Patrick Henry Memorial Foundation's mission is to keep the "Spirit of the Voice of the American Revolution alive" through supporting scholarship and conducting educational programs.

Margaret Henry Penick Nuttle, March 2003. Born in 1913, Margaret Nuttle was a great-great-granddaughter of Patrick Henry. A philanthropist with a love of history, Margaret Nuttle supported several Red Hill projects, including the blacksmith shop's reconstruction. She was also integral in growing the Descendants' Branch by organizing weekend reunion trips. Margaret died in July 2009 at the age of 96.

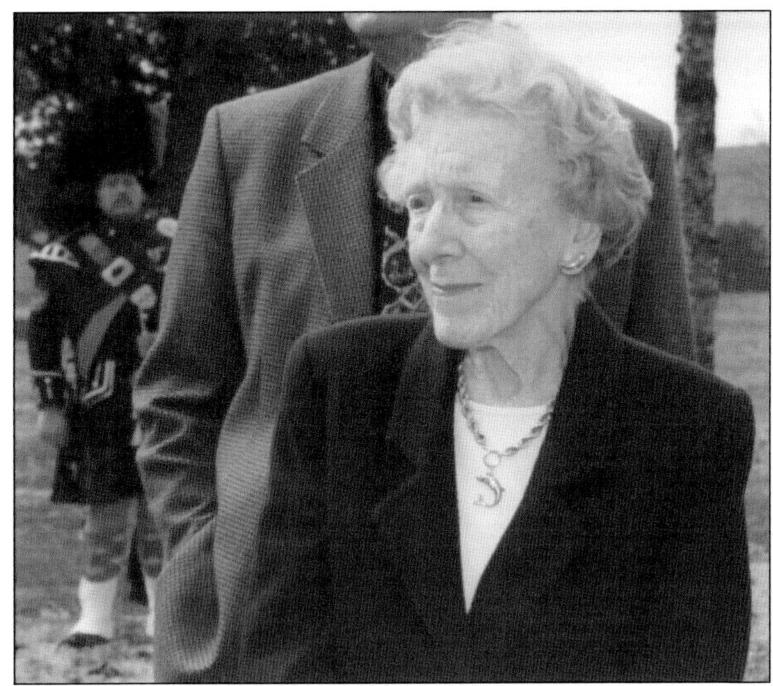

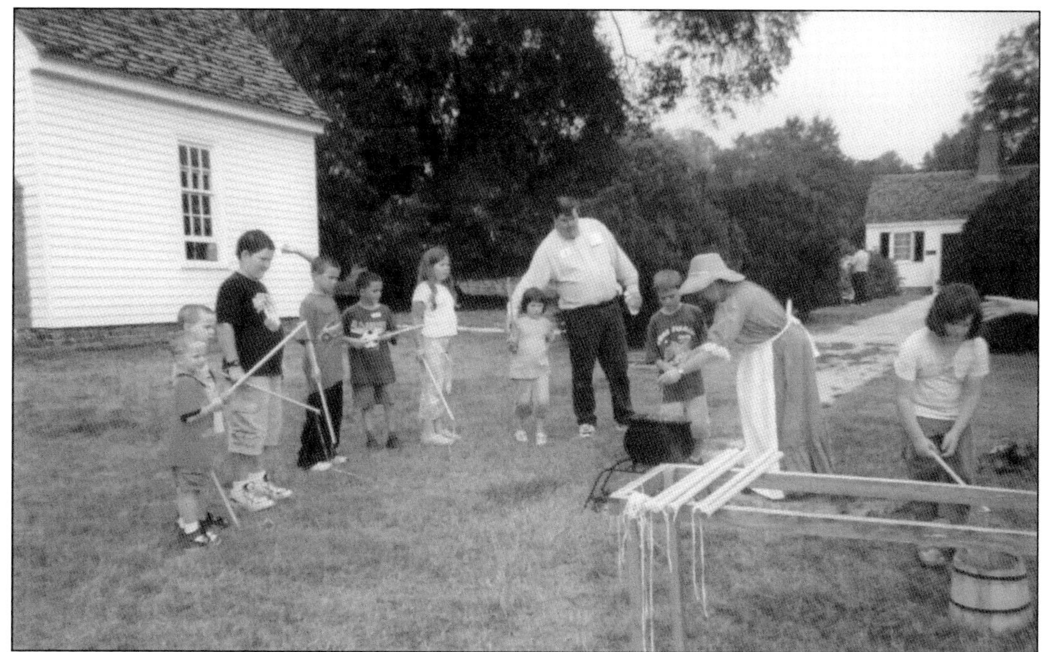

Living History Program, October 2005. Since the early 2000s, Red Hill has hosted Living History Days for area students. The specially scheduled days include hands-on stations that illustrate 18th-century life in Virginia. The Living History Days have grown in popularity; each year, thousands of schoolchildren benefit from their educational experience at Red Hill. Here, students learn the craft of candle-dipping.

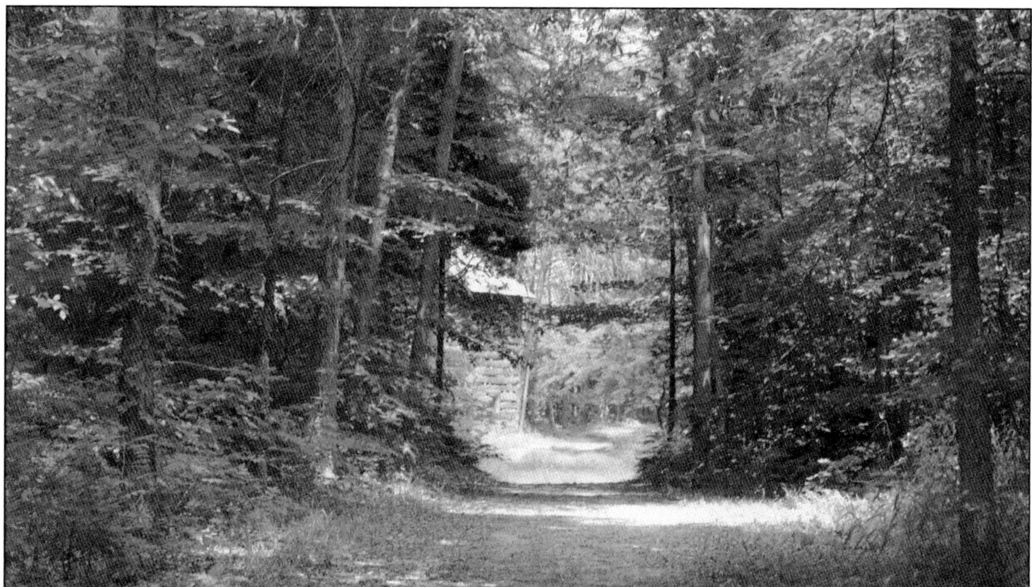

Quarter Place and Tobacco Barn, June 2018. Through a grant in 2018, Red Hill reacquired 77 acres of adjoining property originally part of the land Patrick Henry purchased from Richard Booker in 1794. On this land, referred to as Quarter Place, sits a cemetery that holds the remains of 147 enslaved and freed African Americans. The land purchase has allowed the foundation to preserve and honor this sacred burial site.

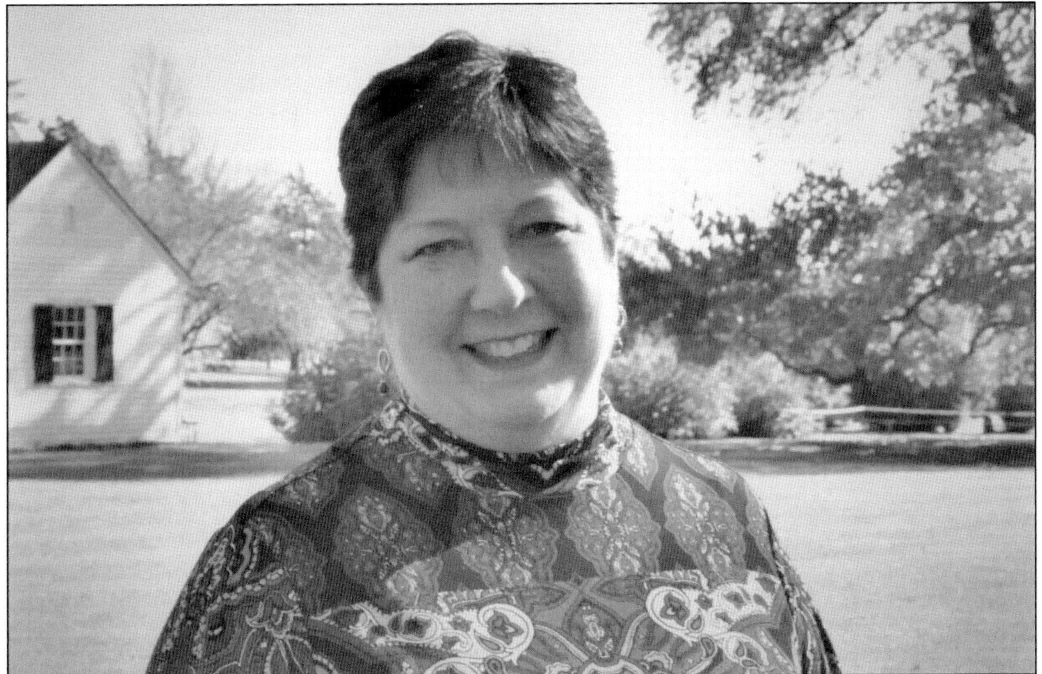

Hope E. Marstin, March 2019. A graduate of Virginia Tech with a bachelor's of science in finance, Hope Marstin started working at Red Hill in 2009. Since then, she has held several positions and was named its first female chief executive officer in 2019. In 2018, Hope received the Hunter-Burley Award from the Small Museum Association. Hope has actively advanced the full story of Red Hill's history.

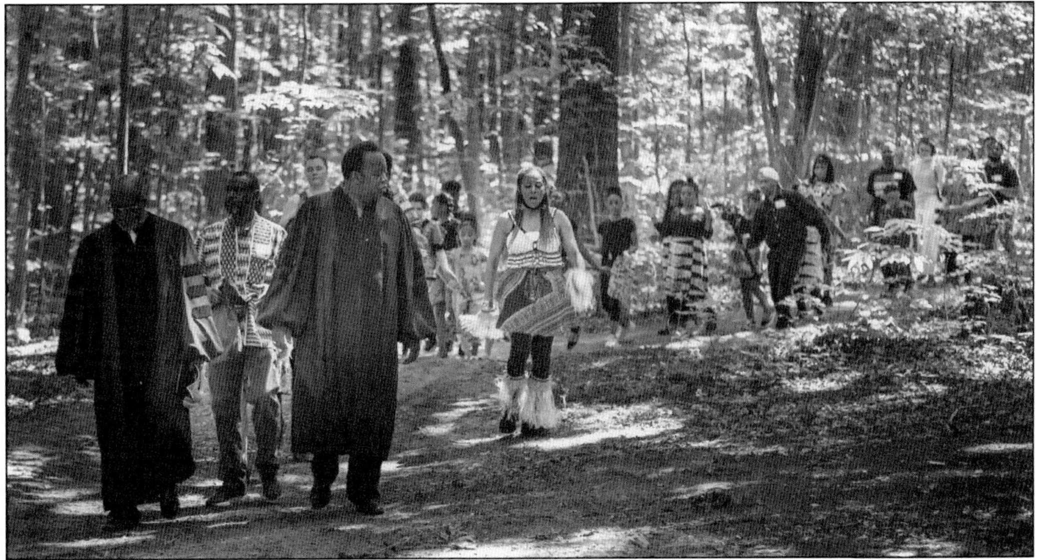

Quarter Place Consecration Ceremony, June 2021. Red Hill hosts guests to consecrate Quarter Place Cemetery. The event, now held annually, includes prayers by local pastors, traditional African songs and dances, and readings of the names of those buried there. The event was the first of its kind to begin to address uncomfortable truths, such as the impact of slavery on the community and the stories of those who were enslaved.

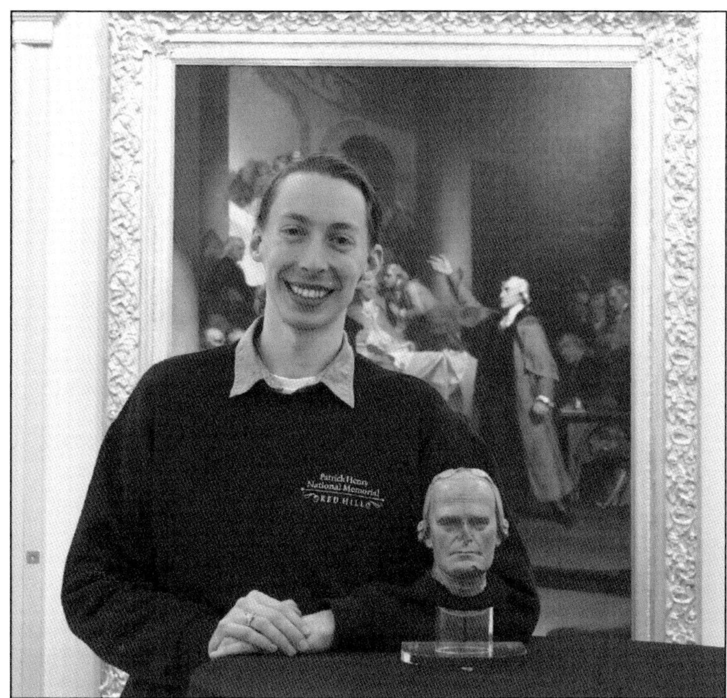

Cody M. Youngblood, 2024. In 2021, Cody Youngblood was hired as the director of historic preservation and collections, the youngest person to hold this position. His curatorial work and innovative research with the museum collection brought an improved analysis of its history, shed light on forgotten stories, and professionalized how historic interiors are furnished and interpreted.

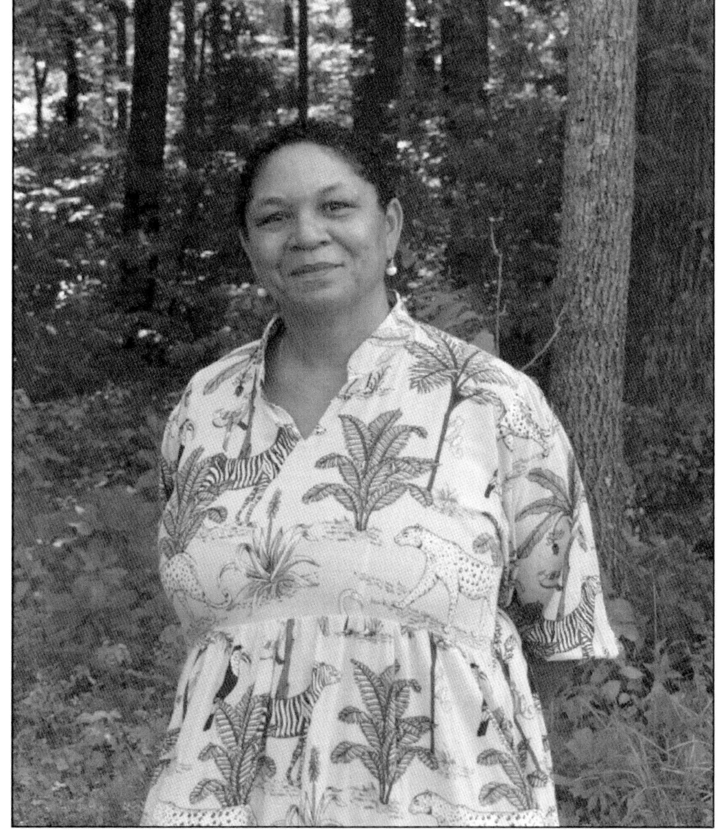

Lisa Beal, June 2024. A descendant of Pollard and Pelton Henry, persons formerly enslaved by John Henry, Lisa Beal made history by becoming the first descendant of people enslaved at Red Hill to join the foundation's board of directors. Her presence brought a more complete, nuanced understanding of Patrick Henry's complex legacy and served as a step toward racial equality and healing.

Bibliography

Carrington, John Cullen, ed. and comp. *Charlotte County, Virginia: Historical, Statistical, and Present Attractions*. Richmond: The Hermitage Press, 1907.

Couvillon, Mark. *Patrick Henry's Virginia*. Brookneal, VA: Patrick Henry Memorial Foundation, 2001.

———. *In Sickness and in Health: The Marriage of Patrick Henry and Sarah Shelton*. Brookneal, VA: Patrick Henry Memorial Foundation, 2021.

Daily, Patrick. *Patrick Henry: The Last Years, 1789–1799*. Brookneal, VA: Patrick Henry Memorial Foundation, 2013.

Deetz, Kelley Fanto. *Bound to the Fire: How Virginia's Enslaved Cooks Helped Invent American Cuisine*. Lexington: University of Kentucky Press, 2017.

Ginsburg, Rebecca, and Clifton Ellis, eds. *Cabin, Quarter, Plantation: Architecture and Landscapes of North American Slavery*. New Haven: Yale University Press, 2010.

Henry Family Papers, Virginia Museum of History & Culture, Richmond, Virginia.

Henry, William Wirt. *Patrick Henry: Life, Correspondence and Speeches*. 3 vols. New York: Charles Scribner's Sons, 1891.

Meade, Robert Douthat. *Patrick Henry: Patriot in the Making*. Philadelphia: J.B. Lippincott, 1957.

———. *Patrick Henry: Practical Revolutionary*. Philadelphia: J.B. Lippincott, 1969.

Morgan, George. *The True Patrick Henry*. Philadelphia: J.B. Lippincott, 1907.

Papers of James Stone Easley, Patrick Henry's Red Hill, Brookneal, Virginia.

Youngblood, Cody. *Historic Furnishings Report: Harrison's Cabin*. Brookneal, VA: Patrick Henry Memorial Foundation, 2024.